COMMUNITY ORGANIZATION CURRICULUM IN GRADUATE SOCIAL WORK EDUCATION

Community Organization Curriculum in Graduate Social Work Education

□

REPORT AND RECOMMENDATIONS

□

By
ARNOLD GURIN

In collaboration with:

JOAN ECKLEIN
WYATT JONES
ARMAND LAUFFER
ROBERT PERLMAN

COUNCIL ON SOCIAL WORK EDUCATION
345 East 46th Street New York, N.Y. 10017

Library of Congress No. 74-129268

Foreword

THIS REPORT, along with several other publications, is the product of a three-year comprehensive study of the community organization curriculum in graduate social work education sponsored by the Councils on Social Work Education.

This volume, entitled *Community Organization Curriculum in Graduate Social Work Education: Report and Recommendations*, includes a summary of the study findings and all of the major recommendations. Other publications resulting from the project include a textbook, *Community Organization and Social Planning* by Arnold Gurin and Robert Perlman (co-published by CSWE and John Wiley and Sons); *Community Organizers and Social Planners: A Casebook*, by Joan Ecklein and Armand Lauffer (co-published by CSWE and John Wiley and Sons); *A New Look at Field Instruction: Education for Application of Practice Skills in Community Organization and Social Planning*, by Jack Rothman and Wyatt Jones (co-published by CSWE and Association Press); and *Students in Schools of Social Work: A Study of Characteristics and Factors Affecting Career Choice and Practice Concentration*, by Deborah Golden, Arnulf M. Pins, and Wyatt Jones (published by CSWE).

Publication of the findings of the community organization curriculum development project, occurs at a significant time in the history of social work education. Major social problems facing our nation underscore the critical need for social work personnel with competence in community organization and social planning. The changes in the curriculum in schools of social work at this time and in the foreseeable future are greater than ever before. The new CSWE Curriculum Policy Statement, approved and issued late in 1969, encourages further curriculum innovations by individual schools of social work.

The study design, the findings, the recommendations and their rationale produced by the Community Organization Curriculum Development Project are described in detail in this report and are incorporated in the other project publications. The recommendations were developed by the project staff with the help of an Advisory Committee. The findings, recommendations, and new resources should be of value to all social work faculty, students, and practitioners. They will be particularly useful to those directly concerned with the practice of community organization and the education of students for these roles and responsibilities. They should also be of interest and use to those schools which do not single out community organization as a specific curriculum concentration.

It is hoped that the faculty of each school of social work will study carefully all the publications of the study and will consider quickly how or which part of new insights and resources coming from this study can appropriately be utilized in enriching and/or revising its curriculum. It is recognized that individual schools will and should utilize the findings and recommendations in different ways.

The Council on Social Work Education and the field owes a debt of gratitude to Dr. Arnold Gurin for his able and creative leadership of this project and to the project staff and the advisory committee for their many contributions.

Thanks are expressed to the Office of Juvenile Delinquency and Youth Development, Social and Rehabilitation Service, Department of Health, Education, and Welfare, whose grant made possible this project. Special recognition should be given to Bernard Russell, former director, and Virginia Burns, staff member, of the Office of Juvenile Delinquency and Youth Development, whose interest and support of the need for a community organization curriculum development study contributed greatly to the initiation and development of this effort.

ARNULF M. PINS
Executive Director

July, 1970

Preface and Acknowledgements

THE REPORT presented in this volume reflects the conclusions and judgments of the staff which conducted the Community Organization Curriculum Development Project of the Council on Social Work Education. In accordance with the policies of the Council in such ventures, the staff takes responsibility for the final product, which is made available to the Council and its member graduate schools of social work and other interested parties for their consideration and use. The Council as an organization, the individual graduate schools of social work, and others who may have an interest in the issues will evaluate for themselves how some or all of the findings and recommendations may or may not contribute to the objectives which are being pursued.

In presenting the product of a collaborative effort, it is difficult to sort out the contributions that should be attributed to the various individuals involved. The project was initiated by an *ad hoc* group of faculty members from schools of social work who were teaching community organization and who, for a period of time, had sought to extend and improve the curriculum of schools of social work in this area. An initial meeting to explore the possibilities of such a project was convened in March, 1963, by Dr. John B. Turner, who was then a professor of community organization and is now dean of the School of Applied Social Sciences at Case Western Reserve University, and Virginia Burns, who was at that time in charge of training programs for the Office of Juvenile Delinquency and

Youth Development, HEW. As a result of that meeting, the Council on Social Work Education assumed responsibility to sponsor a community organization curriculum development project. The Council submitted a proposal to the Office of Juvenile Delinquency and Youth Development of the U.S. Department of Health, Education, and Welfare and received a planning grant for 1963-64.

Professor Meyer Schwartz, now associate dean of the School of Social Work at the University of Pittsburgh, was employed by the Council to direct the planning phase of the Curriculum Project. He and his collaborators made an incisive analysis of the problems and needs with which a curriculum development effort must be concerned and set the stage for the ongoing work of the present Project, which was initiated in June, 1965, with a training grant from the Office of Juvenile Delinquency and Youth Development, HEW.

The Council on Social Work Education arranged to have the Project carried out at the Florence Heller Graduate School for Advanced Studies in Social Welfare at Brandeis University. The staff employed for the project were, or became, members of the Brandeis faculty. It is this staff which carries the responsibility for the final report that is now being presented. As director of the Project, I wish to express my personal appreciation to the members of the staff who grappled earnestly and enthusiastically over a considerable period of time with the complex problems of both practice and curriculum in an ill-defined and rapidly changing field. They brought to the enterprise a variety of backgrounds and talents which helped to make the collaborative process an exhilarating one.

STAFF CONTRIBUTIONS

Robert Perlman, Ph.D., director of Practice Studies for the Project and associate professor of Research at Brandeis, came to the Project directly from a position as associate director of Action for Boston Community Development, one of the earliest community action demonstration programs of the 1960's. He carried primary responsibility for the studies of practice which were conducted by the Project as an integral part of its program. He is also the co-author of the forthcoming textbook, *Community Organization and Social Planning,* which has grown out of the Project's work.

Wyatt C. Jones, Ph.D., research director for the Project and associate professor of Research at Brandeis, a sociologist with extensive experience in evaluative research, had also had direct experience in a community action program. He was associate director of Research for Mobilization for Youth in New York City before joining the Curriculum Project, where he carried responsibility for development of curriculum material and for gathering data in relation to student characteristics and experiences. He is co-author of two on the Project's volumes—*A New Look at Field Instruction:*

Education for Application of Practice Skills in Community Organization and Social Planning and *Students in Schools of Social Work: A Study of Characteristics and Factors Affecting Career Choice and Practice Concentration.*

Joan Levin Ecklein, Ph.D., research associate on the Project staff and now at Boston State College, is a sociologist who had worked for several years on the "West End" study of relocated families in the Boston area. Dr. Ecklein carried major responsibility for the organization of case material out of the data collected by the Project through interviews and field visits and is co-author, with Dr. Lauffer, of *Community Organizers and Social Planners: A Casebook.*

Armand Lauffer, Ph.D., now associate professor at the University of Michigan School of Social Work, made a major contribution to the Project as a research associate despite the relatively short time that he was connected with it, from June, 1967, to August, 1968. During that period he gathered data from schools of social work concerning both general curriculum and the specific content of community organization concentrations. He visited eleven schools of social work and met with administration, faculty, and students, and corresponded with many more. He was responsible for much of the original writing that has gone into this final report and is co-author, with Dr. Ecklein, of the book of case materials previously mentioned.

Jack Rothman, Ph.D., professor and director of the Community Work Program at the University of Michigan, is another collaborator who made a major contribution to this report, although he was not a full-time member of the Project staff. For the summers of 1966, 1967, and 1968, Dr. Rothman was associated with the Project as a senior consultant, concentrating on the area of field instruction. His work is reflected more fully in the monograph on Application of Practice Skills, co-authored with Dr. Jones and mentioned above.

David Jones, O.B.E., was attached to the Project during the academic year 1965-66 while he was visiting the Heller School as a senior Fulbright scholar. Mr. Jones is vice-principal of the National Institute for Social Work Training in London. He made a substantial contribution to the Project's work, especially through his collaboration with Robert Perlman in a study of neighborhood service centers.

Throughout the life of the Project, the staff at Brandeis enjoyed the encouragement and active support of Dr. Arnulf M. Pins, first associate executive director of the Council on Social Work Education, then its executive director since 1966. He also served as associate director of the Community Organization Curriculum Project and helped to guide it on many important issues involving the total field of social work education. Other members of the Council on Social Work Education staff exhibited a lively interest in the Project and contributed useful ideas at various stages in its development. Professor Harold Lewis of the University of Pennsylvania, who is also chairman of the Curriculum Committee of CSWE, provided very helpful consultation during most of 1968 on the relationship of the Project's emerging recommendations to the total curriculum of schools of social work.

A number of other contributions are gratefully acknowledged. Professor Alvin D. Zalinger, now a member of the Sociology Department at Northeastern University, conducted an informal survey during the summer of 1966 of the educational programs of several other professions in the Boston area. He provided the Project with a useful paper on the social science component in professional education.

Professor Violet Sieder of the Heller School faculty at Brandeis University served as a consultant during the summer of 1967 and developed an extensive document on the functions of a community organization practitioner in a direct service agency.

Professor Martin Rein and Professor Richard A. English served as part-time consultants to the Project during the summer of 1968. Professor Rein of Bryn Mawr College Graduate Department of Social Work and Social Research* developed a substantial memorandum on the nature of social policy and the techniques of social policy analysis which represent one of the areas in the curriculum on which recommendations are being made. Professor English of the University of Michigan School of Social Work provided the Project with a useful memorandum on the field of intergroup relations and the nature of community organization practice within it.

OTHER SOURCES

An important source of empirical material which helped to shape the staff's understanding of community organization practice and, therefore, the requirements of the curriculum was provided by the Cambridge Center for Research in the Behavioral Sciences, Inc. The Center conducted about 50 interviews with community organization practitioners and also carried out a feasibility study on the use of self-administered questionnaires to obtain information from practitioners concerning their activities.

Mrs. Deborah Golden, working under the supervision of Dr. Pins with the assistance of Professor Jones, conducted a study of students entering schools of social work in September, 1966. The study will be reported in the volume, *Students in Schools of Social Work,* mentioned earlier. It is a replication and expansion of the 1960 study done by Dr. Pins of the students who entered in that year. Of special interest to the Project is a

* Beginning in September, 1970, Martin Rein will be professor of Social Policy at the Massachusetts Institute of Technology.

comparison of community organization students with those selecting other areas of concentration in the social work curriculum, including factors influencing the students' choice of a social work method for concentration.

Although the contributions made by these various consultants as well as by the full-time staff of the Project have not been recognized individually in the report and may not appear exactly in the form in which their material was submitted, they are fully represented in the final product.

Consultation was obtained not only from those who participated on a staff basis, but also from knowledgeable persons in various positions in both practice and education. An attempt was made throughout the life of the Project to maintain contact with various elements of the field and to test the thinking of the Project staff against the current experience of practitioners and teachers. Reports were rendered regularly to the Board of Directors of the Council on Social Work Education and to its Annual Program Meeting. On these occasions an opportunity was provided for an exchange of views with school and agency personnel. In addition, papers on the project were presented at meetings of the National Association of Social Workers (NASW), National Conference on Social Welfare (NCSW), and other groups, and articles were published in *Social Work Education Reporter* and *Journal of Education for Social Work*, published by CSWE, in *Social Work Practice* issued by *NCSW*, and the *Social Service Review*.

The Project Advisory Committee under the chairmanship of Professor Alfred J. Kahn of the Columbia University School of Social Work played a major consultative role in the Project. The Committee was composed of leading representatives of both practice and education. (See page 197 for list of membership.) During the three years of the Project activities, it met at least once a year for extended reviews of the working papers. Several special workshops for faculty were also held from time to time. A preliminary draft of the final report was reviewed by a group of administrators, curriculum coordinators, faculty members of schools of social work, and members of the CSWE Curriculum Committee in July, 1968.

PUBLICATIONS

While this final report is meant to convey the findings and recommendations of the Project in a comprehensive manner, it does not constitute the entire product of the Project's work. The Rothman-Jones volume on application of practice skills, co-published by CSWE and Association Press, contains considerably more material on the content of practice courses and field instruction than the summary observations included in this overall report. It also contains data concerning students enrolled in community organization concentrations, supplementing the more general information contained in the Golden-Pins-Jones study of students. Community organization concentrators were also the subject of Armand Lauffer's doctoral dissertation, which was undertaken in conjunction with the Project and in fulfillment of his requirements as a doctoral student at the Heller School of Brandeis University.

Another major segment of the Project's work, which was its examination of community organization and social planning practice, is reflected in a textbook entitled *Community Organization and Social Planning*, co-published by CSWE and John Wiley & Sons. It was part of the original plan of the Project to derive curriculum recommenations at least in part from an examination of practice. In addition to the interviews conducted by the Cambridge Center, the Project staff itself made field visits to a variety of projects in different areas of the country, including both voluntary and governmental agencies at various regional levels. The textbooks reflects these studies as well as the distillation of the staff's consideration over a period of time of the literature in the field and the various attempts that have been made to date to develop a conceptual framework for community organization practice.

The curriculum recommendations are based on the same general approaches that are to be found in the textbook which is designed as an important piece of teaching material for the practice courses that are being recommended. *Community Organizers and Social Planners: A Casebook* incorporates the material that was gathered and is also co-published by CSWE and John Wiley & Sons as a companion volume to the textbook. Several of the individual cases in the book will also be issued by CSWE and will be available separately.

An important outgrowth of the Project's examination of practice was its first publication, *Neighborhood Service Centers*, by Robert Perlman and David Jones, issued by the U.S. Department of Health, Education, and Welfare in 1967. That study of six centers, undertaken at the request of the Office of Juvenile Delinquency and Youth Development, HEW, appraised the issues of service delivery and community organization involved in this important aspect of community action and anti-poverty programs.

GENERAL PERSPECTIVE OF REPORT

In introducing this final report, perhaps it would be well to state the general point of view which animates all of the recommendations that are to be presented. This is a point of view that the staff has derived on the basis of the information gathered from all the sources indicated above. However, the conclusions that we have reached are, in the end, matters of judgment. They represent our own evaluation of the information that we have gathered and the product of our deliberations over a period of time. We believe that they are reasonable and considered judgments, but, in the nature of the case, they cannot be definitive. They remain to be tested against actual experience.

The curriculum recommendations are designed to assist the schools in meeting changing and pressing needs. Those needs are made evident partly through the requirements of the field and partly through the expressed desires of the students within the schools of social work. Both the field and the students, each in their own and different ways, reflect the turbulence of the current historical period. There is a general effort on the part of social welfare agencies as well as other groups, organizations, and governmental bodies concerned with social problems to obtain the services of personnel with organizing and planning skills. Because the problems are so urgent and the solutions so uncertain, the need is for professionals who will be innovative, creative, and effective.

There is every indication that social work students, and especially those with an interest in community organization, are a "changing breed." In substantial numbers, they are impatient with what they regard to be the evils of society and tend to see existing bureaucratic structures as helping to perpetuate such evils. They therefore seek to change institutions rather than to serve them, and they challenge the schools continuously to demonstrate that social welfare institutions are relevant to the needs of the times.

While there may be many differences between the needs of the field as perceived by agency administrators and the point of view of the more activist students, there is also a basic compatibility between the two. A changing field must have new personnel who are oriented toward change. The changes which the new students will bring eventually may be far different than those now visualized by agency administrators, but the alternative is stagnation and retrogression which no field can afford.

The critical task for social work education in the immediate future is to capitalize upon the strengths of the "new breed" of students who have both intellectual capacity and emotional dedication. For this to happen the schools of social work must be able to help the students learn how they can translate their abilities and motivations into effective action. The practice of community organization and social planning in social work is one of the channels through which such action can flow.

The schools of social work are being called upon at this time to produce both greater numbers of more adequately educated direct service personnel and also greater numbers of more expert organizing and planning personnel. The Project staff's specific responsibility was toward the latter demand, and it is natural that it should feel the needs in that direction with particular urgency. The issue for the immediate future, as we view it, is for the social work profession to play a growing role, not only in rendering direct service, but in the formulation of social policy and in setting the direction for the expanding field of social welfare services.

The central purpose of the curriculum recommendations presented in this volume is to help the schools of social work to educate a growing number of practitioners whose careers will be oriented toward such broad responsibilities.

There are relatively few guide posts to the successful accomplishment of that very large task. It will call for a great deal of experimentation and for a high degree of flexibility. It is the Project's general conclusion that there can be no single formula for the development of a curriculum under current conditions. Both the field of practice and the students will benefit from a considerable degree of individualization in the curriculum and from a variety of approaches in different schools. There is, however, a central focus which ties all such efforts together and keeps the efforts directed toward the goal of a relevant attack upon social problems. That is the focus on the organizing and planning aspects of social work as an area of specialization which requires a continued expansion and a growth in depth and expertness.

Arnold Gurin
Project Director
CSWE Community Organization
Curriculum Development Project

Contents

Overview of Conclusions and Recommendations

COMMUNITY ORGANIZATION was already established as a methods concentration when the Curriculum Project was initiated. By the terms of the 1962 Curriculum Policy Statement of the Council on Social Work Education, community organization was on a level of parity with casework and group work as an area of concentration. A number of schools were already offering such a two-year concentration, and the number has grown rapidly since then. The charge to the Curriculum Development Project was to strengthen the content of the concentration. The basic notion that students should be prepared for specialized practice in community organization was therefore an *assumption* rather than a finding of the Project.

This assumption was nevertheless examined in the course of the Project's work and tested against empirical observations. Such re-examination has led to the conclusion that the assumption was sound and should be retained as a guideline for curriculum planning.

Practitioners and administrators in community organization and planning agencies have testified to the need for more grounding in relevant bodies of knowledge concerning economic, political, and social forces determining community and social conditions and for more preparation in the necessary skills of organizing and planning for people entering practice in these areas.

Recent developments in schools of social work demonstrate the rapidly growing interest on the part of both students and faculties in programs designed to prepare students for organizing and planning responsibilities. Students entering such programs differ in a number of important characteristics from other social work students. It is likely that many among them have been motivated to enter the social work profession specifically because they could concentrate in community organization.

There also has been a palpable and immediate demand for community organization and planning personnel in a growing variety of settings. Social work is one among several disciplines that are responding to these demands which call for specialized background and skills.

FRAMEWORK OF STUDY OF PRACTICE

The Project has taken an eclectic approach to practice by linking community organization and social planning and by not limiting the field to a particular ideological stance or methodology. The position of the Project staff is that it is important for students to obtain a descriptive and phenomenological grasp of the realities of practice even though there is no coherent overall theoretical structure into which it can be fitted. The settings, functions, and activities that make up the field of community organization and social planning can be described with some unity. They can be conceptualized only partially and in a fragmentary manner.

The framework for the study of practice, as developed by the Project, includes a number of dimensions:

a) Practice is divided by structure and function into three major contexts: voluntary associations, direct service agencies, and allocating and planning organizations.

b) A problem-solving model identifies typical steps in practice which vary in their specific applications in the different contexts. The steps are: problem definition, development of structure, policy formulation, program planning, monitoring, and feedback.

c) Practitioner tasks are divided into "analytical" and "inter-actional" elements, both of which are considered essential to practice.

The Curriculum recommendations are not limited to the methods courses alone. In order to meet the needs of students in community organization concentrations, it was necessary to consider all aspects of relevant content, whether such material has been located within the methods sequence or in other parts of the curriculum. Recommendations are divided into two major categories:

a) *Foundation courses*, which are designed to provide the student with background knowledge that informs and is relevant to practice but is not part of the practice itself, and

b) *Practice courses,* which are designed to equip the student to enter professional practice in community organization and social planning, and to perform at least at the beginning level of such practice. Practice courses include bodies of knowledge that have been absorbed and integrated in such a manner as to make them directly available for use and therefore an element of practice itself. There is, however, a larger body of knowledge that can help to advance practice but has not yet been transformed into principles or elements of methodology. The perspective for a foundation course is the body of knowledge involved. The perspective for a practice course is the use of knowledge for action.

FOUNDATION COURSES

It is assumed that students entering the concentration in community organization and social planning will have had a general base in major areas of social science as well as in elementary methods of social research. The recommended curriculum content in the master's program therefore does not include introductory courses in these areas. The recommendations do however, spell out the kind of background which students should have and suggest ways in which gaps in background might be covered in the master's program through the flexible use of university resources.

The selection of content from the social sciences is guided by the conception of community organization and social planning as representing intervention at the organizational level. Two core courses are recommended:

a) *Social behavior.* Content is drawn from psychology, social psychology, anthropology, and micro-sociology. The focus is on the behavior of people in relation to social systems and includes such subjects as role theory, group dynamics, small group behavior, communication, and decision-making.

b) *Institutional analysis.* Relevant social science knowledge pertaining to institutions is drawn from macro-sociology, economics, and political science. Substantive areas range from sociology of the community, organizational theory, social stratification, and power structure to urban economics and politics.

It is recommended that a wide range of elective courses be made available either by the school or in other departments, permitting the student to obtain greater depth in one of the two areas or to continue to distribute his interests evenly in both suggested areas of social science foundations.

Social science research is a basic tool of the organizer and planner. Foundation courses in research are designed to help students understand the values and uses of research as an effective instrument in problem identification, a device for obtaining needed information, a convenient entrée to the community, and a way of influencing power centers: Two courses are recommended. The first is an introduction dealing with the language and the logic of research, the design of research for different purposes, and the current status of research in social welfare. The second concentrates on methods of collecting and analyzing data and on problems of measurement. Additional courses should be available on an elective basis.

The foundation course in social policy and social welfare is a crucial element in the program of community organization concentrators, since it provides the substantive basis for the expertise which the student must acquire. Content should include a historical and institutional analysis of social welfare, a review of the major contemporary policy issues in social welfare, and methods of policy analysis and evaluation.

PRACTICE COURSES

Practice courses deal directly with the content of the tasks to be performed by the practitioner. Their objective is to integrate knowledge, methodology, and skill. Three core practice courses are recommended: a survey course that is an introduction to the full range of practice in community organization and social planning, a course in methods of organization, and a course in methods of planning.

Each of the core courses is to be based on a combination of learning experiences, integrating class and field instruction. A versatile range of learning experiences is recommended, including role-playing, simulations, programmed instruction, and pre-structured field instruction using a variety of field settings, including both school-sponsored projects and outside agencies.

The core program, including both foundation and practice courses, will occupy about half of the total time available for the master's program. This leaves approximately half the program available for individual specialization.

Specialization is to be reflected in an integrated program of elective courses in social science, research, and substantive, problem-oriented areas of practice combined with a practicum in which the student carries substantial responsibility for a sustained project in some aspects of community organization and social planning.

The recommendations do not constitute a single model, designed to meet the needs of all students and all schools. On the contrary, the breadth of the field and the diversity of student goals argue against such an approach. The recommendations are based on the assumption that schools will vary in their emphasis within the general framework of the community organization curriculum that is being proposed, depending upon their interests and capacities, and that student programs will be individualized in relation to previous background, interests, and career objectives.

Among the options available is the possibility of combining community organization with other aspects of social work practice. Some aspects of the recommended curriculum are very closely related to some of the content in group work concentrations. Others are more closely related to administration and social policy. Combined concentrations along such lines are proposed.

Education for community organization is necessarily interdisciplinary in character. The community organization concentration therefore needs to draw upon resources in the university which may not always be of equal relevance to other concentrations. This flexibility calls for the use of non-social work faculty and for making available course offerings in other departments of the university.

PART I

STATUS OF COMMUNITY ORGANIZATION IN SOCIAL WORK EDUCATION

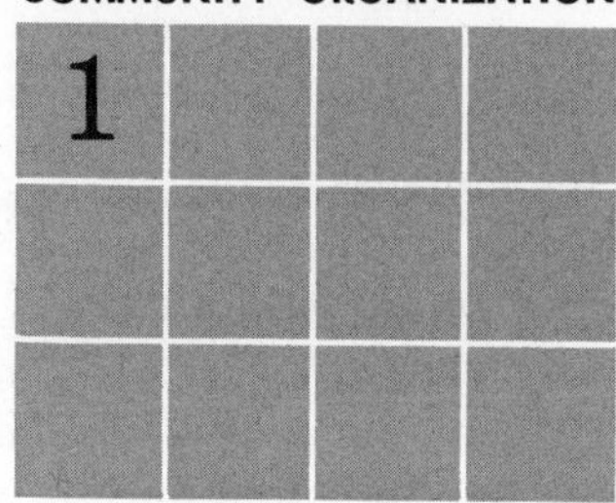

Community Organization in Social Work

THE COMMUNITY ORGANIZATION Curriculum Development Project of the Council on Social Work Education was the outgrowth of developments extending back over a number of years that converged to make it an appropriate and timely undertaking in the current period of social work education. This history will be traced briefly, in order to set the Project's report in its proper context.

The place of community organization in social work is in many ways a microcosm of the stages of development in social work itself. The neighborhood service and social reform activities of early settlement workers represented one of the historical roots of both neighborhood community organization and social group work. Similarly, the Charity Organization Society led both to family casework and to later councils of social agencies and welfare councils. Elements which later became separated into professional methods were, in those days, part and parcel of a common enterprise, in which social objectives and methods were completely intertwined.

As social work has become professionalized there has been a recurring concern with the relationship between the profession's social objectives and its methods or, in the classic formulation of Porter Lee, between social work as "cause" and as "function."[1]

[1] Porter R. Lee, *Social Work as Cause and Function and Other Papers* (New York: Columbia University Press, 1937), pp. 3-24.

EARLY HISTORY

During the period between the two World Wars, the emphasis was primarily on the development of methodology, and, more specifically, on the conceptualization of social casework as a distinctive methodology for helping people. Group work, representing a much smaller segment of the profession, was able to fit into the same general pattern of conceptualization. Both dealt directly with clients, individually or in groups, and thus could identify with prevailing models of major professions like medicine and law, where professional practice is defined in terms of direct service to clients.

Community organization did not develop to the same extent as a distinctive methodology, and its position within the framework of social work practice was for many years ambiguous and problematic. For the most part, its functions were identified as facilitative and ancillary to direct practice with clients. The prevailing view was that such activities as co-ordination, administration, and promotion, while undoubtedly helpful and even necessary, were not distinctive to social work and therefore not at the core of the developing professional method.

As was true of social work generally, those teachers, writers, and practitioners who were concerned with community organization as an area of specialization grappled with the relationship of "cause" and "function." The emphasis shifted from one to the other in different periods, as it did for the profession as a whole. The earliest views of "community organization" as formulated in the early 1920's were rooted in the sociology of the time, which stressed the negative effects of urbanism on social relationships. The focus was ideological rather than methodological, espousing the cause of the organic "Community," defined in terms of participatory democracy.[2] Although there have been many changes through the intervening years in the nature of the social patterns that provide the context for community organization practice, the value of commitment to participatory democracy has been a persistent underlying theme.

Following World War I, the growth of community chests and councils of social agencies provided the major channel for the development of a cadre of professional staff specializing in community organization. These professional workers began to exchange experience, to conduct conferences, and to seek ways of formulating concepts and methodology. The earliest specialized training in community organization was directed to the needs of the chest and council movement. The Lane Report, which was a systematic attempt to formulate a rationale for community organization as a professional method, bore the stamp of the chest and council move-

[2] Edward C. Lindeman, *The Community* (New York: Association Press, 1921).

ment, with its major concern for the co-ordination of the voluntary agencies and its identification with the field of social work.[3]

The Lane Report argued that community organization should be considered an integral part of professional social work, along with casework and group work. It took many years, however, before that point of view was widely accepted. Numerically, community organization workers represented a small minority of professional social workers, and they often had prepared for and had their early experience in other aspects of social work or in other disciplines. As late as 1957, less than two percent of the students graduating from schools of social work had been enrolled in a community organization concentration.

Groups of teachers and practitioners did, however, persist in their efforts to establish community organization as a legitimate method within social work and to encourage its growth. The number of schools offering one- or two-year concentrations grew slowly during the 1950's and accelerated after 1960. The National Association of Social Workers established a Committee on Community Organization which developed bibliographies and working papers designed to help build practice knowledge. Its most important product was a document entitled *Defining Community Organization Practice* which dealt both with the common elements identifying community organization with other social work methods and with some of the distinctive aspects of community organization as a field of social welfare.[4] Formal recognition of community organization as a method of concentration on a level of complete parity with casework and group work came finally in the "Curriculum Policy Statement" adopted by the Council on Social Work Education in 1962.[5]

CURRICULUM REPORT OF 1959

In the late 1950's the status of community organization as a social work method was reviewed and pointed up in the report of Harry L. Lurie that was issued as part of the overall Curriculum Study produced by CSWE.[6] In connection with this present curriculum report, it is instructive to re-examine a number of the judgments made a decade earlier.

---

[3] Robert P. Lane, "The Field of Community Organization," National Conference of Social Work *Proceedings* (New York: National Conference of Social Work, 1939), pp. 495-511.

[4] National Association of Social Workers, *Defining Community Organization Practice* (New York: NASW, 1962).

[5] Council on Social Work Education, "Curriculum Policy Statement" (New York: CSWE, 1962).

[6] Harry L. Lurie, ed., *The Community Organization Method in Social Work Education*, Vol. IV, A Project Report of the *Social Work Curriculum Study* (New York: Council on Social Work Education, 1959).

Lurie recognized the lack of agreement in definitions and concepts of community organization and did not try to resolve them. He also recognized the absence of a general theoretical framework which could serve as a basis for defining practice. He suggested that such a theoretical base might be found in an emerging theory of social change which could perform for community organization the function that a theory of individual behavior had provided for casework.

In the absence of a unified framework, Lurie took an eclectic approach, accepting the use of "community organization" to refer to structure, field, or method, just as "community" might refer to different dimensions of social organization. He found some elements of commonality between community organization and other social work methods, both in common values and shared principles of procedure, but he also stressed the differences. Approaching the matter pragmatically, he noted that there were categories of positions occupied by professional social workers which were termed community organization positions, and that their "distinguising feature . . . is that they are primarily concerned with maintaining and developing the programs and standards of welfare agencies and services rather than directly helping individuals and groups."[7]

Some of the working papers contributed to the Curriculum Project at that time (and reproduced in the Appendix to the report) contained other formulations of the nature of community organization practice. Carter, for example, tried to make a distinction between social work community organization method and other types of activities such as lobbying, negotiating, and public relations, which were part of community organization practice but not distinctive to professional social work. She defined the social work method as a problem-solving process directed "toward improved community integration as well as toward a self determined social work goal."[8]

Distinctions of this type are, however, difficult to define with adequate clarity and to maintain usefully in the light of actual experience. The 1959 Curriculum study placed a certain amount of emphasis on the professional's responsibility for conducting an organizing process. "So far as the community organization worker is concerned," Lurie summarized, "planning the solution involves primarily planning the process whereby the group will be able to function most effectively and expediently to arrive at agreement concerning what needs to be done." Or, at another point, ". . . The ability to organize is the core of the process."[9]

On the other hand, Lurie suggested that it would be arbitrary to draw a

---

[7] *Ibid.*, p. 5.

[8] *Ibid.*, pp. 85-100.

[9] *Ibid.*, p. 41.

line between "working with community" to decide upon needs and programs and the actual development of a program itself. "Both types of procedures are frequently involved in the evaluation and completion of a specific project."[10] Similarly, he found it difficult to draw a sharp line between community organization and administration. Unlike Carter, who sought to distinguish "social work method" from other activities, Lurie concluded that the curriculum must help the student "to understand how administrative and community organization procedures are integral parts of program development and agency operation, and how they may be coordinated in relation to social policy as the fundamental determinant of all communal endeavor."[11]

DEVELOPMENTS OF PAST DECADE

The decade since the appearance of the Curriculum Study in 1959 has shifted the emphasis once more from the concern with professional methodology to the broader social responsibilities of the profession. This shift in emphasis was reflected first in the concern on the part of caseworkers and administrators with the need to adapt services more effectively to the needs of the most deprived segments of the population—"hard core," "multi-problem," and "hard to reach" families. While this condition called for modifications in some of the casework methods being used, it also revealed the lack of co-ordination and continuity of service that were characteristic organizational defects of the health and welfare system. Those concerned with community organization and planning began to focus on these issues. The small beginnings in the voluntary welfare planning field were greatly accelerated by the developments of the 1960's—the civil rights movement and other manifestations of social protest and demands for change, the reawakening of neighborhood organization and action, social experimentation by large foundations and government, the great expansion of governmental health and welfare programs through new federal expenditures, and the development of new social planning structures at all levels of government.

Social work, as a profession deeply involved in human behavior and human services, has been under severe pressure to produce practitioners who can deal effectively with the social problems that have become sharply visible and insistent during this period. While the challenge is addressed to social work as a whole, it is especially pressing in the area of community organization. The side of social work which had been subordinate during its period of professionalization—namely, that side which deals with intervention and change of the social environment rather than the immediate

---

[10] *Ibid.*, p. 10.
[11] *Ibid.*, p. 11.

individual environment or the individual himself—is the one most relevant to the current demands.

In attempting to respond to that challenge, this Curriculum Project has sought to free itself of prior commitments and traditional perceptions of the issues. Its focus has been on the practical issues of how social work can build upon its historical commitment to social reform and its experience in the education of professionals to prepare a new kind of professional for new kinds of tasks. The range of demands facing social work cannot be covered by a single methodology. Earlier formulations which sought to fit community organization into generic social work method are inadequate to the needs of the day. Alternative formulations have therefore arisen. The term planning has come to have equal emphasis with community organization and has sometimes been posed as in opposition to it. Similarly, the community organization worker has been replaced to a degree by the planner, and the roles of organizers and planners are now being defined in much more varied terms than in earlier models, which stressed primarily the enabler as the archetype of the social worker cum community organizer.

Among the newer emphases brought about by the change-oriented action programs of the 1960's is the role of the community organization worker as an advocate, taking leadership responsibility for mobilizing disadvantaged groups to articulate their needs and to make demands upon existing institutions. Workers have adopted strategies of protest and conflict as alternatives to earlier emphases on consensus and negotiation. Simultaneously, on the planning side, social workers, in both practice and education, have been seeking to gain greater sophistication in policy formulation and organizational change. Renewed attention to politics and political influence is a major common theme underlying all recent developments.

EXPANDING SCOPE OF COMMUNITY ORGANIZATION

While the past decade has not produced more coherent theory, it has greatly expanded the scope of community organization and therefore of the social work profession. The numbers and types of positions that fall into the general categories of community organization and social planning grew dramatically during this period, and any listing presented at this time would quickly become outdated. Federal programs have generated planning positions in a larger number of service fields at all governmental levels —federal, state, regional, and local. Community organization positions have proliferated in local communities and neighborhoods, both in specific service fields and in more comprehensive structures which attempts to achieve co-ordination of services and citizen participation. In addition, there are growing demands for technical help from community and citizen groups, protest organizations, churches, and others. The service areas where community organization is a growing factor include not only those traditionally associated with social work (such as public welfare) but housing, education, employment and training, and physical planning.[12]

The Project has developed its recommendations within the context of the opportunities of this evolving situation. It has avoided choosing a theoretical formulation that might lead to the exclusion of certain fields of responsibility. We have attempted to formulate recommendations that would make it feasible for schools to prepare social workers to perform a variety of functions, some of which are quite disparate from one another. Not all students will want or be able to cover this wide range. It is also possible that, over a period of time, social work as a profession may define its responsibilities more narrowly. For the present, however, social workers are represented in the various fields of activity that have been indicated. Social work is, in the final analysis, what social workers do. The growing field of community organization and social planning provides social work with a variety of channels through which the profession can contribute to meeting the urgent needs of the time.

In developing its recommendations, the Project has built upon the existing programs in community organization. Many schools have responded creatively to the changing needs of practice. In that process, they are finding new forms through which to integrate social work's traditional responsibilities both as cause and function.

[12] Melvin M. Webber, "Systems Planning for Social Policy," in Ralph M. Kramer and Harry Specht, eds., *Readings in Community Organization Practice* (Englewood Cliffs, N. J.: Prentice-Hall, 1969), p. 424.

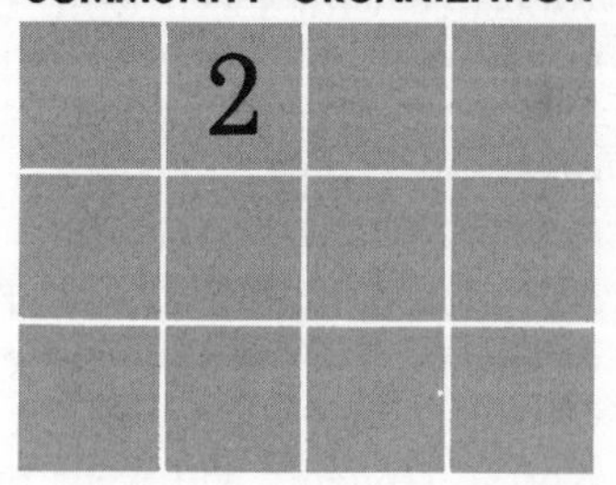

Community Organization Programs in Schools of Social Work: Trends and Issues

IT HAD BEEN ONE of the original motivations of the present Curriculum Project to help to strengthen community organization (c.o.) programs quantitatively as well as qualitatively by devising a curriculum that would help attract more students to the c.o. concentration in schools of social work. Actual developments have run ahead of the Project. A very substantial growth has already taken place in response to the rapid expansion of demand for c.o. workers.

ENROLLMENT IN C.O. CONCENTRATIONS

As of the fall of 1965, the year in which the Project began, there were 442 students enrolled in one- or two-year community organization concentrations in 36 schools.

By the fall of 1969, enrollment had risen to 1125. A total of 30 schools were offering two-year concentrations and an additional 18 schools provided one-year concentration programs. Several others, although not having concentrations, did offer field work placements in community organization.

There is every indication that the c.o. concentration will continue to grow. The concentration was already being offered in 1968-69 on either a

* This chapter is based primarily on material gathered by Armand Lauffer, who also prepared the first draft of the chapter.

two-year or one-year basis in two-thirds of the 72 accredited schools of social work in the United States and Canada. Many of the other schools have plans for providing such a concentration, and most new schools now becoming established are giving a substantial place to c.o. in some form. Furthermore, a number of schools with one-year concentrations are contemplating expanding them to a two-year program.

The situation is somewhat less clear in regard to the size of enrollment in various schools. Recent figures indicate that the pace of growth, which reached a peak of 78 percent in the one-year period from September, 1965, to September, 1966, has tapered off. It is true that enrollment in c.o. concentrations is still growing more rapidly than in other concentrations, but to a lesser extent. Between September, 1968, and September, 1969, the number of c.o. students grew from 1017 to 1125, a rise of 10.6 percent, compared with an overall rise in enrollment of 7.3 percent. (See Appendix I.)

As of September, 1969, community organization concentrators represented 9.0 percent of all full-time students. Before 1960, it had been under 2 percent. While the proportion may be expected to continue to rise, it is difficult to predict what the eventual position will be in regard to relative numbers. As of the academic year 1966-1967, when the Project staff visited a number of schools, those with two-year concentrations were projecting rates of growth which would bring community organization concentrators to anywhere from one-sixth to one-third of the total student body within approximately the next five years.

This growth is taking place spontaneously, as individual schools respond to the pressures of their own situation. There has been no overall study of manpower needs in community organization positions, and therefore no way of establishing general criteria as to a proper distribution of educational resources among the different concentrations. Student demands, market opportunities, and the availability of student stipends have combined to influence schools, independently and spontaneously, to expand their community organization programs.[1] Although c.o. concentrators do not now and may never constitute a majority of all social work students, growth of the magnitude described above represents a major shift in the emphasis of social work education and has far-reaching implications for the future. Since the great majority of social work positions are inevitably in direct service areas, the devotion of even one-sixth of school enrollment

[1] The growth of the field to which schools are responding is reflected in the data reported by the U.S. Department of Health, Education, and Welfare in *Closing the Gap. . . . In Social Work Manpower*, 1965. Table 9 (page 34) shows that the number of social workers (with or without graduate education) engaged in "community services" increased by 186 percent from 1950 to 1960, as compared with an overall increase, in all fields, of 42 percent. The "community" category had a larger percentage increase than any other field of practice.

to students concentrating in areas of policy, community organization, planning, and administration reflects an important commitment. It implies a serious bid on the part of the social work profession to function at the policymaking as well as at the direct service level.

STUDENT CHARACTERISTICS

The growth in c.o. concentrations has a qualitative as well as a quantitative aspect because of the particular characteristics of the c.o. students. The spirit of the phenomenon is captured in the remark of a dean of one of the schools visited in the course of the Project, who said "we have three times as many casework students here as community organization majors, but the c.o. students act as if they were the majority." Others remarked that the c.o. students are particularly active in student organizations and vocal in demanding changes. "They perform a valuable and needed function," remarked one chairman of a c.o. concentration, "challenging the faculty to remain contempoary, to review and re-evaluate programs, curricula, and traditions."

The Golden-Pins-Jones study of students entering schools of social work in 1966 identified some of the specific characteristics of the c.o. concentrators.[2] The sex ratio was exactly the reverse of what it was for total enrollment—60 percent of the c.o. concentrators were male, and 40 percent were female. In the total student body, only 40 percent were male. Also striking was the fact that 20 percent of all c.o. students were black which in 1966 was more than twice the ratio that existed in either casework or group work. The percentage of black students in community organization had doubled between 1960 and 1966, while their proportional representation in casework and group work had declined somewhat.

Although the c.o. students did not differ from those in other concentrations in regard to grade-point average, a higher proportion of them came from selective colleges and universities. A number of indices show that community organization concentrators have more background than other students in community and organizational activities. More of them came to social work through their contacts among relatives and friends in general community activity rather than through social work per se. They were more involved in political and civil rights movements and labor unions. A larger proportion had worked in VISTA, the Peace Corps, or anti-poverty programs. They also differed in a number of attitudes toward social work, indicating a commitment particularly to the social action objectives of the profession, which they identified with the c.o. concentration.

---

[2] Deborah Golden, Arnulf M. Pins, and Wyatt C. Jones, *Students in Schools of Social Work: A Study of Characteristics and Factors Affecting Career Choice and Practice Concentration* (New York: Council on Social Work Education, 1970).

STUDY OF PROGRAM TRENDS

The Project gathered written materials from all the schools of social work concerning their approaches to community organization. Project staff made visits to eleven schools offering c.o. concentrations and conducted sessions with faculty members in different parts of the country. Two questionnaires were administered to c.o. students and faculty: one on a limited exploratory basis, and another on a more comprehensive and systematic basis. In addition, the study of 1966 entering social work students was used to explore in detail the factors influencing students' choice of method concentration.[3]

This chapter draws upon all these sources and from subsequent impressions in order to summarize the state of affairs in the schools offering c.o. concentrations. Much of what is reported here covers the programs at the time they were studied intensively (1966-1967 academic year). Since then, a number of these schools have shifted emphasis and revised curricular objectives. Some of the shifts will be noted but cannot be described in the same detail. Since programs are changing very rapidly and are under continuous study and reconsideration, no publication of such material can hope to be current. The reports presented here nevertheless illustrate trends and problems.

COMMUNITY ORGANIZATION METHODS COURSES

On superficial examination, there was considerable similarity in the content of c.o. curricula offered at various schools during the 1966-67 academic year. Since the literature on community organization was relatively limited, bibliographies, at least for introductory courses, tended to include the same basic works. On the other hand, there were significant differences from school to school, both in the extensiveness of their c.o. offerings and in the emphasis given to one or another area of content. These differences reflected the relationship between the c.o. sequence and the total program and the relative size and importance of the c.o. concentration. In schools where the c.o. concentrators were a larger proportion of the total student body, there were larger numbers of courses required specifically of the c.o. concentrators, separately from other students.

C.o. methods courses differed in the extent to which they included foundation knowledge from the social sciences which does not deal with methods per se. In many schools, the c.o. courses had become the vehicle for carrying the social science content that was not available elsewhere in the curriculum. In 1966 as much as 75 percent of methods class time

---

[3] *Ibid.*

might be given to providing the student with the political, economic, and sociological knowledge base needed for development of macro-level intervention strategies. Recent curriculum revisions have been in the direction of greater emphasis on "practice" content, but the volume of social science material is still considerable.[4]

Schools also differ in the concepts which they use for the definition and analysis of practice. Such differences affect the number and titles of courses offered in a sequence. For example, one school defines c.o. practice as differing at the neighborhood, organizational, and the inter-organizational levels. Field work assignments and classroom content parallel each other along these lines. Another school differentiates "community practice" into three distinct but complementary forms: action, development, and planning. Some schools concentrate on work with individuals in small groups or in their neighborhoods during the first year, and on intervention strategies directed at large and complex organizations during the second. Others spend the entire first year introducing students to the history, philosophy, and background of c.o. practice. The latter part of that year may be spent on an analysis of the worker's roles and the tasks he is called upon to perform. The content of the second year is then focused on agencies, formal structures, power structure, social systems, etc. Some schools reverse this pattern. A number of schools try one order of sequencing of courses one year and then reverse it the next, searching for an effective ordering of the learning process. Some faculties do not feel they can teach their students to perform adequately along the entire spectrum of responsibilities identifiable within the compass of community organization. One school, for example, concentrates explicitly on urban problems. Its courses focus on those concerns more closely related to students of government, urban planning, and politics than to students in group work or casework. Another school is experimenting with a first-year focus on a particular field—housing. It will develop laboratories, field experiences, and faculty-led seminars within this subject area. While several schools only mention planning as part of community organization, others offer both an introductory course in planning and at least one advanced seminar in the "tools of planning."

---

[4] On behalf of the Project, in the summer of 1966 Alvin D. Zalinger conducted a study of several professional schools in the Boston area. He found that there was generally much more teaching of social science, as such, in schools of social work than in other professional schools. Zalinger's working paper, which is available in the Project files, was based on catalogue material and interviews with faculty of the following programs: Harvard University School of Public Health and Graduate School of Education; Massachusetts Institute of Technology Department of City and Regional Planning; Boston University School of Education, Public Health Nursing, Psychiatric Nursing, Public Communication; Boston College, School of Nursing, School of Education. Additional discussion of Zalinger's findings will be found in Chapter 3.

THE INTRODUCTORY COURSE[5]

In 1966-67, an introductory course was usually offered to c.o. majors exclusively, although a parallel course might be required or offered as an option for caseworkers and group workers. Today, introductory courses tend to be open to all students jointly. In general, the areas of content include most of the following units:

1. Definitions of community organization and introduction to the parameters of practice.

2. The history and philosophy of c.o. practice (which places community organization as a method within the profession of social work).

3. A variety of practice theories which underlie current approaches, including community development, planning, and social action material as drawn from social work, social psychology, political science, and non-professional social action sources.

4. An introduction to social theories and social processes, the content of which depends in part on how these will be handled in later c.o. courses or in other departments at the school.

5. A more specific area of social theory which receives considerable emphasis is focused on the community. Attention is given to community institutions and subsystems (e.g., government, education, family, social welfare) and to community power structure and decision-making. In a number of schools, such topics account for at least a third of the first semester and may be the only concentrated exposure to community theory given the student in his two years at the school.

6. Introduction to c.o. tasks and processes such as leadership development, committee work, public relations, budgeting. At least half of the schools examined leave this to a later course on the "how" rather than the "what" of c.o. practice.

7. The settings in which c.o. practice occurs from neighborhood *ad hoc* groupings to complex and formal organizations.

8. Variations in c.o. practice with the corresponding worker's roles ranging from "enabler" to "expert" to "advocate."

Each school places its own emphasis on each of the above areas, and in some schools, not all of them will be covered during the first semester. In others, two or three of these units may be alluded to in a single lecture while another unit may take up as much as half the course sessions.

---

[5] These units were abstracted from data collected in 1966-67. Course outlines have changed since then, primarily because of the availability of newer texts and reference materials.

Community organization is generally presented as a problem-solving process and, for this reason, some schools use the introductory course to expose the student to a variety of social problems, in particular those most evident in urban-metropolitan areas.

In most of the schools studied, courses included a combination of two types of materials. The first type is closest to "practice theory." The other type of material is less directly oriented to practice. It is drawn primarily from the fields of sociology and political science, has appeared mostly since 1960, and serves to introduce the student to theories and processes which provide a foundation for practice theory.

The "change agent" concept developed by Ronald Lippitt *et al.* exemplifies the first type.[6] It found favor in the later 1950's and early 1960's with those faculty members who wished to justify the role of the community organizer in terms that paralleled the therapist, caseworker, and group worker. The notion of a "change agent" acting as an enabler to help a "client system" to deal adequately with stress and change fitted well into principles of social work and was widely adopted.

Also widely adopted was Murray Ross's approach which focused heavily on achieving a "process objective," although he too recognized general and specific content objectives as integral aspects of community organization practice.[7] At the time of the Project's survey of schools, the Ross model was generally viewed by c.o. faculty as being limited in that it reflected only one of many approaches to dealing with practice problems. The Lippitt model, though more widely employed, was found wanting in explicitness regarding community structures and forces. Further, Lippitt's model of change agent called in by a client system to enable it to deal with a problem or set of social phenomena no longer reflected the realities of practice. Reliance upon these two works has become much less prevalent in the past few years, with the growing emphasis upon other approaches to community organization, such as "advocacy," and with the appearance of important additions to the literature.

Research, fact-finding, and data analysis received more attention in c.o. courses than in other methods. Close to half of the schools surveyed assigned quasi-research projects during the first semester or quarter. Several included field or laboratory types of experiences in their introductory courses, which included such assignments as a "foot survey" of a neighborhood, gathering data on the incidence of social problems, or descriptions of structure and data on operations of an agency.

The ways in which schools structure the introductory course reflect

---

[6] Ronald Lippitt, J. Watson, and B. Westly, *The Dynamics of Planned Change* (New York: Harcourt, Brace & Co., 1958).

[7] Murray G. Ross and Ben Lappin, *Community Organization: Theory Principles and Practice* (New York: Harper and Row, 1967), 2nd edition.

either explicitly or implicitly their assumptions concerning the learning process. Most schools use a didactic approach, dealing initially with the background of c.o. practice. Sometimes this simply is done historically. Others however, move more directly to a review and critique of the assumptions which underlie c.o. practice, using history only as a tool in beginning to construct a theoretical framework for practice. This approach leads to an early emphasis on delineation of practitioner roles and strategies in relation to goals, clients, and problems.

In a number of schools, faculty expressed concern with the problem of student motivation and the limitations of the didactic approach in achieving the immediate "engagement" of the student. Laboratory exercises have been used to meet this need. In one or two schools attention was given first to the student's immediate experience in his initial exposure to c.o. practice, with theory and history coming later in the first year.

COMMUNITY DEVELOPMENT COURSES

All schools teach something about community development, but few schools have special courses devoted exclusively to this subject. Several schools do, however, offer advanced courses that are titled community development. In one such course, the focus is on community development in the context of national planning. Another school looks at community development internationally and in both the urban and rural United States. A few students are placed in rural settings or with migrant farm laborers.

Aspects of community development are included in c.o. courses in a variety of ways. Several schools compare and contrast the concepts and methods of c.o. practice as between urban and rural settings, or between the United States and other countries, especially those that are underdeveloped. Comparisons are made in relation to the nature of problems and goals, the goal-setting process, participatory democracy, relationship to national resources, and the like. One school included community development in a context which combined social and economic aspects of urban development abroad with rural development in the United States. Some schools include community development somewhat arbitrarily (as if it did not fit in anywhere else) in a course that also covers sections on social problems and on community processes.

On the other hand, one of the few schools that required a full semester entitled "Community Development" included content on the use of small group methods, participation, representation, and similar topics that are covered in other schools under other c.o. labels.

It is apparent that many of the difficulties in conceptualizing the place of community development in the curriculum stem from the different ways in which the term is defined. Community development has come to mean the following things at different schools:

1. National social development programs.

2. Work with rural communities, mostly in non-industrialized countries, on the U.N. model.

3. Work with indigenous population groups regardless of location (including urban slums in the United States).

4. The Ross model of community organization process.

SOCIAL PLANNING COURSES

Of eleven schools whose courses were examined in some detail, five presented "planning" in separate and distinct courses at the time the survey was made. Most of the other schools included planning content in more general c.o. courses, mostly in the second year.

The most unusual program was one in which five distinct courses on planning were offered. The first course, in Social Planning Design, was organized on the basis of small groups of students who were attached to a real community situation and assigned to develop complete plans for the use of specified "clients" or "target groups." Such plans were to include statements of value assumptions, relevant theoretical and empirical knowledge, choice of strategies and methods, and mechanisms for evaluation. The completed plan was then presented to the appropriate agency or organization. Other courses in the planning sequence included Administration of Social Agencies, Urban Planning (given jointly with other graduate departments), Critique of Practice (an examination of operational problems in planning settings), and Planning Implementation. The latter focused on the interactional tasks in which the planner must engage during the process of developing a plan and after the parameters of the plan are set. It often followed the Social Planning Design course.

The other schools offering distinctive planning courses generally limited them to one or two during the two years. These tended to be survey courses covering both conceptual models of planning and specific tools of planning, such as fact-finding, goal development, client analysis, public relations, program budgeting, legislative processes, etc. Usually these were placed within the framework of a problem-solving process, following a series of steps.

Where planning was treated not as a separate subject but as part of other community organization courses, as was true in most cases, there was a great deal of variation in the amount of attention given planning and in the point of view and emphasis presented. Planning tended to be taught either as a methodology which cuts across a number of practice settings or in relation to a number of specific structures in which planning is practiced. Thus, several schools still provided an entire course on the structure and operations of health and welfare councils. In one school, materials on planning were included in an analysis of social work and other professions.

In some c.o. methods courses, special assignments were given calling for the exercise of planning skills, such as examining a service program in relation to a set of problem conditions or designing proposals for demonstration projects. Planning was combined with community development in one school and with administration in another. To a limited extent (at the time of the survey), schools had worked out arrangements with other departments in their universities for joint offerings in the planning area or for the availability of electives in other departments. Departments being used in this way included architecture, physical planning, public health, and politics and international affairs.

Planning is also learned through field work. Most schools provide some kind of planning assignments in field work settings. Those settings that have come into use more recently include urban renewal agencies, city planning commissions, and the offices of political officials.

SOME EMERGING PATTERNS AND INNOVATIONS

The foregoing summary suggests the diversity of emphasis and approach in curriculum content. When course outlines and interviews with faculty over the Project's three-year life span are compared, certain common themes do nevertheless emerge. It might be more accurate to perceive these as "tendencies" rather than trends. They are somewhat more discernible in the innovations of a few schools than in an across-the-board analysis of the programs of all schools with c.o. concentrations. These tendencies consist of changing emphasis in the content being taught, and in the organization or structuring of education experiences. They may be summarized as follows:

1. The planning, policy formulation, and goal-setting aspects of the practitioner's responsibilities are receiving increasing emphasis, to the point that some schools are developing courses geared almost exclusively to these tasks.

2. Some schools are finding it difficult to prepare students for all the exigencies of practice, preferring to help a student concentrate his learning experiences in a selected area of practice (work with neighborhood groups, administration and program development in service agencies, or agency coordination and central planning). This particular area is then viewed against the backdrop of the others.

3. Macro-level social theories and social science concepts are becoming increasingly important. Theoretical background material is drawn primarily from sociology (organizational analysis and community analysis particularly) and political science (especially urban politics). Psychodynamic, psychiatric, and developmental theories have been deemphasized. On

the other hand, new approaches are being sought to give students requisite knowledge and insights about human interaction and group behavior. Micro-level concepts and theories tend to be drawn increasingly from socio-psychological and socio-behavioral areas of knowledge.

4. Research, particularly with reference to data analysis and usage, is being emphasized as an integral part of a c.o. concentration. Special research courses, sections, and seminars may be required of c.o. students above and beyond those required of other students.

5. Similarly, a convergence of approaches to structuring or organizing the content of learning experiences seems very much in evidence. These might be summarized as including the following:

a. Overlapping assignments between courses are given at a number of schools. Thus, readings and student assignments may be planned in coordinate fashion between a policy and planning course, or between research and administration and planning.

b. C.o. students are frequently given the option to "proficiency-out" of a course, in particular to choose from among a number of social and behavioral science electives. Some of these may be offered outside the school of social work in graduate departments or in other professional schools such as criminology, urban studies, or public administration.

c. By the same token, students from other professional schools and disciplines may take courses at the school of social work. Where a school is conducting a training center, some students in other disciplines may participate in field assignments. Faculty may have joint appointments or may be on loan from other schools. Joint teaching is becoming more common.

d. Perhaps the most dramatic innovations are found in the structuring of learning for skills application. Community observations and field laboratories conducted by school-based faculty are being used in some schools in the first year.

FIELD INSTRUCTION

Field instruction is a crucial element in the community organization concentration, as in all of social work education. It is dealt with in detail in a separate monograph which places field instruction in a larger context of training for "skills application" through a variety of methodologies.[8] Two general trends in field instruction were identified by the Project staff during the data gathering process:

1. A shift toward school-based and faculty directed field instruction as against agency-based field placements.

2. Attempts to achieve greater integration between the content of class instruction and the learning experiences in the field.

[8] Jack Rothman and Wyatt Jones, *A New Look at Field Instruction: Education for Application of Practice Skills in Community Organization and Social Planning* (New York: Association Press, 1970).

Almost all schools were found to be seeking ways to extend faculty direction and control over the content of field experience. With a few exceptions, they either had or were developing full-time faculty positions to coordinate and support the work of field instructors. A summary of emerging trends may be helpful. These do not reflect developments in every school, but do suggest the variety of approaches being explored.

1. The range of settings being used for field instruction is expanding. Neighborhood settlements and welfare councils and federations which have been the most prevalent placements for c.o. students no longer account for the largest proportion of students. Growing numbers are placed in community health and mental health, public welfare, employment and vocational training, public schools, housing and urban renewal, city and state planning, labor unions, intergroup relations, civil rights, welfare rights and other "cause" organizations, as well as on staffs of political officials.

2. Faculty supervisors hired by and responsible to the school supervise all field work students and may also have classroom teaching responsibilities. Some supervisors are attached to specific agencies and may be given administrative responsibilities within those agencies. Others may function as "roving supervisors" working with students assigned to a number of agencies or settings.

3. Field or skill laboratory units are conducted directly by the school for at least part of the first year. Laboratory objectives are to introduce the student to community problems, to neighborhood concerns, to serve indigenous population groups, and/or to develop specific skills.

4. Just beginning to develop at the time of the survey were training centers to be operated directly by the school. These were usually neighborhood multi-service centers which were to serve as training sites for students in all methods concentrations. One was a joint venture with VISTA.

5. Some schools were using "satellite" field assignments. Under this plan, students are assigned to field work agencies where they are supervised by agency staff members or by university faculty. Since no agency or single assignment can provide a student with all the experiences relevant to his needs and interests, "satellite" assignments are made that may last anywhere from two weeks to an entire year. These may be in other agencies and around very specific types of tasks or issues. A student, for example, may be made the recorder of a legislative committee, may participate in budgetary hearings of the community welfare council, or may become engaged in crisis intervention at the outbreak of racial violence. The satellite assignment is tailor-made under faculty supervision to fit the particular needs and interests of the individual student.

On several issues of field work organization and structure, faculty differ widely, depending on their assumptions and viewpoints regarding educational methods.

A number of c.o. faculty, for example, urge the development of block placements. They point out that students working with indigenous groups cannot be effective on a two- or three-day-per-week basis. Action may take place on a weekend or on a day when the student is attending classes. The heavy demands of the field often result in a student's putting in forty or fifty hours per week, including early mornings, late evenings, weekends, etc. Other faculty members disagree. They point out that "process" takes a good deal of time. Block placements are too short. The specific nature of a student's placement may call for a flexibility in hours, but it often takes months before a process comes to fruition.

Some schools are beginning to experiment with both approaches, using block placements in relation to student interests and needs and concurrent placements in the light of the realities of a particular setting. Other schools are experimenting with summer block placements but run into considerable difficulties around student financing. One school begins its first year with eight weeks of field laboratory and ends its program with two months of block placements. This pattern is being considered by other schools as well.

A number of schools build their students' first-year experience around "work with individuals and small groups" at the neighborhood level. Second-year assignments are in large-scale bureaucracies and formal organizations, such as welfare councils, public welfare departments, or planning commissions. Faculty at these schools argue that effective planning and coordination efforts require an intimate understanding of social problems as they affect people at the neighborhood level. Field placements, in such cases, parallel classroom work.

Other educators point out that students do better with an overall perspective and that the first year's learning experience ought to be in a planning setting with highly structured, limited responsibilities. Frequently, adherents to each of those positions argue that all students should have both types of experiences, turning them into sequentially ordered requirements. Again, other educators disagree, pointing out that not all students will want or need experiences in all kinds of settings. Those who are interested primarily in neighborhood work, they argue, ought to have the opportunity of having two years of neighborhood experience, albeit at different levels. They take the position that curriculum objectives must be planned individually around the needs, interests, and capabilities of each student.

A major disagreement concerns the ordering of learning experiences. A number of faculty feel that students should progress from simpler to more complex tasks, from dependence on faculty direction to independent self-directed work and inquiry, from skill learning to problem-solving, and from lower to higher levels of responsibility. These assumptions lead to starting with observation experiences, moving only gradually to the assumption of responsibility in a work assignment.

Proponents of the counterargument point out that students learn best from real-life situations and that most effective learning comes inductively out of experiencing and doing. Students are not only given early client contact and work responsibilities, but may become totally involved in a problem area prior to formal classroom or laboratory learning experiences.

CLASS AND FIELD

A key issue brought to the attention of the Project staff relatively early in its explorations of curriculum trends and developments was the problem of relationship between classroom teaching and field instruction. It was highlighted as an issue first in the spontaneous comments obtained through a relatively informal survey of student opinion conducted among c.o. concentrators in the spring of 1966 and then elaborated in interviews and visits with c.o. faculties in the subsequent year. Widely noted was a lack of integration between class and field instruction, due to the different frames of reference in which the respective instructors tended to operate. Students observed that the concepts they were learning in the classroom from theoretically oriented instructors seemed to have little relevance to the tasks in the field. On the other hand, field instructors expressed both skepticism as to the relevance of the classroom teaching (one described it as too "global"), while also expressing a sense of inadequacy due to their own lack of familiarity with some of the newer theoretical literature.

That this is a generally recognized problem which is being tackled actively by the schools is evidenced in data gathered by the Project in its second and more systematic survey in the spring of 1967. At that time, a majority of students indicated that active steps were being taken by their schools to achieve a better integration between class and field instruction. Some of the measures designed to improve integration included observation and laboratory experiences, field instruction centers, and the like. In formulating its recommendations, the Project has built upon these developments in suggesting a more consistent emphasis on campus-based field instruction. It is nevertheless important to recognize that the issue of integration is a complex one and will not be easily resolved.

The shortcomings of which both students and faculty are aware and the problems that they identify relate not simply to the issue of coordination between class and field but, more importantly, to the quality of the entire educational program. At times, the field learning experience is found lacking. Even more frequently, the classroom instruction is found lacking in challenging and relevant content. Indeed, students frequently find greater stimulation in the field experience, not necessarily because of the quality of the instruction which is given in that setting, but simply because it provides an exposure to the realities of social issues and an opportunity for action.

Greater integration of class and field instruction, a process now apparently well under way, may therefore be secondary to the larger issues of the content of the curriculum, both in class and field. At the time of the survey, schools were beginning to feel student pressures. These have since become more insistent and well-organized. The major targets of student criticism were: (1) the lack of sufficient emphasis on social action, (2) the over-emphasis on what they viewed as "traditional social work content" in the c.o. curriculum, and (3) the neglect of other areas of knowledge they considered more important, such as political science, economics, urban affairs, and social philosophy. Community organization practice courses were criticized as lacking in depth and being based on inadequate concepts and literature. One of the most consistent comments was the desire for greater freedom and more options in pursuing individualized study programs that would meet their interests more adequately.

FACULTY

The c.o. concentration shares with all of social work education the problem of a severe shortage of faculty. While the problem may be no more serious in community organization than in other sections of the curriculum, it is aggravated by the rapid growth of the concentration and the great changes in the content of the program. The rise in c.o. enrollment, the introduction of c.o. courses or concentrations in many schools for the first time, the introduction of new concepts from the social sciences into the teaching of community organization, and the rapid appearance of new practice settings are some of the major factors which complicate the issues of staffing. The problems are both quantitative and qualitative.

At the present time, faculty are recruited both from academic and practice backgrounds. While there is general agreement that both advanced theoretical and research training and substantial experience in practice are highly desirable, schools are rarely able to find all these qualities in available candidates. At the time of the Project's survey, the shortages were so severe that there was no clear trend in regard to preference for one or another type of background. Schools adapted themselves to the limited choices available to them.

Two types of faculty members, however, tend to predominate. One is the seasoned practitioner who is relatively new to teaching; the other, the younger faculty member with advanced education, but with relatively little community organization practice experience. As doctoral programs expand, there is a slow growth in a third type—experienced practitioners who obtain advanced degrees and then enter teaching for the first time. A fourth type of faculty member is the experienced teacher who has taught previously in other sequences, such as group work, policy, or administration, and moves into the teaching of community organization either as the result of the development of his own interests or in response to the needs of the school, or both.

To the extent that a trend is discernible, it seems to be in the direction of stressing the academic component, at least in regard to the teaching of classroom courses. In the great majority of cases among the schools that were surveyed, classroom instructors had earned their doctorates or were enrolled in doctoral level studies. In many instances, the doctorates are not in social work. Even those that are in social work do not necessarily contain a specialization in community organization. They may be based on theoretical and research studies with as much or even more relevance to other social work methods as to community organization.

Emphasis on the Ph.D. points to the conscious effort on the part of schools to bring a more theoretical emphasis to the teaching of community organization and to integrate the school's overall program more fully into the academic framework of the university. As that process continues, it brings into sharp focus the general issues of relationship between theory and practice, as well as the integration between classroom courses and field instruction.

The relationship between classroom instructors and field instructors poses a problem of faculty organization in the school. Are both class and field instructors to be part of the academic community? How should their responsibilities and positions differ? Several different patterns now exist, sometimes more than one in a given school.

At one pole, there is full integration of classroom and field instruction within a single faculty. All faculty are full-time and they all have threefold responsibilities: classroom teaching, supervision of field instruction units, and advising and administrative responsibilities. This pattern is still quite rare.

More typical is a faculty made up entirely of full-time members and clearly divided into two types—classroom instructors and field instructors. The latter may supervise field instruction units operated directly by the school or carry liaison responsibilities to field work placements and agency-based field instructors. A common difficulty in this pattern emerges from the status differential between the two categories of faculty members. The classroom instructors tend to have doctorates in hand or in process, are eligible for tenure, and have full faculty status in the university. The field instructors, while enjoying status within the school of social work, may not be able to qualify for the equivalent status in the larger academic community.

Most prevalent at the time of collecting this information was the more traditional model of faculty organization which is based on a coordinator of field instruction who is a full-time faculty member and who works with part-time field instructors who are generally agency personnel, recruited and trained by the director of field instruction. While they may have nominal faculty status, they are agency employed. Occasionally, they may receive a token stipend from the university.

A major problem in this approach stems from the lack of clarity in the distribution of responsibilities between the faculty member responsible for field instruction in the c.o. sequence and the overall school director of field instruction. Who is to determine the suitability of certain agencies for placement of students and the appropriateness of particular individuals as field instructors? The criteria for the selection of acceptable field placements in the other methods are frequently inapplicable to community organization. Community organization is practiced in settings which do not necessarily employ social workers, where methods and strategies are not typical of other social work approaches, and which may lie outside the traditional parameters of the welfare field.

Usually c.o. field instructors have few concerns in common with field instructors in casework and group work. "When we get together, it's a disaster," remarked the chairman of one c.o. sequence; "Our c.o. field instructors are usually agency executives involved in such disparate activities that they have little enough in common with each other. They won't sit still in meetings geared to casework practitioners." At another school, it was impossible to bring c.o. field instructors together as they had so little in common. One was a Democratic mayor, one a Republican state representative, the others included a migrant farm organizer who spoke only halting English, an MSW from a settlement house, an indigenous organizer for a welfare clients organization, a welfare council director, and an architect.

Most of the schools develop "mixes" of different patterns of faculty structure and assignments. No school is fully satisfied with its present arrangement, and all those with which the Project has had extensive contact indicated continuing re-examination of these issues.

RELATIONSHIP OF THE C.O. SEQUENCE TO THE TOTAL SCHOOL PROGRAM

It seems an understatement to say that the introduction of new c.o. sequences in recent years has created many tensions. A new sequence may result in polarization of the faculty. At one of the schools visited, a casework instructor expressed concern that the c.o. faculty were teaching their students inappropriate and "unethical" ways of conducting themselves. A more commonly heard criticism had to do with the rapidity with which c.o. faculty was moving into new areas. The direction of the movement may have been considered good, but it was too rapid for other departments and other faculty members to keep up. Often the rapidity of change is a strategic decision. "If we were going to be really innovative we had to make the basic structural changes in our first two years," reported the chairman of a new sequence. Yet excessively rapid change may result in alienation and separation from the rest of the curriculum.

On the other hand, the introduction of a new c.o. sequence has also served as an opportunity for re-examination and change on the part of the entire school, as indicated in the following comments:

> It points out which courses are worthwhile, which ones are dead wood, and which ones need changing.
>
> It makes more rapid integration of social science materials into other courses (an integration which might have come about eventually but not as rapidly).
>
> It brings back into sharp focus the issues of generic vs. two or multi-track curricula.
>
> It provides new and exciting options for students in terms of new courses and new role models.

A number of unresolved issues were identified in regard to the relationship between the course content in the community organization and other sequences. There are two aspects to this issue: (1) the integration of social science, research, social policy, and other social work methods into the c.o. concentration; and (2) the integration of c.o. content into the other practice methods. Many questions are raised about these relationships, but no consistent patterns have emerged.

During the lifetime of the Project, there was a tendency for curricula in schools of social work to become less prescribed and to permit more exemptions from general courses (if competence in the area could be demonstrated). A wider choice of electives within the school of social work and sometimes also in other departments is also prevalent. The result of this trend makes it possible for c.o. concentrators to select certain courses in other sequences applicable to their needs while foregoing others. There are some schools where no particular sequence of behavioral science is required of all students. Instead, c.o. concentrators can select among a number of behavioral science offerings which are considered relevant. However, this is far from general, and most schools still have a substantial number of core requirements that are common to students in all the methods. At most schools, all students are also required to take one or more introductory methods courses outside of their own concentrations. At some schools, all students take a "general methods" seminar.

The variety of approaches used to introduce students to other methods has more of a "catch as catch can" aspect to it than any sound logic. Part of the prevailing confusion arises out of an indecision at many schools about whether community organization is to be regarded as a method or as a field. Should non-c.o. students be taught *about* community organization, or *how to practice* community organization? Are there appropriate c.o. tasks that all caseworkers must prepare to undertake? If so, where are such methods to be taught—within a casework course or in a "c.o. for caseworkers" course?

An interesting side issue pertains to new relationships between schools of social work and other units at the university. With the development of new c.o. programs, relationships are being formed with schools of law, graduate political science departments, urban studies centers, schools of planning and architecture, departments of international relations and government affairs. In a number of cases, social work faculty hold joint appointments or teach in other schools, and instructors in other schools teach courses at the school of social work. At times, c.o. students and faculty have shown more interest in segments of other professions than in other specializations within social work. This has added to the tensions within their own schools.

There seems to be no question that such interdisciplinary relationships will expand in line with general trends in all the human service fields. As yet these developments are at an incipient stage. Their full implications are not yet apparent. Only as new sequences take shape do the policy issues crystallize. "Does this (c.o.) sequence actually belong in a school of social work?" was a question posed by faculty members in other sequences during the Project's early days. It has been dealt with in many schools and by many concerned faculty. The question is legitimate, but it might be better phrased. "Does this sequence belong in *our* school of social work?" indicates the responsibility of each school to determine its specific focus within an expanding range of social work practice forms. Most schools have answered affirmatively.

PART II
CURRICULUM CONTENT: FOUNDATION AREAS

Introduction

THE FOLLOWING THREE CHAPTERS present recommendations for content in the foundation areas of social science, social research, social welfare, and social policy.

As indicated in the preliminary overview, the distinction between foundation and practice areas is based essentially on the degree to which relevant knowledge has or has not been integrated into practice. In the foundation areas, students are expected to become acquainted with areas of knowledge that they will draw on and, hopefully, add to as practitioners, but which they shall have to integrate into practice in their own way.

The aim of the foundation courses should be to provide the student with enough grounding in each of the areas so that he can be sophisticated in following the literature after leaving school. The courses should also provide an experience in performing the tasks of adaptation from background knowledge to practice—an ongoing task in which the student will continue to engage.

Any foundation area, by definition, may be appropriate for all social work students, not only for c.o. concentrators. The content that we have recommended is, however, geared to the particular needs of those concentrators, and we have not undertaken to deal with the total subject matter in each of the areas. The degree to which courses need be designed separately for c.o. students will vary with the size of the school and the different kinds of specializations available. It is our general view that the differences might be greatest in the social science area and least important in the social welfare-social policy area, with research somewhere in between and perhaps most variable from school to school.

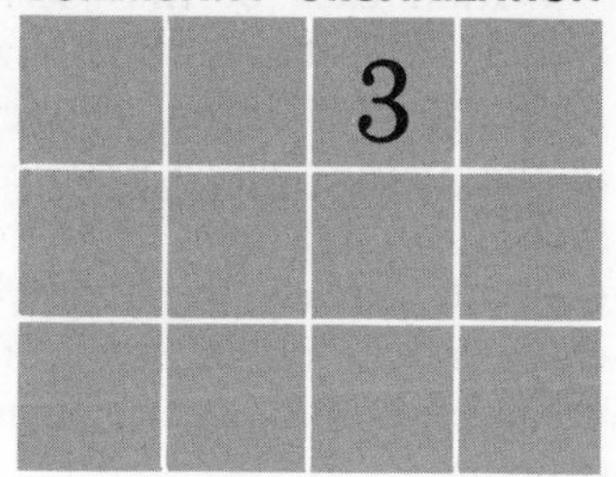

Social Science Foundations

THE RELATIONSHIP of social science knowledge to social work in general and to community organization and social planning in particular is a continuing concern of educators. It has been a major aspect of developments in social work education during the past two decades, in both doctoral and master's level programs.[1] In fact, the prevasiveness of social science content in social work education makes it difficult to describe this emphasis in isolation from other components of the curriculum. In most schools, social science content is used in a variety of ways: as bases for building practice theory, as guides to policy and strategy, or as sources of substantive knowledge relevant to practice.[2] In addition, as pointed out by Thomas, social science background is employed in social work education to promote a scientific stance and a commitment to empirical research.[3]

[1] Orville G. Brim, Jr. (ed.), *Knowledge Into Action: Improving the Nation's Use of the Social Sciences*. Report of the Special Commission on the Social Sciences (Washington, D.C.: Science Foundation, 1969).

[2] Ernest Greenwood, "Social Science and Social Work: A Theory of Their Relationships," *Social Service Review*, 27 (March, 1955), pp. 20-33; and "Relationship of Science to the Practice Professions," *Journal of the American Institute of Planners*, XXIV (July, 1958), pp. 223-232.

[3] Edwin J. Thomas, "Selecting Knowledge from Behavioral Science," in *Building Social Work Knowledge: Report of a Conference* (New York: National Association of Social Workers, 1964), pp. 38-47, also in *Behavioral Science for Social Workers* (New York: Free Press, 1967), pp. 417-424. Also see: Thomas (ed.), *The Socio-Behavioral Approach and Application to Social Work* (New York: Council on Social Work Education, 1967).

Within each of the social science disciplines there are a number of specific subject areas that have particular relevance to social work practice. Although they cannot be viewed as "practice theory," they constitute the ground within which practical experience in community organization and social planning can begin to plant its theoretical roots. Some familiar examples already represented in existing curricula at various schools include, among others: group dynamics, community analysis, urban politics, urban economics, social organization, bureaucracy, and community power structure.[4]

The recommendations of the Curriculum Project in the area of social science are based on the expectation that practice theory and practice knowledge will continue to develop and that, increasingly, the social science component of the curriculum will be incorporated into practice courses. To the extent that this is already the case, the recommended practice courses are designed to reflect the changing and growing body of relevant social science material. Social science foundation courses constitute more general bodies of background knowledge that are considered relevant to practice, although the precise relationships have not yet been articulated.

PREREQUISITES

The recommendations on foundation courses in the social sciences are based on the assumption that most students entering schools of social work at the present time will have a reasonably good undergraduate background in the basic social sciences and that the courses offered at the graduate level can be advanced courses in areas selected for their potential relevance to social planning and c.o. practice. It is therefore recommended, as a general approach, that a background in social science be considered a prerequisite for the c.o. concentration in the master's program. A general guide in this would be to require an undergraduate major in one of the social sciences (anthropology, economics, political science, psychology, social psychology, or sociology) and introductory courses in all or most of them.

This guide, however, should not be applied rigidly. It is suggested as a norm to be used in making decisions, on an individualized basis, in the admissions and advising process. It is recognized that not all applicants necessarily have the background suggested and that a number who lack such background nevertheless may be highly desirable students on the basis of their academic capacity and motivation. While an undergraduate background in the social science is the most likely route by which students will move toward professional social work, other types of undergraduate educa-

---

[4] Roland L. Warren, "Application of Social Science Knowledge to the Community Organization Field," *Journal of Education for Social Work*, 3 (Spring, 1967), pp. 60-72.

tion may very well provide an equally good foundation.[5] Thus, a student who has performed successfully as an undergraduate major in the sciences, mathematics, philosophy, or literature, and who, through subsequent personal development, thinking, and experience decides upon a career in social work, may bring to his graduate work talents and points of view that can be valuable to both his own practice and the development of the field.

Assuming that the primary emphasis in the selection of students is on ability and motivation rather than on specific academic background, schools need to provide some mechanisms for fitting students into the program of advanced courses in the social sciences. There are several ways in which this can be done within the framework of the concept of prerequisites, depending upon the individual student. One is through the waiver of prerequisites on the basis of demonstration that the student has acquired the necessary background without having had formal courses. Some students, although lacking formal course work, may have covered substantial material in social science areas through their own reading and could demonstrate their ability to profit from more advanced courses in a number of areas. Others may be able to reach the minimum required level through a program of supervised reading that can be accomplished within the period between acceptance for admission into the school and the beginning of the first year's work. The determination of the level of the student's competence is probably best left to criteria and methods established by members of the faculty responsible for the teaching of the advanced social science courses, since it is they who know what background is assumed in the construction of their courses.

For those students whose lack of background would seem to require more formal preparation, schools should be able to avail themselves of course offerings within the university that provide an introduction to relevant social sciences, selectively utilizing these to fill the major gaps in the background of specific students. In general, it would seem to be expeditious for schools of social work to use university facilities for this purpose rather than to provide a battery of introductory courses under their own auspices. Particularly relevant are brief courses or pro-seminars that some graduate departments offer to their own students who have deficiencies in their undergaduate studies.

Prerequisites are, by definition, antecedents to the graduate program and not part of the program itself. It would follow, therefore, that any work undertaken by the student to compensate for the lack of prerequisites would not earn academic credit in the graduate program or would be required in addition to the normal graduate credit requirements. Implementation of such a policy will pose some administrative and fiscal problems,

[5] D. Golden, A. Pins, and W. Jones, *Students in Schools of Social Work: A Study of Characteristics and Factors Affecting Career Choice and Practice Concentration* (New York: Council on Social Work Education, 1970).

since it may, in some cases, call for a longer period of study. However, if all of the options outlined above are explored, the number of such instances should be relatively small and the problems minimal. The alternative of tailoring graduate work in the social sciences to the least common denominator of student background should be avoided.

SELECTION OF SOCIAL SCIENCE KNOWLEDGE

The central problem in defining the social science content that is to be included in the curriculum for students concentrating in community organization and social planning is the issue of selection. It is obvious that not all areas of all social sciences are equally relevant to the practice of social work in general or to specific fields of social work practice.[6] Before presenting the Project's recommendations for the content considered most relevant to practice in the light of our proposed framework, we shall comment briefly on the issue of selection itself.

Aptekar, in discussing these issues in relation to doctoral programs, suggests a paradigm for the selection of social science knowledge that calls for the specification of the links among three sets of phenomena:

A. Realms of study—social science areas such as anthropology and sociology, economics political science, etc. as well as professional areas such as medicine, education, and business.

B. Scope of social welfare and social work—social development, welfare and health planning, administration, social work practice, teaching, and research.

C. Educational needs of the student—for theory, factual knowledge, and application.[7]

The test of relevance proposed by Aptekar is the ability to state what a given course in one of the realms of study will contribute—either in the area of theory, factual knowledge, or application—to the ability of the student to cope with specified areas of social welfare and social work practice.

> In the kind of made-to-measure programming which would characterize the course of study for any particular student, if it were worked out in some such manner, the principle of search for relevance and complemen-

---

[6] Alfred Kadushin, "The Knowledge Base of Social Work," in Alfred J. Kahn (ed.), *Issues in American Social Work* (New York: Columbia University Press, 1959), pp. 39-80; Harriet Bartlett, "The Place and Use of Knowledge in Social Work Practice," *Social Work*, 9 (July, 1964), pp. 36-46; LaMar T. Empy, "Sociological Theory and Social Action," *Social Problems*, 12 (Summer, 1966), pp. 56-67.

[7] Herbert Aptekar, *Relevant Knowledge in Advanced Education for Social Work, Papers in Social Welfare*, 16 (Waltham, Mass.: Brandeis University, 1967).

tarity might be concretized. The student in social welfare who is interested in urban renewal might be directed towards courses in practical politics in urban communities. One who is interested in certain types of health programs, however, might be considered to have more need for an understanding of environmental biology. The one who plans a teaching career might find little of pertinence in either type of course, but instead find study in educational psychology of very great value.[8]

Aptekar's paradigm points to the kinds of decisions that need to be made in the process of selection, even though it will not always be possible to translate each specific element of social science knowledge into a corresponding element of social work practice theory or principle. As indicated above, the Project's recommendation is that, to the extent that such complete integration can be achieved, the theoretical elements should be built into the practice courses themselves. Short of such integration, Aptekar's criteria can help to determine whether a given body of knowledge has the potential to contribute to the illumination of practice. The criteria call for a specification not necessarily of the end product but at least of the area in which the contribution is to be sought.

Additional criteria that can be helpful in the process of selection and which supplement the criteria proposed by Aptekar are offered by Thomas, Lauffer, and others.[9] Thomas summarizes the contributions of social science to social work education as follows:

1. Scientific stance;
2. The process of conceptualization or use of conceptual tools;
3. Substantive knowledge about human behavior and social forces;
4. Methodological techniques for empirical research.[10]

For present purposes, points 2 and 3 in the above list are particularly relevant. Issues of research will be dealt with in the next chapter, while the development of a scientific stance is assumed as pervading the entire curriculum. The two realms of content as identified by Thomas in these two points parallel Aptekar's elements of theory and factual knowledge in his listing of the educational needs of the student.[11]

---

[8] *Ibid.*, p. 14.

[9] Thomas, "Selecting Knowledge . . . ," *op. cit.*; Armand Lauffer, "The Social Science Component in Professional Education for Community Organization in Social Work," (New York: Council on Social Work Education [unpublished paper], 1967); and Joseph Bensman, and Arthur Vidich, "Social Theory in Field Research," in Maurice Stein and Arthur Vidich (eds.), *Sociology on Trial* (Englewood Cliffs: Prentice-Hall, Inc., 1963), pp. 163-172.

[10] Thomas, *Socio-Behavioral Approach* . . . (1967), pp. 3-13.

[11] Aptekar, *op. cit.*

The process of conceptualization involves the classification of factual information on the basis of definitions and concepts that are assumed to contribute toward explanation and prediction. Factual information devoid of conceptualization does not yield scientifically based substantive knowledge nor do the concepts without empirical verification. In much of the social science that is potentially relevant to social work practice in community organization and social planning this integration of conceptualization and substantive knowledge has been achieved only in very limited areas. In recognition of this situation, selection for the curriculum should include not only verified substantive knowledge but also conceptual frameworks, while unproven as regards their ability to yield knowledge, still offer ways of looking at phenomena that may enable the practitioner to order his observation in a more useful manner.

Lauffer has suggested a number of different ways in which this process might be performed.[12]

1. The use of closed theoretical systems of the logical-deductive type from which the practitioner may attempt to order and explain all social reality.

2. The more open use of codified and systematically related theories pertaining to a complex of related problems or set of social realities.

3. The successive application of unsystematized theories from various sources, used sequentially for heuristic purposes.

In social work education today there are probably few proponents for the first approach, and there are no such systems available except possibly Freudian theory and Marxist theory in their classical forms. However, there may very well be in the faculties of schools of social work proponents of both the second and third approaches and wide differences of opinion among them.

Codification, the second approach, has much to recommend it. It does not presuppose a grand theory for either the social sciences or for the profession, nor does it limit itself to the confines of a personality system, a social system, or a cultural system. It is developed around a concern about a complex of problems, such as those that typically form the focus of certain forms of practice, for example, family instability, group disintegration or anomie, poverty, delinquency, etc. It then goes on to examine, for their usefulness and relevance, the specific and discrete theories that have been used to explain or inform action with regard to these problems. In making comparisons, or identifying overlaps and convergencies, different levels of generalization and different perspectives are codified into paradigms and models that permit a more comprehensive point of view. The new perspective is then presented for the practitioner to judge whether or not it is useful in problem solving.

---

[12] Lauffer, *op. cit.* The following discussion is a summary of Lauffer's paper.

In recent years, this approach has been reflected in the use of theories about "opportunity," "powerlessness," and the "culture of poverty" to provide a conceptual framework for community action programs.

There are, however, some distinct disadvantages to this approach. Once a set of concepts has been codified, there is a tendency to limit the perspectives to which the student is exposed. Problems and practice methods tend to be defined increasingly by the codified theoretical paradigm, which may lead to consistency in practice, but at the price of limiting the practitioner's ability to experiment and to discover new dimensions of the problems at hand. Systematic or codified theory is general, and this is its advantage. But practice problems are situational. They are specific, and must be dealt with in specific and individual terms.

The heuristic and unsystematized approach begins with the specification of a particular problem, not simply an awareness of a complex of problems. The problem at hand, for example, might be a growing disparity between an agency's stated goals (those specified in its mandate) and the way in which it actually directs the use of its resources. The precipitating factor might be vocal demands for change in services by a potential or actual client group. The practitioner, using a heuristic approach, would begin by asking himself what he knows empirically about the particular situation, and then what knowledge or theory from other sources might make it possible to comprehend and order the data and to direct the gathering of more data where necessary.

He might go to Selznick, for instance, for examples of organization penetration and cooptation, to Etzioni for insights about the disparity between ideal and real goals, or for understanding how organizations institute compliance.[13] Blau and Scott might inform him of how the principal beneficiaries of an organization act to control it, while Thompson and Levine *et al.* might further inform him of the inter-organizational exchange processes.[14] Price might offer propositions on the influence of external factors on the organization's effectiveness, and Warren's analysis might lead him to search out the sources of horizontal and vertical inputs and their effect on the choice of consensus as opposed to conflict strat-

---

[13] Philip Selznick, "An Approach to a Theory of Bureaucracy," *American Sociological Review*, VIII (February, 1943), pp. 47-54; "Foundations of the Theory of Organizations," *American Sociological Review*, XIII (February, 1948), pp. 25-35; *TVA and the Grassroots* (Berkeley: University of California Press, 1949); and also Amitai Etzioni, *A Comparative Analysis of Complex Organization* (New York: Free Press, 1961); and *A Sociological Reader and Complex Organizations* (New York: Holt, Rinehart and Winston, 1969, second edition).

[14] Peter Blau and W. Richard Scott, *Formal Organizations: A Comparative Approach* (San Francisco: Chandler Publishing Co., 1962); and Sol Levine and Paul E. White, "Exchange as a Conceptual Framework for the Study of Interorganizational Relationships," *Administrative Science Quarterly*, 5 (March, 1961), pp. 583-601.

egies.[15] Banfield and Wilson might direct him to new sources of personal influence and Katz and Lazarsfeld to those of political influence; Merton might lead him to focus on alienation, ambivalence, and the latent functions of changing goals; while Gouldner and Argyris, in different ways, might lead him to examine the behavior of the actors within the agency.[16]

Thus, different theories are used heuristically, rather than formally, in successive fashion, each yielding different data, each suggesting different strategies. As new data and new insights are evoked, the problem tends to be reformulated until the formulation becomes operational—that is, until the researcher-practitioner-planner can use it to undergird and direct his action strategy. The theories may still be re-used at this point to ask how an action strategy might have differed had it been informed by a different theoretical perspective. Thus, while the problem tends to be modified by successive applications of theory, even the final formulation remains tentative, an alternative preferred to others but not the only possible action strategy.

The "heuristic" approach to the use of unsystematic theory has a number of inherent limitations. First, very few theories yield more than a limited number of plausible explanations. Most are helpful, at best, in the conceptual and analytic phases of problem-solving. Secondly, their very specificity and situationally bound perspective give them limited usefulness in producing generalizations about phenomena or in the formulation of practice principles.

The experienced teacher and practioner will note that there are great similarities between the use of unsystematic theories and the use of a codified theoretical perspective. Both have heuristic values, yield follow-up data, and enable the practitioner to conceptualize the problem prior to strategy formulation. Both also have their hazards and limitations. For purposes of curriculum building, codification runs the risk of over-selectivity, while the less systematic approach offers little guidance for making choices. While it provides a useful stance towards knowledge, it offers few specifications of relevance for practice.[17]

---

15 James L. Price, *Organizational Effectiveness: An Inventory of Propositions* (Homewood, Ill.: Richard D. Irwin, Inc., 1968); and Roland L. Warren, *The Community in America* (Chicago: Rand McNally & Co., 1963).

16 Edward C. Banfield and James Q. Wilson, *City Politics* (Cambridge, Mass.: Harvard University Press, 1963); Elihu Katz and Paul F. Lazarsfeld, *Personal Influence* (Glencoe, Ill.: Free Press, 1955); Robert K. Merton, *Social Theory and Social Structure* (revised edition, New York: Free Press, 1957), and Merton *et al.* (eds.), *Reader in Bureaucracy* (New York: Free Press, 1952); Alvin W. Gouldner, *Patterns of Industrial Bureaucracy* (New York: Free Press, 1954), and *Studies in Leadership* (New York: Harper and Row, 1950); Chris Argyris, *Integrating the Individual and the Organization* (New York: John Wiley & Sons, 1964), *Interpersonal Competence and Organizational Effectiveness* (Homewood, Ill.: Richard D. Irwin, Inc., 1962), and "The Individual and Organization: Some Problems of Mutual Adjustment," *Administrative Science Quarterly*, II (June, 1957), pp. 1-24.

17 Alvin W. Gouldner, "Theoretical Requirements of the Applied Social Sciences,"

The search for a unified theoretical perspective and the grouping or codification of theories pertaining to certain areas of practice will continue. Some social work educators will continue to search for a unified theory base that will enable their students to come away with some perspective they can call social work's. Similar attempts are in evidence in the social science disciplines and across disciplinary lines.[18] The curriculum should reflect these efforts, while avoiding premature theoretical closure that may lead to practice doctrine rather than practice theory.

For a final note on the issue of selecting social science knowledge, we can refer again to Thomas, who suggests some preliminary and provisional criteria.[19]

1. Content relevance—referring to the subject matter and the level of human aggregation to which it is addressed (individual, group, organization, community, society).
2. Knowledge power—which can be determined according to three features: validity, predictive potency, and variable or explanatory potency.
3. Referent features—that is, to what in the real world is the knowledge applicable; how accessible is this empirical indicator to action approaches; and to what extent is it manipulable, what is the cost of that manipulation, and its ethical implications.

In the recommendations that follow, criteria of content relevance and applicability have played a prominent part. The issue of "knowledge power" is an important consideration to which the student must be exposed in the sense of being educated to identify the level of knowledge with which he is dealing and to look for more adequate verification of propositions offered as a basis for action strategies. This should not preclude, however, his exposure to untested propositions and his tentative use of theories that still lack adequate verification.

A COMPARATIVE NOTE

The problems of selection are not unique to social work.[20] As part of the work of the Project, a limited study was made by Zalinger of the social science components in the curriculum of a number of schools in the

---

American Sociological Review, 22 (February, 1957), pp. 92-103. Also in W. G. Bennis, *et al.* (eds.), *The Planning of Change* (New York: Holt, Rinehart and Winston), pp. 83-95.

[18] Eugene J. Meehan, *Contemporary Political Thought: A Critical Study* (Homewood, Ill.: Dorsey, 1967); and Mustafa Sherif and Carolyn W. Sherif, *Groups in Harmony and Tension* (New York: Harper and Row, 1953).

[19] Thomas, "Selecting Knowledge . . ." (1964).

[20] Henry C. Hightower, "Planning Theory in Contemporary Professional Education," *Journal of the American Institute of Planners*, XXXV (September, 1969), pp. 326-329.

Boston area.[21] While he found that there was relatively little teaching of basic social science courses as such, there was a large volume of courses on specific topics or sub-fields within the social sciences that met the needs of the particular school. In general, these offerings conformed to the two major criteria suggested in the Project's recommendations—namely, that they be at an advanced rather than introductory level, and that they be selected on the basis of relevance to practice.

The offerings were found to be of two general types. One type represented a specific area in a specific social science. For example, group dynamics is taught very widely in professional schools concerned with preparation of students for supervision and administration. Many schools teach selected topics in social psychology or aspects of human growth and development that are pertinent to a particular program (e.g., child development in some programs of schools of nursing). In this type of course the professional school is not necessarily re-fashioning the social science area to its needs, but simply exposing students to an existing body of social science knowledge that it considers useful for their professional education.

The second type of course is quite different. Here, a deliberate attempt is made to integrate elements of social science knowledge, usually across discipline lines, into a foundation course geared to the specific field of practice. For example, one of the schools of education offers a course entitled Social Foundations of Education that is based for the most part on an anthropological approach and develops the implications for education of such topics as culture, class, and socialization.

While the second type of course would necessarily be given within the professional school itself, the specialized course in various disciplines may be found both in the professional schools and in university departments. Many patterns were found within the small number of schools examined. Schools varied both as to the numbers of social science offerings that students were required to take and as to the number provided under their own auspices, through joint offerings with other departments, or by allowing credit for courses taken in other departments.

Also of interest is Zalinger's finding that most of the professional schools provided a considerable number of distinct programs, sometimes even reflected in different degree titles, representing sub-specializations. Thus, a school of education offers master's degrees in elementary school administration or secondary school administration; a nursing school has programs for clinical specialists, as distinct from a program in administration and supervision, or teaching; and a school of public health has divisions for environmental health, epidemiology, maternal and child health, among others. We shall return to this issue of sub-specialization as it

[21] Alvin D. Zalinger, "The Social Science Component in Professional Education," Community Organization Curriculum Development Project (New York: Council on Social Work Education, 1967) (unpublished paper).

applies to social work at a later point in this report.

While the experience of other professional schools is not necessarily an appropriate guide to curriculum building in social work education (especially in the current period of widespread reexamination of all professional education), it is nevertheless of interest to note that the Project was able to draw upon the experience of other fields in two respects. One was the availability of a number of patterns for the organization of social science offerings; the other was the evidence of flexibility in gearing curriculum to the different needs of students in professional fields that try to encompass a wide range of functions.

RECOMMENDATIONS ON CORE COURSES

Within the framework of the total curriculum, which includes both the integration of some social science concepts into practice courses and the opportunity for students to select advanced courses in various social science disciplines, it is recommended that schools also experiment with the development of core courses in which contributions from various disciplines are brought together as a foundation for practice in community organization and social planning. To the extent that these courses are applicable to other concentrations, they may, of course, be open to all students.[22]

This recommendation is offered with some reservations and cautions stemming from recognition of the difficulty of the task that it involves. No adequate models are available at this time for automatic adoption into the curriculum. Each faculty will therefore need to exercise its own creativity in constructing such courses, should it decide to do so. The recommendation is made in the hope of stimulating faculties to undertake the task, despite the difficulties, because of the benefits that can be derived from such an effort. One of the benefits will be in helping faculties to think through the relationship between areas of knowledge and practice and thus to contribute to the growing body of practice theory. It will provide one of the points at which students can be helped to integrate the learnings which they derive from the disparate areas of social science to which they may be exposed. It will also offer students a direct experience in the different ways in which theory can be related to practice, along the lines discussed above.

A part of this experimentation should include the development of interdisciplinary teams of instructors. However, the core courses should not

[22] For useful earlier proposals relating to social work education more generally see: Bernt H. Lund, "The Teaching of Social Science in Schools of Social Work," *International Social Work*, 3 (January, 1960), pp. 1-8; and Herman D. Stein, "Issues in the Relationships of Social Science to Social Work Education," *International Social Work*, 4 (January, 1961), pp. 10-18.

be conducted by having various lecturers give one or a few sessions on topics in their field of specialization. What is intended, rather, is that two or perhaps three instructors, from different backgrounds, collaborate in constructing and conducting a course that reflects a genuine pooling of their specialized areas of competence into an integrated framework.

At this stage of development, it is the Project's view that the number of core courses should be limited, and that they should constitute a minor rather than the dominant part of the student's learning in relevant social science areas. As a general scheme, it is proposed that two courses be considered, each of which has a relatively distinct central theme. One way of doing this, which will be explicated below, is to divide the subject matter into "macro" and "micro" elements, with one course in *Social Institutions* and another in *Social Behavior*.

In the past, most of the emphasis in the application of social science knowledge to social work practice has been on the behavioral rather than institutional side. That is a natural emphasis in view of the central concern of social work practice with service at the individual and family levels. Thus, the major contributions have come from individual and social psychology which, in our terminology, falls into the area of "micro" social science.

Among the many examples that could be cited, it is sufficient to note the incorporation of role concepts into casework theory, the wide use of small group theory and research in group work and community organizations, and the development of social-behavioral theory as a proposed general framework for social work practice.[23]

It is noteworthy in this connection that the selection of concepts and materials from the social sciences that have both "micro" and "macro" levels has been much heavier on the "micro" side.[24] This has been the case with respect to sociology, anthropology, and political science.[25]

Social work has been interested in that part of anthropology which focuses on the influence of culture on behavior and personality. In the study of formal organizations and bureaucracy, considerable attention has been given to the special problems of the role of the professional within an organization. The study of social change has used primarily the frame-

---

[23] See: Bruce J. Biddle and Edwin J. Thomas (eds.), *Role Theory: Concepts and Research* (New York: John Wiley & Sons, 1966); Marvin Silverman, "An Assessment of Knowledge in Social Group Work Through a Review of the Literature," *Social Work*, 11 (February, 1966), pp. 56-63; Edgar F. Borgatta, "Role and Reference Group Theory" in L. S. Kogan (ed.), *Social Science Theory and Social Work Research* (New York: National Association of Social Workers, 1960); and Thomas (ed.), *The Socio-Behavioral Approach* . . . (1967).

[24] Henry S. Maas, "Use of Behavioral Science in Social Work Education," *Social Work*, 3 (January, 1958), pp. 62-69; and Merlin Tabor and Iris Shapiro, "Social Work and its Knowledge Base: A Content Analysis of the Periodical Literature," *Social Work*, 10 (October, 1965), pp. 100-107.

[25] Grace L. Coyle, *Social Science in the Professional Education of Social Workers* (New York: Council on Social Work Education, 1958).

work of small group theory, thus focusing on planned changed efforts in interpersonal relations rather than on changing organizational systems. Similarly, the gleanings from political science have been primarily in the area of political influence where personal interactions play a major role.

The emphasis on "micro" social science is due not only to the balance of interests within social work but also to the state of development of the social sciences themselves. During the past two decades of social work's "rediscovery" of the social sciences, the emphasis in the latter has been overwhelmingly in the behavioral area. Particularly important is the great expansion of social science research during the same period, very largely within a behavior framework. As a result, there is a vast body of both theoretical and research literature upon which to draw for the "micro" areas, but very much less to call upon in the "macro" fields.[26]

It is only in the very recent period that some reversal has begun to appear. Currently there is a growth of interest and expanding literature that focuses on large-scale social systems rather than on small group interactions or on the individual within the system. Two types of literature are particularly relevant in this connection, both probably reflecting the impact on social science interests of contemporary social problems. One, as typified by Etzioni's *The Active Society*, is a return to an older sociological tradition of studying whole societies, but with the focus on the possibilities and processes of planned social change.[27] Another type of literature, equally relevant to the issues of community organization and social planning, is more substantive and problem oriented.[28] Particularly prevalent are works in the field of urban problems, where various disciplines are drawn upon to contribute to a better understanding of the most critical problems of contemporary American society.[29]

SOCIAL INSTITUTIONS

The central purpose of a course focusing on social institutions would be to help the student understand the systems in which social problems are embedded as well as the processes of change that take place within such systems. General conceptual frameworks for the study of social systems, as represented primarily in the work of Parsons and his col-

---

[26] A. Paul Hare, *Handbook of Small Group Research* (New York: Free Press, 1962); and A. Paul Hare, Edgar F. Borgatta, and Robert F. Bales, *Small Groups: Studies in Social Interaction* (New York: Alfred A. Knopf, 1965, rev. ed.).

[27] Amitai Etzioni, *The Active Society* (New York: Free Press, 1968).

[28] Herbert J. Gans, *People and Plans: Essays on Urban Problems and Solutions* (New York: Basic Books, 1968); and Howard E. Freeman and Wyatt C. Jones, *Social Problems: Causes and Controls* (Chicago: Rand McNally & Co., 1970).

[29] Howard S. Becker, *Social Problems: A Modern Approach* (New York: John Wiley & Sons, 1967); Leonard J. Duhl (ed.), *The Urban Condition* (New York: Basic Books, 1963); Leo F. Schnore and Henry Fagin (eds.), *Urban Research and Policy Planning* (Beverly Hills, Calif.: Sage Publications, 1967); and Gans, *op. cit.*

laborators, are useful in providing paradigms for understanding the attributes of systems such as the allocation of functions and the interrelationship of the whole system and its several parts.[30] One of the functions of the course would be to examine such schemata critically in order to clarify both their contributions and limitations, and also to compare a number of approaches to system analysis that stem from different disciplines.[31] The major focus of the course, however, should not be on conceptual schemata (which might be pursued in depth by some students on an elective basis), but on the substantive knowledge concerning "macro" social systems that can be drawn from the different disciplines.

A framework for the integration of a broad range of social science material in this institutional category (i.e., "macro" level social science) can be found in the study of community, which is a particularly appropriate focus for a foundation course in a professional curriculum for practice in community organization. The concept of community to be employed here is, however, a broader one than the prototype of the rural village or urban neighborhood that has been the focus of most of the work in community organization and community development.[32]

If we look upon the community in Warren's terms as a nexus for "locality relevant" functions within the framework of the larger society to which it is bound both totally and in its different parts in a system of vertical relationships, then materials from different social science disciplines can provide insights for its analysis.[33] Ecology provides a foundation for understanding spatial and temporal factors; demography for understanding the distribution of population characteristics; social structure for viewing the interaction of groups of different characteristics, values, and ideologies; and political and economic analysis for locating the processes

[30] Talcott Parsons, *Structure and Process in Modern Societies* (Glencoe, Ill.: Free Press, 1960).

[31] Robert Chin, "The Utility of System Models and Development Models for Practitioners," in W. G. Bennis (ed.), *The Planning of Change* (New York: Holt, Rinehart and Winston, 1961); Gordon Hearn, *The General Systems Approach: Contributions Toward a Holistic Conception of Social Work* (New York: Council on Social Work Education, 1969); and Gerald Rabow, *The Era of the System: How the Systems Approach Can Help Solve Society's Problems* (New York: Philosophical Library, 1969).

[32] George A. Hillery, Jr., *Communal Organizations: A Study of Local Societies* (Chicago: University of Chicago Press, 1968); and Roland L. Warren (ed.), *Perspectives on the American Community: A Book of Readings* (Chicago: Rand-McNally & Co., 1966).

[33] A few selected sources which seem particularly relevant are: George W. Theodorson, *Studies in Human Ecology* (New York: Harper and Row, 1961); Thomas R. Ford and Gordon F. DeJong (eds.), *Social Demography* (Englewood Cliffs, N. J.: Prentice-Hall, 1970); James M. Beshers, *Urban Social Structure* (New York: Free Press, 1962); Arthus L. Steinchcombe, "Social Structure and Organizations," in James G. March (ed.), *Handbook of Organizations* (Chicago: Rand McNally & Co., 1965), pp. 142-193; and Robert L. Heilbroner (ed.), *Economic Means and Social Ends: Essays on Political Economics* (Englewood Cliffs, N. J.: Prentice-Hall, 1969).

for the allocation of power and the distribution of resources within communities as well as for locating the sources and directions of potential change.

In attempting to understand those aspects of the operation of the economic system which are most relevant to the concerns of social workers in community organization and social planning, a number of key issues should be identified for intensive exploration. One such question is that of income distribution. The course should provide some exposure not only to the facts concerning income distribution and its trends but to the processes in the economic system that determine the nature of income distribution within a society.

Another major issue relates to manpower and employment. The extensive debates that have taken place in the United States concerning the impact of technology upon employment and the difference between "structural" and "frictional" unemployment should be reviewed against the conflicting evidence in order to indicate areas of agreement and disagreement within the field of economics and the methods of analysis that lead to the different positions. The problems of youth employment are particularly important.

A third suggested area relates to the allocation of resources. The course should seek to draw upon economic analysis for guides to the understanding of the relationship between social welfare services and the operation of the market. Recent literature within the field of economics that has emphasized investment in "human resources" and extension of public services represents one point of view that is particularly congenial to the values of social work.[34] It should, however, be examined in relation to alternative viewpoints that argue for greater reliance on market mechanisms. Here, again, the effort should be to understand the basis on which these different positions rest and to separate value judgments from technical decisions.

In the course of examining these issues, it will become clear that all policy choices provide benefits in some areas and costs in others, and involve consideration of which values and whose values are to be given priority at a particular point in time; therefore, no choice can be made strictly on technical grounds. The course should examine how economic decisions are made at present and the extent to which central decisions at the national level act as constraints upon the operations of the economic system in the local community. It should also present various viewpoints on how decisions should be allocated for optimum functioning of the

[34] James N. Morgan, M. H. David, W. J. Cohen, and H. E. Brager, *Income and Welfare in the United States* (New York: McGraw-Hill, 1962); Margaret E. Gordon, *The Economics of Welfare Policy* (New York: Columbia University Press, 1963); and Charles Z. Schultze, *The Politics and Economics of Public Spending* (Washington, D. C.: Brookings Institutions, 1968).

system, and the potential effects on changes in existing mechanisms.

As in the case of the economic system, several key issues in the area of politics would be selected on the basis of their particular relevance to the concerns of practitioners in community organization and social planning.

Perhaps the most fundamental question to be asked in regard to the political system is the way in which it distributes power among the different elements in the population. The questions might be put in the terms used by Lasswell in his classic volume, *Politics: Who Gets What, When, How*.[35] The perspectives of political science and sociology can be brought to bear on these questions. Lehman has analyzed the "macrosociology of power" in terms of two processes—influence and social control.[36] Influence is an upward process turning inter-member power into systemic or political power in the competition for scarce utilitarian resources; social control is a downward process using the coercive resources of power to regulate inter-member power in setting, pursuing, and implementing goals for the entire system.

The linkages between economic power and political power need to be traced as they appear differently on the national scene and in local communities. One of the limitations of the literature on power structure is that it has dealt primarily with power structure at the local community level and in relation to decision-making in matters that are primarily local in scope. There has been less consideration of the ways in which political power is exercised over national decisions. In order to deal with the latter issue it is necessary to examine some of the basic political mechanisms in the country and the ways in which they operate. This refers to political parties, how they are constituted, and how their decisions are influenced. Existence of a considerable body of knowledge concerning voting behavior helps in the understanding of these processes, especially when political behavior is linked with an examination of major groupings in the society and their stratification along class and ethnic lines.[37]

From the sociological disciplines, this course should draw upon the more recent literature alluded to earlier, which deals with larger social systems and substantive social problems. A number of topics are par-

---

[35] Harold D. Lasswell, *Politics: Who Gets What, When, How* (New York: Mentor Books, 1961).

[36] Edward W. Lehman, "Toward a Macrosociology of Power," *American Sociological Review*, 34 (August, 1969), pp. 453-465.

[37] For comprehensive data on voting behavior, see: A. A. Campbell, *et al., The American Voter* (New York: John Wiley & Sons, Inc., 1960). A few recent works dealing with power and influence from somewhat different viewpoints are: Robert A. Nisbet, *Community and Power* (New York: Oxford Universitly Press, 1969); Terry N. Clark, *Community Structure and Decision Making: Comparative Analysis* (San Farncisco: Chandler, 1968); and William A. Gamson, *Power and Discontent* (Homewood, Ill.: Dorsey, 1968).

ticularly relevant. One, for example, is social stratification viewed not in terms of the influence of class on behavior, but in relation to the allocation of resources and power among different segments of the society. Attention should be given to both ethnic groups and social class and to the relationship between them as alternative and complementary determinants of status and power. Another relatively neglected area that belongs within the framework of a course focusing on the analysis of social institutions is migration. The differences between rural and urban communities, and the factors leading to migration from one to the other, need to be explored; also the impact of population movements on social structures and on social problems in areas both of in-migration and of out-migration.

Also, of growing importance, is the issue of social movements, how they are generated, the process of their growth and development, and their role in bringing about social change in major social institutions.[38] The study of social movements should include both the ideological and structural elements, and should be tied into an analysis of the relationship of both to the economic system and to political forces. The study of social movements in terms of their ideologies is based on an analysis of the nature of values and value systems; the processes through which they are generated within the society; and their growth, reinforcement, and change over time. Social movements are, however, not merely the product or expression of ideology. They also represent groupings that have specific locations within the social structure and especially in its economic and political systems. The relationship of social movements to these systems—both as products of the conditions generated by them and as factors for change—are part of this analysis.

SOCIAL BEHAVIOR

In view of the much more extensive development that has taken place in sociology and social psychology in the area of groups and small social systems rather than in larger social structure and total societies, there is a vast body of literature from which to draw for the behavior course.[39] Therefore the problems of selection are more difficult. Such a course must be based upon the development of a limited number of central topics or themes. The suggestions which follow may be too many to encompass within a single course but are offered as possibilities from which the instructor may make choices.

---

[38] For varying social science perspectives on social movements, see: William Bruce Cameron, *Modern Social Movements: A Sociological Outline* (New York: Random House, 1966); Barry McLaughlin (ed.), *Studies in Social Movements: A Psychological Perspective* (New York: Free Press, 1969); and Rudolf Heberle, *Social Movements: An Introduction to Political Sociology* (New York: Appleton-Century-Crofts, 1969).

[39] One example of a selection of materials for social work teaching is: Herman D. Stein and Richard A. Cloward (eds.), *Social Perspectives on Behavior* (Glencoe, Ill.: Free Press, 1958).

A starting point might be a consideration of the central problem in social psychology and indeed in the social sciences generally—the relationship of the individual to society. The classical literature in sociology has dealt with this problem, and it remains an unsettled issue parallel to some of the classical problems in metaphysics and epistemology, which have recurred through the centuries in different forms.[40] There are, nevertheless, a number of major philosophical orientations that can be reviewed as a way of identifying the theoretical problems and providing a framework for the examination of more specific topics. The kinds of questions to be clarified in this general review are: the nature of "social facts," the problem of reductionism in the social sciences, the meaning of explanation at the social level, and the continuity or discontinuity between the study of individual behavior and the study of group or organizational behavior.[41]

A more empirical basis for examining these issues can be found in two substantive areas, both of which are highly relevant to practice in community organization and social planning. The first is the general field of socialization within which special attention can be given to deviant behavior. The second area is the field of small group theory and research that has yielded a body of substantive knowledge concerning the processes of interaction among individuals within a group setting.

Consideration of socialization and deviant behavior can be organized in relation to the different stages of the individual life cycle. Classical theories relating to the socialization process in the early years of infancy and childhood have been supplemented recently with additional concepts and studies that view the socialization process as continuing throughout the individual's life.[42] Erikson's widely used framework of the tasks to be solved at different stages of the life cycle provides a basis of examining the elements in the social structure that impinge upon these different stages.[43] Merton's interpretation of anomie provides a general orientation for understanding the relationship of social structure to socialization and attempts to explain deviant behavior in terms of dysfunctional elements within the social structure.[44] His seminal ideas have produced a body of

---

[40] Philip H. Phenix, *Realms of Meaning: A Philosophy of the Curriculum of General Education* (New York: McGraw-Hill, 1964), pp. 126-137.

[41] Neil J. Smelser and William T. Smelser (eds.), *Personality and Social Systems* (New York: John Wiley & Sons, Inc., 1963).

[42] Orville G. Brim, Jr., and Stanton Wheeler, *Socialization after Childhood* (John Wiley & Sons, Inc., 1966); John A. Clausen (ed.), *Socialization and Society* (Boston: Little & Co., 1968); and Nevitt Sanford, *Self and Society: Social Change and Individual Development* (New York: Atheneum, 1966). For discussion of social problems in a life cycle framework, see: Freeman and Jones, *op. cit.*

[43] Erik H. Erikson, *Childhood and Society* (New York: W. W. Norton, 1963), 2nd edition.

[44] Merton, *Social Theory* . . . (1957).

theory and research on deviant behavior that has been influential in the formulation of action programs.[45]

From this broad view of the interaction between the individual and the social structure, a review of selected material from the study of small groups can help bring into sharper focus the specific processes of group formation and functioning.

The study of small groups includes knowledge as to the ways in which groups are formed and the relationship of their formation and continuity to the individual needs of their members. The processes whereby groups identify their goals and create norms and values have been the subject of some of the major work in social psychology and the course should provide an opportunity to examine the contributions of such social psychologists as Sherif and Lewin.[46]

Another major subject is the distribution of roles within the group and the reciprocal relationship between role behavior and group performance. Particularly relevant here is the extensive work that has been done on the subject of leadership.[47] The view of leadership that has emerged from small group theory and research illuminates the interrelationship between individual personality and social processes.[48] The research makes it clear that leadership is not a single concept but takes various forms depending upon the group situation. Equally important are the findings that demonstrate various types and styles of leadership and their relative effectiveness under different sets of conditions.[49]

It is a natural progression to move from the study of small groups to consideration of the subject of formal organizations. Here, too, there is a body of both theory and empirical research that has yielded a number of important substantive findings.[50] One of the leading themes in this area is the relationship between the formal and informal structure within organizations and the ways in which these bear on the functions of the organizations and influence their performance. Merton's theoretical formulation concerning "manifest" and "latent" functions has been explicated

---

[45] Richard A. Cloward and Lloyd E. Ohlin, *Delinquency and Opportunity, A Theory of Delinquent Gangs* (Glencoe, Ill.: Free Press, 1960).

[46] Sherif and Sherif, *Groups in Harmony* . . . (1953); and Kurt Lewin, *Field Theory in Social Science* (New York: Harper and Row, 1951).

[47] Cecilia Gibb, "Leadership," in Gardner Lindzey (ed.), *Handbook of Social Psychology*, Vol. II (New York: Wesley Publishing Co., 1954).

[48] George C. Homans, *Social Behavior, Its Elementary Forms* (New York: Harcourt, Brace and World, 1961).

[49] Linton C. Freeman, *Patterns of Local Community Leadership* (Indianapolis, Ind.: Bobbs-Merrill Co., 1968).

[50] Blau and Scott, *Formal Organizations* . . . (1962); and Daniel Katz and Robert L. Kahn, *The Social Psychology of Organizations* (New York: John Wiley & Sons, Inc., 1966).

through the study of organizational processes. The extent to which the goals of formal organizations are achieved or displaced is related to differences between these functional levels.[51] Additional knowledge is also available concerning the ways in which communication takes place within organizations and the relationship of communication to organizational decision-making and performance.[52]

Another major theme is the analysis of the functions of formal organizations within society and their place in systems of relationships involving individuals, primary groups, formal organizations, and larger social systems. One can begin with the classic definition of bureaucracy developed by Weber and trace modifications in that theory that have resulted from recent research.[53] One of the interesting lines of inquiry has been the work of Litwak and his associates in studying the distinctions between the functions of formal organizations and primary groups.[54] Another recent development of particular import for community organization is the focus on interorganizational relationships.[55] In this area, new concepts have been introduced that deal with additional dimensions that arise in the interaction among formal organizations.

Finally, a course on social behavior might also draw upon the work in political science that emphasizes behavior rather than institutional aspects. Extensive research in voting behavior has produced substantive findings on the ways that people in different positions within the social structure behave politically.[56] This research has also revealed some of the processes

---

[51] Merton, *op. cit.*

[52] Eugene Litwak, "Policy Implications in Communication Theory with Emphasis on Group Factors," *Education for Social Work, Proceedings of the Seventh Annual Program Meeting* (New York: Council on Social Work Education, 1959); and Harold Guetzkow, "Communications in Organizations," in James G. March (ed.), *Handbook of Organizations* (Chicago: Rand McNally & Co., 1965).

[53] Max Weber, *The Theory of Social and Economic Organization*, translated by A. M. Henderson and Talcott Parsons, with an introduction by Talcott Parsons (New York: Free Press, 1947); and Peter Blau, *Bureaucracy in Modern Society* (New York: Random House, 1956).

[54] Eugene Litwak and Henry J. Meyer, "A Balance Theory of Coordination between Bureaucratic Organizations and Community Primary Groups," *Administrative Science Quarterly, II* (June, 1966), pp. 33-58; Eugene Litwak and Jose Figueira, "Technological Innovation and Theoretical Functions of Primary Groups and Bureaucratic Structures," *American Journal of Sociology*, 73 (March, 1968), pp. 468-481; and Eugene Litwak and Ivan Szelenvi, "Primary Group Structures and Their Functions: Kin, Neighbors and Friends," *American Sociological Review*, 34 (August, 1969), pp. 465-481.

[55] Levine and White, "Exchange as a Conceptual Framework . . ." (1961); and Roland L. Warren, "The Interorganizational Field as a Focus of Investigation," *Adminstrative Science* Quarterly, Vol. 12, No. 3 (December, 1967), pp. 396-419.

[56] Herbert Hyman, *Political Socialization: A Study in the Psychology of Political Behavior* (New York: Free Press, 1969).

whereby voting behavior in the larger society is influenced.[57]

It would be possible in this section of the course to bring together several strands of related subject matter that have been developed in different branches of social science, primarily political science, sociology, and social psychology. Thus, sociological studies have explored the ways in which attitudes and behavior with respect to larger social issues are mediated through patterns of personal influence.[58] Among the useful products of this research are typologies, such as the division of community leaders and sources of influence into "cosmopolitans" and "locals."[59] A contribution of the literature on community power structure is the identification of the basis within the social structure and in the control of resources upon which personal influence may rest.[60] Also of relevance here is the material from social psychology that deals with processes of communication and attempts to identify the factors that determine how a message is perceived, accepted, acted upon, or rejected.[61]

SOCIAL SCIENCE ELECTIVES

It is obvious from the range of content suggested for the core courses that even a limited number of topics cannot be explored in great depth. The risk of superficiality is high in such an approach and one must guard against this. The experimentation should make clear that core courses are not meant as substitutes for advanced courses in specific social science areas but as supplements to them. Obtaining requisite depth in specific social science area is one of the objectives of the curriculum. The student concentrating in community organization and social planning, therefore, should be offered social science electives on as wide and flexible a basis as possible within the resources available to the school. A deliberate effort also should be made to encourage students to take advantage of courses available in other departments of the university.

The outline of the proposed core courses as presented above suggests

---

57 Robert J. Pranger, *The Eclipse of Citizenship* (New York: Holt, Rinehart and Winston, 1968).

58 Dorwin Cartwright, "Influence, Leadership, Control," in James G. March (ed.), *Handbook of Organizations* (Chicago: Rand McNally & Co., 1965); and Katz and Lazarsfeld, *Personal Influence* (1955).

59 Merton, *Social Theory . . .* (1957); Gouldner, "Theoretical Requirements . . ." (1957); and Alvin W. Gouldner, "Cosmopolitans and Locals: Toward an Analysis of Latent Social Roles," *Administrative Science Quarterly*, II (December, 1957), pp. 281-306; II (March, 1958), pp. 444-480.

60 Nelson Polsby, *Community Power and Political Theory* (New Haven, Conn.: Yale University Press, 1963).

61 Litwak, "Policy Implications . . ." (1959); and Hugh Dalziel Duncan, *Communication and Social Order* (New York: Oxford University Press, 1969).

the areas in which appropriate electives might be located. The division between social institutions and social behavior affords a framework for making meaningful selections. Individualization of student programs is recommended to the end that electives may be related to the specific interests and career goals of the student. It is generally desirable that a student have some exposure both to "macro" and "micro" levels of social science material since the practice of community organization and social planning as projected in these curriculum recommendations presupposes concern with all levels of social systems. However, different students may very well elect to specialize in one area while others may wish to pursue both to a relatively equal extent. All such options should be available. The following list is a suggestive rather than an exhaustive indication of the kinds of courses that might be available as electives under the two broad categories suggested for the organization of social science material.

Social Institutions:	*Social Behavior:*
Urban economics	Deviant behavior
Urban politics	Personality and culture
Race and ethnic relations	Patterns of socialization
Social change	Group dynamics
Social movements	Small group interaction

Beyond such specific subjects there may be more general courses that cut across substantive areas within individual social science disciplines and offer broader conceptual frameworks that are potentially relevant to practice. It is possible, for example, that certain courses outside the traditional social science departments but located in departments of philosophy or history or in interdisciplinary institutes may contribute usefully to the student's preparation for practice. In this connection, it should be recalled that the educational task is to prepare students not only for existing practice situations but to enable them to adapt to changing conditions and to explore innovative situations. The challenge is for a continuing search within the educational program for bodies of knowledge and ways of thinking which, even though they cannot be related immediately to practice, nevertheless provide the student with additional stimuli toward the development of his own thinking. Thus, for example, it might be desirable for some students to gain a grounding in philosophical and mathematical frameworks for further study in systems analysis, communication, and decision-making.

There are obviously limits to what an individual student can absorb within a two-year program and to the amount and range of subject matter that even a highly flexible program can encompass. Limitations on the number and scope of electives will be imposed necessarily by the facilities that are available in the university, by the interests of faculty members, and by their capacity to relate themselves to other university resources and to the interests and abilities of their students. The central purpose of the foundation electives should be to stretch all of these potentialities as far as possible, but on a planned and individualized basis and within the realistic limitations imposed by a professional program.

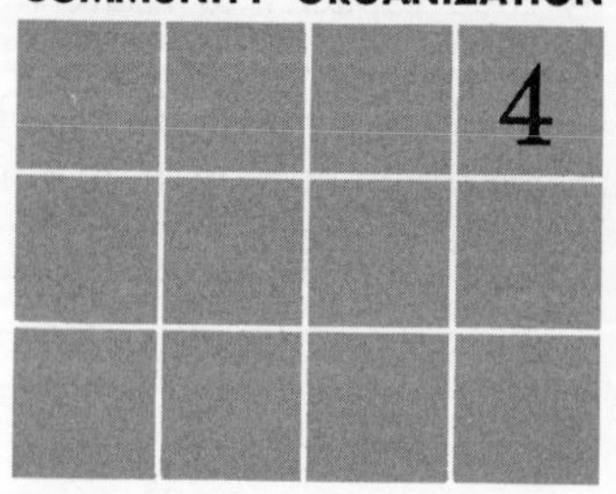

Social Research

THE RECOMMENDATIONS of the Project with respect to the inclusion of social research as a foundation area parallel those that were offered in regard to social science. As in Chapter 3, the emphasis is placed on advance courses, with topics selected for their potential relevance to the specific functions of community organization and social planning.

The distinction made between "foundation" material and that which is built into practice itself pertains to the consideration of research as well as to the preceding discussion of social science. The practice of community organization and social planning involves considerable use of fact-finding and employs a variety of research techniques that will be reflected in the recommendations for practice courses. The present chapter deals, however, with more general background work in social research that is of potential usefulness and relevance to practice although not an integral part of it.[1]

Sophistication in the area of research appears to be one of the clearly indicated needs for practitioners who are called upon to deal with problems of organization, policy, and planning. It may be argued that similar sophistication is desirable for all students. Schools that adopt this position may very well establish a uniform social research sequence for all students, regardless of their method of concentration. As in the previous chapter,

[1] Peter Rossi, "Theory, Research and Practice in Community Organization," in C. Adrian, *Social and Community Action* (East Lansing, Mich.: Michigan State University Press, 1960).

the issue will be approached in this report from the point of view of students concentrating in community organization and social planning, with whatever special focus that seems to require.

Perhaps a further word needs to be said about what is meant by "sophistication" in research. In discussions of the goals of the research sequence in social work education, the position is frequently taken that students should be educated to be "consumers" rather than "producers" of research.[2] A sharp distinction of this type does not seem useful for the community organization concentration.[3] The level of sophistication necessary is one that goes well beyond the ability to read research articles in relevant social science journals and to understand the methodology used, although this goal is important. The practitioner will need to do more than that. Increasingly, his practice is likely to involve him in the planning and organization of research activity in order to deal with practice problems. He needs, therefore, to be experienced in the uses of research and knowledgeable in the relationship of research to policy and administration.[4] One of the responsibilities he will carry in practice is active collaboration with researchers. In order to help formulate research questions, engage in data collection, and supervise researchers, he will need to be able to communicate with them in their own language.

It is doubtful that this type of sophistication can be achieved without direct involvement by the student in learning some specifics of research methodology. To that extent, the goal of the research courses should be to prepare the student to "do" research, and not only to consume it. While the master's program may not be adequate to prepare fully qualified research specialists, it should aim to make it possible for at least some of the students who have the interest and ability to begin a specialization in research that could be pursued both in practice and in later doctoral studies. Research concentrations are still relatively rare in social work master's programs. In the view of this report, research has a place as an area of concentration within the community organization program. In schools that offer research as a separate methods concentration, the research sequence may still be combined with a focus on community organization and social planning.

In setting the "doing" of research as one of the objectives of the students' program, it does not follow that any particular pattern of learning exper-

---

[2] Tony Tripodi, Phillip Fellin, and Henry J. Meyer, *The Assessment of Social Work Research* (Itasca, Ill.: F. E. Peacock, 1969).

[3] Sidney E. Zimbalist, "What Model for Community Welfare Research?" in David Fanshel, *Research in Social Welfare Administration* (New York: National Association of Social Workers, 1962).

[4] David Fanshel (ed.), *Research in Social Welfare Administration* (New York: National Association of Social Workers, 1962).

ience is necessarily prescribed. It leaves open such questions as whether there should be a thesis requirement, and whether, if there is a thesis, it should take the form of an individual or group research project. Different learning experiences may lead to the same goals. More important than the format is the content of the learning experience. The objective should be to provide the student with an opportunity to perform, alone or in collaboration, a number of the crucial steps in standard research methodology. The recommendations on course content that follow are framed with this general purpose in mind.

PREREQUISITES

The observations made earlier concerning prerequisites in the social sciences are also applicable to research. In view of the abilities and backgrounds of students now entering schools of social work, it should be possible to assume more preparation in the research area than has been true in the past. It is therefore desirable to build the curriculum in the master's program on such assumptions, requiring make-up or remedial work for students who do not fit the norms rather than setting the standards at too elementary a level.

The research prerequisite would assume that the student is thoroughly familiar with such fundamentals as the use of scientific method in social research; some of the common types of research methodologies used (surveys, community studies, experiments, etc.); the logic of research design; general statistical concepts such as probability, measures of central tendency and dispersion, and methods of tabular presentation. These prerequisites could be satisfied by two undergraduate courses, one in elementary statistics and one in methods of social research, or by a demonstration of comparable proficiency.

All such topics would of course reappear in the graduate courses, but at a more advanced level and within the context of problems and issues that are of specific concern to various fields of social research.

Specific implementation of prerequisites, as discussed earlier, should take place through the flexible use of a number of alternatives. These may include qualifying examination (if courses have not been taken), short-term make-up courses or tutorials, summer courses, programmed instruction, or the addition of such courses to the students' normal load. In the case of research, it may be necessary to undertake more individualized planning than in other areas, due to the wide range and inconsistency of undergraduate research courses in different colleges. As in the case of social science prerequisites, the best approach would be for the instructors in the research courses in the graduate school of social work to set the specific prerequisites for their courses and to evaluate whether individual students have adequate preparation for them.

CORE COURSE

Assuming the general background as discussed in the above section on prerequisites, the courses within the master's program can focus more specifically on research within the field of social welfare. It is recommended that the curriculum include a basic course in the problems and methods of research in social work and social welfare. This core course will have two central functions: (1) to introduce the students to social work research as a field of activity and to help him understand its functions, problems, and methods of procedure; and (2) to provide the student with a beginning experience in performing some of the activities of social work research. In many instances, such a course will be available within the curriculum for all students and will not require any special provision for those concentrating in community organization.

We are speaking of one course rather than two, although it is possible to divide the content into units that could be organized into separate courses. There would seem to be some advantages in keeping these two objectives bound together within a single course, so that the student learns to use methodology within the context of the problems of the field. The outline of specific content units that follows is based on an integrated approach. It visualizes a single course continuing throughout the year (two semesters or three quarters).

CONTENT

1. *The Scientific Method and Its Applications.* Assuming that the student will have been acquainted as an undergraduate with the basic elements of scientific method and the logic of inquiry that underlies it, these will be reviewed in regard to the special problems of social research.[5] This review will provide an opportunity to examine recurring questions concerning benefits and limitations of the application of models of inquiry developed in the natural and social sciences to the field of social welfare and to the specific problems of applied fields of social action, such as social work.[6]

One aspect of these issues is the relationship of values to knowledge

[5] Abraham Kaplan, *The Conduct of Inquiry: Methodology for Behavior Science* (San Francisco: Chandler, 1964); and Scott Greer, *The Logic of Social Inquiry* (Chicago: Aldine, 1969).

[6] Henry A. Maas, "Use of Behavior Sciences in Social Work Education," *Social Work*, 3 (January, 1958), pp. 62-69; and *Five Fields of Social Service: Reviews of Research* (New York: National Association of Social Workers, 1966); Ernest Greenwood, "Social Science and Social Work: A Theory of Their Relationship," *Social Service Review*, 29 (March, 1955), pp. 20-33; and Leonard S. Kogan (ed.), *Social Science Theory and Social Work Research* (New York: National Association of Social Workers, 1960).

and to the methods of seeking knowledge.[7] Traditional formulations as to the distinction between value judgments and methods of scientific investigation have been challenged in recent years by the critics of the assumptions of "value-free" science. As far back as Marx and Weber, a "sociology of knowledge" type of analysis has been used to indicate the influence upon social theory of biases related to the culture and social position of the theoretician or investigator. The general method that has been relied upon to protect against such influences has been the more rigorous use of the scientific method. The latter-day challenge is, however, more pervasive. It argues that the social sciences and the methodologies they use reflect implicit value positions that define and limit the problems to be considered.[8] This criticism has important implications for social work, which is based on a set of values expressed through explicit goals for social change in specified directions. An examination of the values built into the scientific method and their relationship to the action goals of social work is therefore relevant.[9]

The purpose of this review is not to negate the importance of the scientific method for social research generally and for the specific research needs of the field of social welfare. On the contrary, the purpose is to help the student gain sophistication in the understanding of the specific method, including an ability to evaluate the contentions of its critics and the proposed alternatives. The bibliography should include basic works that set out the elements of the scientific method in specific application to the social sciences, as well as more recent critiques, such as contrasting views of Nagel and Maslow.[10] Understanding the limitations of the scientific method should be seen as a device for the more effective use of this important framework for the systematic study of problems of social phenomena.

2. *Theory, Research, and Practice.* Issues in the application of theory to practice have been discussed in Chapter 3 in relation to the social science components of the curriculum. Additional elements in the relationship of theory to practice come into focus in regard to research and are therefore pertinent for inclusion in the foundation course on research methods.

A number of basic works in social research provide classification schemata

[7] Robert S. Lynd, *Knowledge for What?* (Princeton, N.J.: The University Press, 1939).

[8] Herbert C. Kelman, *A Time to Speak—On Human Values and Social Research* (San Francisco: Jossey-Bass, 1968).

[9] Ernest Greenwood, "The Science of Practice and the Practice of Science," and Ronald Lippitt, "Value-Judgment Problems of the Social Scientist in Action Research," both in Bennis *et al.*, *The Planning of Change* (New York: Holt, Rinehart and Winston, 1961).

[10] Ernest Nagel, *The Structure of Science* (New York: Harcourt, Brace and World, 1961); and Abraham H. Maslow, *The Psychology of Science* (New York: Harper and Row, 1966).

for describing the categories of research.[11] For example, distinctions are made among basic, applied, and program or administrative research. Another popular way of classifying studies is to categorize them as exploratory, descriptive, and experimental or hypothesis testing. These typologies and others suggest gradations in the relationship between the research problem and a body of theory. The distinctions are useful analytically, and it is one of the aims of the course to help the student understand the uses and limitations of each type of research and the procedures that are appropriate to each level. On the other hand, the boundaries among such categories are frequently fluid, and the student should gain an appreciation of how they interact in the process of problem formulation and research design. Thus, it has been observed that theory may arise as a serendipity out of research activity and not only through the logical pursuit of theoretically based propositions.[12] Even more complex and subtle are the interactions between basic and applied research, each of which may be grounded in part on theory and in part on concern for a solution to a practical problem. The purpose of reviewing the distinctions that exist in the world of research should be not to limit the focus of the practitioner but rather to enlarge his vision. He should be able to see the contributions that can be made to the solution of a practice problem by research based on theoretical premises and also the contributions that research addressed to a specific problem can make to the more general advancement of knowledge.[13]

In this course particular attention should be paid to the process of problem identification, which is both a key to research design and a critical issue in the relationship of theory to practice. All instructors who have helped students undertake theses or dissertations know the difficulties that they encounter in defining a meaningful and researchable problem. The course should provide an opportunity for direct experience in performing that task, thereby demonstrating how bodies of theory, past research, and practice experience, can all be probed as sources of research questions.[14]

In order to function at any point within the researcher-practitioner chain, the student will need some familiarity with what might be called the "language of variables." Included under this rubric are such topics as

---

[11] Tripodi et al., *op. cit.*

[12] Alvin W. Gouldner and S. M. Miller, *Applied Sociology: Opportunities and Problems* (New York: Free Press, 1965); and Barney G. Glazer and Anselm Strauss, *The Discovery of Grounded Theory: Strategies for Qualitative Research* (Chicago: Aldine, 1967).

[13] Tripodi et al., *op. cit.*; and Hans L. Zetterberg, *On Theory and Verification in Sociology* (Totowa, N. J.: Bedminster Press, 1965).

[14] Robert K. Merton, "Notes on Problem-Finding in Sociology," in Robert K. Merton, Leonard Bloom, and Leonard S. Cottrell (eds.), *Sociology Today: Problems and Prospects* (New York: Basic Books, 1959).

the definitions of and distinctions among assumptions, concepts, and hypotheses; different orders of variables and their interrelationship (e.g., independent, dependent, and intervening); the operationalization of variables; the meaning of probability, the distinction between association and causality; and some of the general problems of measurement.

3. *Methodologies.* Under this heading, the course will review the different types of study designs that can be employed, the methodologies available, and a number of more specific techniques that can be used. Exercises should be provided to introduce the student to the actual utilization of such methods.

However, it is not intended that there be a mere cataloging of research methodologies. The purposes of the research and the problem being addressed (as it relates to theory and practice) provide the framework for clarifying the criteria for selecting a particular methodology. Each has assets and limitations that are to be explicated.

While it will not be possible within a single course to cover all aspects and varieties of research methodologies in depth, it is desirable that the course provide a broad view of the methodologies available and avoid excessive emphasis on one or another approach. Some instructors may be oriented primarily toward survey research, others to field or laboratory experiments, and others to participant observation. Opportunities for more intensive study of a number of such methodologies should be available through electives. In this course, however, it is important that the student gain a sense of the availability of a repertoire of approaches serving different purposes and, therefore, all having potential usefulness in dealing with different kinds of problems that grow out of practice.

A distinction is to be made here between methodologies, which are larger units of operations, and techniques, which are more specific operations that may be used in more than one methodology. For example, interviewing and questionnaire construction are techniques that may be used in a survey methodology, a field observation study, or a hypothesis-testing experiment.

For the sake of clarity, it is suggested that a scheme for the classification of social research methodologies should distinguish between the purpose of the research (in regard to its theoretical level), the basic design of the research, and its setting. This would be encompassed in a three-dimensional classification scheme as follows:

1. The purpose, or theoretical framework, of the research is either exploratory or hypothesis testing.
2. The design of the research is either experimental or descriptive.
3. The setting of the research is either in a natural setting (field) or in a simulated setting (laboratory).

This three-way classification of research methodologies—by purpose, design, and setting—yields eight different types of studies. They may be visualized in the following diagram:

Purpose	Design and Setting			
	Experimental		Descriptive	
	Field	Laboratory	Field	Laboratory
Exploratory	1	2	3	4
Hypothesis-testing	5	6	7	8

Examples should be provided in the course of all eight types of studies encompassed by this scheme. Students should obtain some appreciation of the particular problems associated with each, as well as the advantages of each from the point of view of both feasibility and validity.

Another dimension that is of particular importance to community organization and social planning is the issue of the unit of analysis. In most social research, studies are made of individuals or characteristics of individuals and conclusions reached from research regarding group characteristics or "social facts" are derived from these measurements. A long-standing issue, both in social research and in social theory, is the question of how to define a "social fact" apart from the characteristics of individuals making up a social group. For the c.o. student, this general issue takes a specific form in the need to become acquainted particularly with the problems associated with studies that have organizations and communities rather than individuals as their unit and/or object of analysis.[15]

The study of organizations poses difficult problems of conceptualization and measurement with which the student will be concerned as a practitioner and to which he should be introduced in this course. A growing literature of organizational research deals explicitly with problems of conceptualization and methodology.[16] For example, the student should gain some knowledge of what is involved in defining the organizational characteristics that he is trying to study and the measurements that are appropriate to them. As the literature indicates, an organizational characteristic can be defined in terms of the aggregate of traits of its

[15] Karl E. Weick, "Laboratory Experimentation with Organizations" (pp. 194-269); and W. Richard Scott, "Field Methods in the Study of Organizations" (pp. 261-304); both in James G. March (ed.), *Handbook of Organizations* (Chicago: Rand-McNally & Co., 1965).

[16] Allen H. Barton, *Organizational Measurement and Its Bearing on the Study of College Environments* (New York: College Entrance Examination Board, 1961).

members, or it can be defined as some collective element such as organizational performance. Increasingly, the approach to organizational and community studies is a comparative one, which means that the measures, whether of characteristics of members of the collectivities being studied or of some attribute of the collectivity itself, need to be conceptualized in such a way that they can be compared from setting to setting.[17] Within the course a number of organizational studies should be reviewed in order to illustrate the different ways in which these problems may be approached.[18]

4. *Sources of Data.* Within the types of studies outlined above, a variety of data sources are used. Most of the emphasis in social research methodology and in teaching has been placed on the individual respondent answering structured or open-ended questions, either through self-administered questionnaires or interviews. The course should include substantial consideration of this major source of data and the methodological and technical problems involved. The students should become acquainted with a number of the problematic issues such as interviewer bias, the effect upon the responses of different ways in which the questions are formulated, and numerous other issues that have been discussed extensively in the literature on survey research.[19]

The existence and potentialities of other sources of data have not been treated as extensively and should be given adequate attention within the course. Both direct observation and the use of documentary materials are particularly important in community and organizational studies. In community studies, for example, extensive use should be made of census material that provides at least a starting point for examination of many community characteristics that have a bearing on social problems and ways of intervening in them.

The use of observation techniques is particularly important in organizational studies. The student should become acquainted not only with some of the classical approaches of anthropological investigation, and participant observation but also with the highly structured techniques that have been developed in the field of small research, notably interaction process analysis.[20] There has as yet been relatively little use of such syste-

---

[17] Bert E. Swanson (ed.), *Current Trends in Comparative Community Studies* (Kansas City, Kansas: Community Studies, 1962); and Stanley H. Udy, Jr., "The Comparative Analysis of Organizations," in March, *op. cit.*, pp. 678-709.

[18] Tripodi, Fellin *et al., op. cit.*

[19] Charles Y. Glock (ed.), *Survey Research in the Social Sciences* (New York: Russell Sage Foundation, 1967).

[20] John W. Bennett and Gustav Thaiss, "Survey Research and Sociocultural Anthropology," in Glock, *op. cit.*; Matilda W. Riley, *Sociological Research: I. A Case Approach* (New York: Harcourt, Brace and World, 1963); M. Dalton, "Preconceptions

matic observational approaches in the field of social welfare, but this is an area in which further work will undoubtedly be done, and in which future practitioners in community organization and social planning may well be involved.[21]

5. *Data Analysis.* The course should include a very substantial component of training in the techniques of data analysis. This should include direct exposure to some of the routines of processing data through the steps of recording, editing, coding. The approach to such routines is not to be limited to the mechanics of the operation to be performed, but should be organized in such a way as to help the student learn the importance of each step in the process of carrying out a research project, the ways in which errors can occur and how to safeguard against them, and efficient ways of organizing the various operations involved.

Within this course there can be only an introduction to the methods of data analysis. However, an attempt should be made to cover a number of different types of analysis in order to introduce the student to the varied repertory of methods that can be drawn upon in community and organizational studies. Both quantitative and qualitative methods of data analysis should therefore be included. The coverage of the course should also extend to the analysis of secondary data obtained from governmental departments, research surveys, and data banks, as well as from social agencies. There are examples available of the use of census and other types of governmental statistics for the illumination of social policy issues, as for example in the extensive studies recently conducted on poverty in the United States.[22] A focus on the methodological approaches involved in such studies will be helpful as background to the more specific consideration given in practice courses to the data being used in community action programs.

Since research in the organizational field tends to make use of documentary material, the course should include some consideration of methods of analyzing documents and particularly the techniques of content analysis. Also of importance here are the methods that have been developed for the

---

and Methods in 'Men Who Manage,'" in P. E. Hammond (ed.), *Sociologists at Work* (New York: Basic Books, 1965); George McCall and J. L. Simmons, *Issues in Participant Observations: A Text and Reader* (Reading, Mass.: Addison-Wesley, 1969); Paul A. Hare, Edgar F. Borgatta, and Robert F. Bales, *Small Groups: Studies in Social Interaction* (New York: Alfred A. Knopf, 1965); Edgar F. Borgatta (ed.), *Social Psychology Readings & Perspective* (Chicago: Rand McNally & Co., 1969).

[21] Arthur J. Vidich, Joseph Bensman, and Maurice R. Stein, *Reflections on Community Studies* (New York: John Wiley & Sons, Inc., 1964).

[22] Herman Miller, *Rich Man, Poor Man: A Study of Income Distribution in the United States* (New York: Crowell, 1964); and James N. Morgan, M. H. David, W. J. Cohen, and H. E. Brager, *Income and Welfare in the United States* (New York: McGraw-Hill, 1962).

systematic recording and analysis of data obtained through direct observations by the researchers themselves.[23]

One of the key elements involved in the use of multiple and complex technologies that are typical of community and organizational studies is the problem of subjecting qualitative data to quantitative analysis. Special attention should be given to the use of different types of scales that have been developed, particularly those utilized in the study of attitudes and opinions.[24]

While this introductory course in research methods is not to be considered a course in statistics, it does have to include some introduction to the types of statistical procedures that are available for data analysis, the logic on which they are based, and the types of problems to which they are applicable. The course should therefore include consideration of the characteristics of parametric and non-parametric statistical procedures, descriptive statistics, and the basic elements of correlational analysis and analysis of variance. It should also include information on measures of significance and the logic on which these are based.

In general, the purpose of the background courses in research will not be statistical training as such but rather an understanding of the concepts and principles underlying statistics so as to provide the student with some sophistication in the ways in which statistical analysis can be used. The dilemma is, however, that it is difficult to convey this understanding without exposing the student to some direct experience in the manipulation of data and in the practical use of statistical techniques. If the assumption is correct on which this course is based—namely, that the student has had, as an undergraduate, at least an elementary course in statistics and therefore has mastered some of the basic concepts and routines—this core course on a graduate level should try to take him at least a short step further in mastering some of the techniques of significance testing, measurement, and data analysis. The objective necessarily must be quite limited leaving it to elective courses to provide at least some of the students with more intensive training in this area.

In view of the major role which the age of computers is now playing in all social research, it is very desirable that even this introductory course provide the student with a beginning exposure to the understanding of computer technology. The teaching of statistics and research both in schools of social work and in many social science departments tends today to be somewhat obsolete. The techniques taught are rooted in older methods of

---

[23] R. C. North, O. R. Holsti, M. G. Zaninovitch, and D. A. Zinnes, *Content Analysis* (Evanston, Ill.; Northwestern University Press, 1963); Eugene J. Webb, Donald T. Campbell, Richard D. Schwartz, and Lee Sechrest, *Unobtrusive Measures: Nonreactive Research in the Social Sciences* (Chicago: Rand-McNally & Co., 1966).

[24] Charles M. Bonjean, Richard J. Hill, and S. Dale McLenore, *Sociological Measurement: An Inventory of Scales and Indices* (San Francisco: Chandler, 1967).

data analysis that require operations (such as the grouping of data) which are no longer required for machine handling. The course should try to reflect the way in which most studies are now done, and to focus on the kinds of research questions that can be asked and the form in which they need to be asked in order to take advantage of new technology.

At the same time, the limits of current technology should be made clear and its appropriate use emphasized. One of the dangers to be guarded against is excessive reliance upon complex computer technology which may at times be too elaborate for the kinds of investigations being undertaken. Another potential difficulty is the tendency to formulate research questions in terms that are suitable to the technology, even though these may not be the most important issues to be pursued at the present state of knowledge concerning the problem under investigation.

6. *Research in Social Welfare.* While the emphasis in this core course is on the teaching of research methods, such instruction can be related specifically to the content of research studies in the field of social welfare. The course should illustrate through the reports of actual studies the specific problems of methodology that arise and how the researchers attempt to solve them. While the course will thus serve to introduce the student to important studies in social welfare and social work, it will be only one of the channels through which this goal is accomplished. Each course taken by the student, whether in the field of social welfare, the profession of social work, practice methods, or specific problem areas will presumably include a review of the research literature relevant to that course. The emphasis in this core course on research methodology is not on the findings within the substantive field but rather on the problems inherent in the methodologies themselves.[25]

It is possible to divide the areas of research in social work and social welfare into two very broad categories. One is focused on special problems (and the people affected by them) which are the targets of social work and social welfare. The other area deals with methods of intervention. Both categories include a variety of specific purposes and subject areas that can be sampled in this course.

Research on populations, target areas, and social problems can be carried out at various points on the continuum from descriptive studies to those that involve hypothesis and theory testing. A large number of studies are of the descriptive type, attempting to develop a coherent and meaningful picture of population characteristics and the distribution of social problems. At the other end of the continuum are studies that seek to establish causal relationships among a multiplicity of variables in a social problem.

[25] Norman Polansky (ed.), *Social Work Research* (Chicago: University of Chicago Press, 1960); Maas, "Five Fields . . ." (1966); and Phillip Fellin, Tony Tripodi, and Henry S. Meyer, *Exemplars of Social Research* (Itasca, Ill.: F. E. Peacock, 1969).

Such research follows a general epidemiological model and is geared toward the identification and specification of the "population at risk." The student should be trained in the use of census data and other types of general population studies as a framework for identifying social problems and obtaining basic knowledge concerning their distribution.[26] This exposure will provide a foundation for the more intensive training in the use of community studies that he will obtain in the practice course.

As in the case of studies of social problems and population characteristics, research in the area of social work and social welfare intervention also takes place at different levels of theoretical development. One type of research based on social welfare operations involves the systematic use of service data in order to illuminate both the needs to be served and the nature of the activities to be performed.[27] This is the general area of administrative research that will be dealt with in greater depth within the context of practice courses since it is an intrinsic element of social planning. However, preliminary consideration can be given to this field of research within the framework of the general course on social research methods. The course should touch upon emerging developments in the use of agency data and the integration of such data into the more general studies of population characteristics. One example is the development of social data banks at the local community level. Another is the growing interest in a system of social indicators that will facilitate longitudinal and comparative studies of the incidence and prevalence of social problems.[28]

Since social welfare research must ultimately seek to contribute to the determination of the effectiveness of intervention efforts, considerable emphasis in the course should be given to the field of "evaluative" research. There is a substantial literature in this field both within social work itself and in related areas.[29] A number of common problematic issues run through all of this research. All evaluative studies need to define the outcome objective of the intervention effort and to find operational definitions that are

---

[26] Herman Turk, *A Method of Predicting Certain Federal Program Potentials of Large American Cities* (Los Angeles: Laboratory for Organizational Research, University of Southern California, 1967).

[27] David G. Gil, "Developing a Qualitative-Quantitative Service Accounting System," *Child Welfare*, 44 (January, 1965), Brandeis Reprint Series No. 9; and Paul Schreiber, "Statistical Data in Social Work and Social Welfare," *Encyclopedia of Social Work* (New York: National Association of Social Workers, 1965).

[28] Raymond E. Bauer, *Social Indicators* (Cambridge, Mass.: Massachusetts Institute of Technology Press, 1966); Eleanor B. Sheldon, and Wilbur E. Moore (eds.), *Indicators of Social Change: Concepts and Measurements* (New York: Russell Sage Foundation, 1968); and U.S. Department of Health, Education, and Welfare, *Toward a Social Report* (Washington, D.C.: U.S. Government Printing Office, 1969).

[29] Elizabeth Herzog, *Some Guidelines for Evaluative Research*, U. S. Department of Health, Education, and Welfare, Children's Bureau Publication No. 375 (Washington, D.C.: U.S. Government Printing Office, 1959); and Edward Suchman, *Evaluative Research: Principles and Practice in Public Service and Social Action Programs* (New York: Russell Sage Foundation, 1968).

appropriate to that objective. They must then resolve the problem of how to isolate the intervention variable from all of the other elements in the situation that have an effect upon the outcome. Complex as these problems are in the study of clinical forms of intervention, they become even more difficult in the field of community organization and social planning. Intervention at the organizational level characteristically has a multiplicity of objectives with the consequent difficulty of defining or specifying the outcome that is desired. In addition, the relationship between the intervention effort and the outcome is difficult to establish because of the numerous influences that may be operating simultaneously in the problem situation.

Some studies focus not on the outcome of intervention efforts but on the intervention process itself. Many aspects of the treatment process, whether in social casework or other forms of therapy are not well understood and therefore there has been an investment of research in observing and analyzing what practitioners do in order to isolate and conceptualize the elements within practice.[30]

7. *Research and Action.* A great deal of attention has been paid to the relationship between social research and social policy, the more general relationship between research and action, and the role relationships between reseachers and administrators or policymakers. Much of this literature deals with individual treatment and therefore deals with such issues as confidentiality, the ethical problems involved in using treatment for research rather than therapeutic purposes, the selection of people for treatment on the basis of research rather than clinical criteria, and the conflict of values between clinicians and researchers. A social planner and administrator should be aware of these issues because it may very well be part of his responsibility to participate in the development of research projects on clinical problems. However, he will be more directly concerned with relationships between research and action in the organizational area.

Here, again, much of the discussion can and should be reserved for the courses on practice, since it is in that context that one can deal best with the integration of research and its use as a tool in the practice of community organization and social planning. However, the subject can be introduced and discussed generally within the research course. The context for its discussion is an analysis of the conditions required for doing research within an organizational structure devoted to goals of action; and the interaction between researchers and organizers and planners in the various stages of research.[31]

---

[30] Lilian Ripple, Ernestina Alexander, and Bernice Polemis, *Motivation, Capacity and Opportunity: Studies in Casework Theory and Practice*, Social Service Monographs, Second Series, No. 3 (Chicago: School of Social Service Administration, University of Chicago, 1964).

[31] Roland L. Warren, *Social Research Consultation—An Experiment in Health and Welfare Planning* (New York: Russell Sage Foundation, 1963).

For example, one of the critical questions is the interaction of the two types of personnel in the process of problem identification. Both planners and policymakers on the one hand and researchers on the other have a responsibility for identifying and defining problems as a basis for research. The student should be helped to understand the different perspectives which the respective practitioners bring to bear on this issue and the problem of translating the frame of reference of one to that of the other. The policymaker should be able to state his problem in terms that will define the knowledge needed to determine policy and action. On the other hand, the form in which it is stated is not necessarily one that can be used by the researchers in order to develop a viable research design. It therefore becomes the investigator's responsibility to reframe the question in researchable terms. Obviously there is need for collaboration between the two types of professionals if the research problem as finally formulated is to meet the necessary conditions of both.

In addition there are a number of other issues that involve the general climate of the setting in which research is undertaken and the wider environment on which the research project is dependent for support and resources. It would be well in this course to introduce the student to the real world of research operations—the agency settings in which research tends to be done, the university setting in which the researchers frequently are based, and the inter-relationships between the two. Also of value is an examination of the relationship among various disciplines within a research undertaking and some of the typical problems of establishing effective working relationships among them, taking cognizance of the different frames of reference from which they operate.[32] Not to be neglected are the problems arising from the need to finance research and the relationships of researchers to funding sources both public and private.

A number of problematic issues that are typical of applied research in the field of social welfare might be examined. Several of these revolve around the conflict of interest between sponsoring organizations and researchers. These are reflected most acutely in situations where research findings run counter to the views of administrators, raise questions about the validity of some of the things that the agency is doing, or may in other ways have a negative effect upon the public relations or even the financial security of the sponsoring body.

A more general issue is the utilization of research findings for program and planning purposes.[33] Emphasis is usually placed upon the conflict aspects of the question of utilization. The problems of utilization are, however, broader. A basic problem is the difficulty of providing all of the

---

[32] Mustafa Sherif and Carolyn W. Sherif (eds.), *Interdisciplinary Relationships in The Social Sciences* (Chicago: Aldine, 1969).

[33] Human Interaction Research Institute, *Utilization of Applicable Research and Demonstration Findings* (Los Angeles: Human Interaction Research Institute, 1967).

connections that are required between the findings of research and the specific program measures that might be derived from those findings.[34] Research, unless it is highly specific fact finding built into the administrative apparatus, does not deal in a very direct way with the questions on which planning, policy, or administrative decisions need to be made. The function of research is to increase the fund of knowledge that could be drawn upon in order to make such decisions. However, such knowledge may or may not be relevant to the action-decisions involved. Or, what is more important, an additional element of creativity is required in order to ferret out its possible relevance.[35]

A most important task for future development, therefore, is to find ways whereby there may be effective collaboration between researchers and action people in integrating knowledge and practice. It will be noted that this brings us back to a general issue that was discussed in the chapter on social science as well as in earlier sections of this chapter on research. It is the underlying theme of the integration of knowledge and practice to which, in large measure, the entire social work curriculum is addressed.

There are several models that can be studied as illustrations of forms of collaboration between the researcher and the sponsoring agency. One is the individual consultant operating from a base outside the organization but serving as a critic, analyst, and research planner on behalf of the organization.[36] Another is to build the research capacity right into the administrative framework of the sponsoring agency. A third is for the sponsoring agency to contract with an outside organization such as a university or a specialized research organization to undertake a project on its behalf.[37]

All of these patterns, and others, have their examples in real life. All of them have advantages and limitations that have been discussed in the literature.[38] There is the beginning of conceptualization as to where one or another of these models might be most appropriately used, depending upon the kind of problem that is being tackled as well as the environmental and organizational conditions that provide the framework for the research undertaking.

---

[34] Aaron Rosenblatt, "The Practitioner's Use and Evaluation of Research," *Social Work*, 13 (January, 1968), pp. 53-59.

[35] Herbert Halpert, "Communication as a Basic Tool in Promoting Utilization of Research Findings," *Community Mental Health Journal*, Vol. 2 (1966), pp. 231-236.

[36] Warren, *op. cit.*

[37] Fanshel, *Research in* . . . (1962).

[38] Robin Williams, "The Strategy of Socio-Medical Research," in Howard E. Freeman, Sol Levine, and Lawrence Reeder (eds.), *Handbook of Medical Sociology* (Englewood Cliffs, N.J.: Prentice-Hall, 1967); and Edward A. Suchman, *Evaluative Research: Principles and Practice in Public Service and Social Action Programs* (New York: Russell Sage Foundation, 1968).

METHODOLOGY OF THE COURSE

The course as outlined above is very extensive in its coverage and also quite diverse in the character of the information being covered. It will therefore call for several different approaches in the construction of learning experiences. It should be both a didactic course based on lectures, readings, and discussion; and a laboratory course in which students undertake exercises in order to acquire some beginning skills in research methodology. The different sections of the course as outlined above lend themselves with differing degrees of appropriateness to one or another of these teaching approaches.

As has already been indicated, much of the teaching can be based on a careful and detailed critique of existing research with particular emphasis on the methodological aspects. It might be both feasible and useful to develop "case histories" of research projects that would illustrate many of the issues outlined above, including not only problem formulation and research methodology, but also the relationship between research and social welfare objectives as reflected in every step of the process from research design to the application and utilization (or non-utilization) of results.[39]

The training in skills can be achieved by designing a number of exercises that will be closely related to segments of the course. A diversity of exercises should be included. Some can be very brief and highly specific but structured so as to help the students master a particular technique. The manipulation of data for purposes of analysis is an example of this type of task. Students might be given a body of census data and required to devise different ways of analyzing the material in order to obtain data needed for practice decisions. Similar brief exercises might be undertaken in the data collection and data processing areas—as in the construction of a questionnaire and a code book or the ordering of a single computer run using a standard program. It would be highly desirable to tie a number of such experiences together through the use of a laboratory, in order to expose the student to the wider world of research, to give him an opportunity to experience directly the inter-relationships of steps in the research process, and to reduce his fear or anxiety about the mysteries of research. Since the course is to cover a full year, a plan could be made at early sessions for students to undertake a project that would be sustained through the entire period. This could be done either on an individual or a group basis. It would be designed so as to carry the student through major areas of research design, and perhaps even implementation. Reporting would be

[39] Fellin, *et al.*, *Examplars of Social Research* (1969).

phased so that the student has specific tasks to complete at different points in the year.

A number of models exist for the organization of teaching programs in the research area. The group projects that have been conducted at schools of social work as a subtitute for the individual thesis provide this kind of framework, as do also the research centers in a number of universities that are essential resources for social science departments.

ELECTIVE COURSES

It is desirable that the program in community organization and social planning allow the opportunity for advanced research courses.

It is difficult to lay out a plan for such offerings because the central recommendation is that these be available on a very flexible basis for use by students in relation to their particular interests and career goals. The general recommendation is, however, that there be an expectation within the community organization concentration that a larger proportion of the students will be encouraged to gain further grounding in research methodolgy (beyond this one-year core course) as part of the "foundation course" component in the curriculum. As a general rule, it might be anticipated that virtually all students would take an additional one-semester elective course in research methodology and that a substantial portion will take at least two such courses.

While there are many courses with different emphases that might be appropriate, the general approach should be to make available courses that provide opportunities for intensive training in particular methodologies. Some of these offerings that would be relevant and useful include: advanced courses in statistical methods with particular emphasis on multivariate analysis and computer technology, in simple design and execution of surveys, in field observation and participant observation, in the study and measurement of organizational behavior, or in the analysis of small group behavior. In addition, some courses that deal with substantive fields of interest may be primarily methodological in their focus and would also be suitable alternatives. Of particular interest to students of community organization and social planning should be courses in demography, epidemiology, ecology, economic analysis, and voting behavior.

In the research area it is particularly desirable to apply the general principle that informs all of these recommendations of drawing upon the wider resources of the university beyond the school of social work itself. The school may wish to develop courses in research and methodology in a number of limited areas that reflect a major emphasis in its overall program. However, for the most part it is contemplated that the students will choose their elective courses in research from the social science departments of the university (including the statistics department) or from interdisciplinary institutes or research centers sponsored by many universities.

Those schools of social work that conduct doctoral programs will probably have a richer complement of research courses to offer than those that are limited to the master's level. These schools are also likely to have a system of established relationships with other resources in the university that can be drawn upon for this purpose.

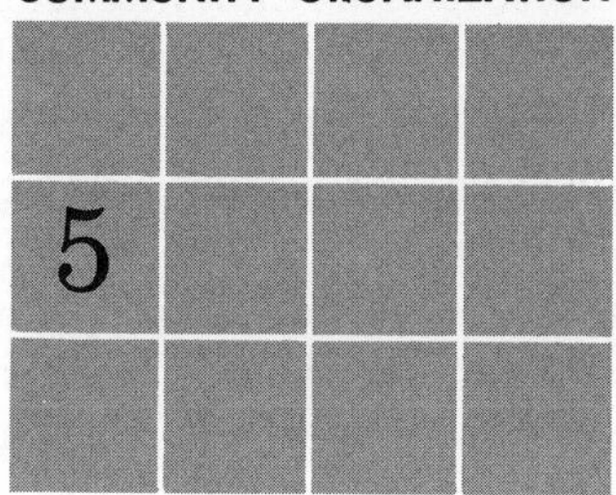

Social Welfare and Social Policy*

INTRODUCTION

IN ACCORDANCE with the overall distinction that has been made in the curriculum recommendations between foundation and practice courses, social welfare and social policy have been grouped together in this chapter as a foundation area.

Several introductory observations are in order. Since this is a foundation rather than a practice area, it is not necessarily limited to concentrators in community organization but has general applicability for all students, regardless of their methods concentration.

The social welfare policy and services sequence as it now exists in the curriculum of many schools of social work contains content of relevance to the practice of community organization and social planning. The recommendations contained in this chapter are not meant to substitute for such content but to comment and elaborate on some aspects which have particular salience as foundation elements for the c.o. concentration. The recommendations are in line with recent trends to shift the emphasis in

* This chapter is based in part on two papers prepared for the Project by Martin Rein entitled, respectively, "The Boundaries of Social Policy" and "Policy Analysis." Further discussions of the issues raised by Dr. Rein will be found in his recent book, *Social Policy: Issues of Choice and Change* (New York: Random House, 1970).

the sequence from a descriptive approach to the social welfare field to a more analytic approach in which issues of social policy are highlighted.

Concentrations in social policy have begun to appear in several schools of social work. There will be further discussion in the concluding sections of this report on ways in which concentrations in social policy, community organization and social planning, and administration might be related to one another. At this point, it may be sufficient to note that the c.o. concentration, as we envisage it, necessarily calls for a substantial component of social policy. This in no way negates the possibility of a social policy concentration. Indeed, the existence of a concentration in social policy would greatly contribute to the effectiveness of the c.o. concentration and would almost inevitably result in some degree of joint programming between the two.

The topic which involves the greatest degree of overlap between the two areas is policy analysis. Social policy courses and sequences which provide students with training in methodology of social policy analysis would be, in our framework, practice courses. Policy analysis is an integral part of the problem-solving scheme which we are employing as a frame work for the practice of community organization and social planning.

It does not seem necessary to resolve this boundary issue, since the study of social policy can be enriched through being approached from different perspectives. The outlines of practice courses that will be presented in Part III clearly show how policy considerations are used within the community organization-social planning context. Schools which offer social planning analysis elsewhere in their curriculum will be able to judge whether the material is sufficiently comparable so that the social policy course may, in effect, serve as one of the units in the c.o. concentration —perhaps in place of the proposed course in planning methods (Chapter 8) or one of the specialized courses (e.g., social development or urban planning) in Chapter 9.

However, on the basis of the curriculum as it now stands in most schools of social work, the social welfare-social policy sequence will most likely deal primarily with the field of social welfare and the substantive issues of social policy and very little with methodology. It is on this assumption that detailed consideration of policy analysis has been incorporated into the proposed practice courses in our recommendations for the c.o. concentration.

We shall limit our observations in this chapter to an indication of elements within the areas of social welfare and social policy which seem particularly important for the student in community organization and social planning. The chapter will touch upon the following topics:

1. Conceptual framework for the study of social welfare and social policy;
2. Content of the social welfare field;

3. Social policy issues;

4. The place of professional intervention.

Before proceeding to a brief discussion of each of these topics, a few prefatory notes are in order.

THE PERVASIVENESS OF VALUES

Value issues and value judgments pervade all aspects of the curriculum. They have been raised in the discussion of social science foundations and will be discussed again within the framework of the practice courses. The social welfare-social policy area, however, is the segment of the curriculum in which the value issues can be studied most extensively and systematically. It is generally recognized in the field of social policy, even more than in social planning, that value issues are fundamental to the entire subject. Rein, in a paper prepared for this Project, follows Titmuss in arguing that social policy is concerned with social purposes and objectives rather than with technical analysis of costs and benefits.[1] "What is needed," he writes, "is not so much good methods . . . but good questions (which implies a social philosophy)." While he goes on to add that "A sound scientific methodology will, of course, be a vital component of the efforts to answer relevant and important questions," it is the identification of the questions that is the heart of the matter, and the questions are based on values.

To say that value issues are fundamental and pervasive to the subject of social policy is not necessarily to argue that there is a uniform, consistent value base underlying the field of social welfare or the practice of professional social work. No such assumption is being made, and it is indeed one of the functions of the course to probe the explicit value assumptions underlying practice, going beyond the rhetoric of ideological value statements to the examination of actual institutions and behaviors. Some specifics are suggested below in discussion of each of the topics outlined earlier.

HISTORY AND PHILOSOPHY

History and philosophy provide perspectives that are much needed in the study of social welfare and social policy, and should be represented somewhere in the curriculum, either within the social welfare and social policy courses or as separate offerings. From the standpoint of the c.o. concentration, history is important as a way of understanding not only the background but also the nature of issues in which planners are currently involved or likely to be in the future. Such matters as the relationships

[1] Richard M. Titmuss, *Commitment to Welfare* (New York: Pantheon Books, 1968).

of social welfare to the more general social forces of the times (what we call later, in the discussion of planning, the "societal context"), the social functions of welfare institutions as instruments both of social change and social control, etc., have contemporary relevance. Historical perspective also helps to sort out issues which have a unique relevance to a time and place as against those which reflect recurring dilemmas that need to be re-evaluated periodically. For example, the relationship between welfare and work may be seen as part of the historical era of industrialization from which value commitments have been inherited that may not be appropriate to the present situation. On the other hand, a question such as the universal vs. selective criteria for social welfare provisions may be identified as a recurring issue.

Although history is reasonably well represented in the course offerings and bibliographies of schools of social work, there has been relatively little use of contributions from philosophy.[2] Yet the perspective is an important one if the issues of value that were mentioned earlier are to be considered properly. There is need to clarify and evaluate the relationship of social welfare to issues such as freedom and equality, which are classical concerns of philosophy. This is an area in which schools would be well-advised to make further efforts at faculty enrichment and interdisciplinary collaboration, for the sake, we are certain, not only of the c.o. concentrators but of all social work students.

INTER-CULTURAL COMPARISONS

Another important perspective is the international one. The tendency has been, until recently, to limit the teaching of social welfare and social policy primarily to the British and North American experience. As concepts develop concerning the relationship of social welfare to the broader cultural, economic, and social institutions of the society, comparisons of social welfare in societies which differ in their social structure and value systems become increasingly relevant. The work of the United Nations provides a continuous source of information on the development of social welfare systems in countries throughout the world. The number of individual studies is also growing.[3]

---

[2] For an unusual collection of philosophically oriented articles, see: John S. Morgan (ed.), *Welfare and Wisdom* (Toronto: University of Toronto Press, 1966).

[3] A few examples include: Alvin Schorr, *Social Security and Social Services in France* (Washington, D.C.: Government Printing Office, 1965); J. A. Ponsioen (ed.), *Social Welfare Policy* (The Hague: Mouton & Co., 1963); Barbara Rodgers, J. Greve, and J. S. Morgan, *Comparative Social Administration* (London: George Allen and Unwin, Ltd., 1968); and Bernice Q. Madison, *Social Welfare in the Soviet Union* (Stanford, Calif.: Stanford University Press, 1968).

CONCEPTUALIZATIONS OF SOCIAL WELFARE

One purpose of the sequence is to examine different ways of understanding the societal functions and context of "social welfare" and its relationship to economic and political systems. Some of this can be done historically, as in the work of Wilensky and Lebeaux and others.[4]

Titmuss has suggested three "models for conceptualizing the functions and social purposes of social welfare: welfare as a residual burden; welfare as complementarity; and welfare as an instrument of equality."[5] These three approaches all refer to the relationship between social welfare and the functioning of the economy. The residual burden concept looks upon welfare as a series of measures to compensate for breakdowns in the normal functioning of the economy, with the presumption that the economy itself will, for the most part, act as the normal and adequate channel for the distribution of society's goods and services. The "complementarity" notion sees the field of social welfare as handmaiden to the economy and therefore ties social provisions to the presumed needs of the economy to promote production and saving. The concept of equality places social welfare in the position of being an instrument of the society for redistribution of resources. It thus becomes one of the basic integrating institutions of the society.[6]

Earlier formulations of the functions of social work and social welfare have also focused on the difference between "residual" and "institutional" conceptions.[7] That distinction continues to be a useful way into the kinds of analysis that are pertinent to the present period in which the boundaries of the field of social welfare are expanding and its "institutional" aspects are becoming more widely recognized.

Another set of disinctions offered by Titmuss is helpful in demonstrating

[4] Harold L. Wilensky and Charles N. Lebeaux, *Industrial Society and Social Welfare* (New York: Russell Sage Foundation, 1958); Roy Lubove, *The Struggle for Social Security 1900-1935* (Cambridge, Mass.: Harvard University Press, 1968); Samuel Mencher, *Poor Law to Poverty Program: Economic Security Policy in Britain and the United States* (Pittsburgh, Pa.: University of Pittsburgh Press, 1967); Karl Palanyi, *The Great Transformation* (Boston, Mass.: Beacon Press, 1957); and Clarke A. Chambers, *Seedtime of Reform: American Social Service and Social Action, 1918-1933* (Minneapolis, Minn.: University of Minnesota Press, 1963).

[5] Titmuss, *op. cit.*, p. 16.

[6] In elaboration of these models, not yet available in published form, Titmuss has pointed out that the institutional model is not necessarily beneficent; this depends upon the values of the society. The general point, however, is that social welfare does have a redistributive function, whether recognized or not. When not recognized, it can lead to redistribution in the form of greater benefits to those less in need, although the intent may be quite the opposite.

[7] See, for example: Helen L. Witmer, *Social Work* (New York: Farrar and Rinehart, 1942); Wilensky and Lebeaux, *op. cit.*, pp. 130-142; and Alfred J. Kahn, *Social Services as Social Utilities*, unpublished paper prepared for XIIIth International Conference of Social Work, Washington, D.C., September, 1966.

that "welfare" as a societal function is not limited to the field of social welfare as we normally define it. He identifies three types of welfare: social welfare, fiscal welfare, and occupational welfare.[8] Social welfare refers to measures taken by the society to deal with states of dependency that are recognized as collective responsibilities. (The definition of social welfare will be pursued further on in this chapter.) Titmuss makes the point that there are other ways in which society meets dependencies without recognizing them explicitly either as dependencies or as transfer payments, in the way that social services are recognized.

One of these other ways is fiscal welfare, which refers to various forms of tax exemptions and allowances authorized by the fiscal laws of the state; another is occupational welfare, which refers to the growing volume of social benefits that function as part of the labor market and are incorporated into the relationships between employer and employee. They constitute social costs both in the form of loss of government revenue and prices paid for goods. The point here is that decisions on welfare benefits are being made at public cost but through private agreements.

From these broad perspectives, which need constantly to be kept in mind as part of the total view of social planning in relation to allocation of resources, program evaluation, etc., we turn to the more specific questions involved in defining the boundaries of social welfare as a specific field.

CONTENT OF SOCIAL WELFARE FIELD

The inherent difficulties of conceptualizing the subject are complicated by differences in terminology which have developed in different countries. Thus, the field of study which is generally called "social welfare" in the United States is called "social administration" in Great Britain. There is no uniformity in the use of the terms "social welfare," "social services," and "social work." In the terminology used by the United Nations and also by Great Britain, "social services" is a very broad category which embraces health services, education, housing, and a number of other fields, as well as public assistance and family and child welfare. On the other hand, in the United States "social services" is used in a much more limited sense to define the kinds of activities in which there is a personalized service to individuals and families, whereas "social welfare" has been used as the broader term to cover both social services and other systems (e.g., health, education, etc.) concerned with social needs.

With appropriate translations in terminology, it is useful to draw upon the work that has been done in England in the field of "social administration." Richard Titmuss, summarizing the status of that subject as of 1967,

---

[8] Richard M. Titmuss, *Essays on "The Welfare State"* (London: Unwin University Books, second edition, 1963), p. 42.

writes: "I happen to believe that as a subject, social administration has begun to develop a body of knowledge and a related set of concepts and principles."[9] While foregoing the effort to develop a firm definition of the subject, Titmuss offers the following description of its interests and perspectives.

> Basically, we are concerned with the study of a range of social needs and the functioning, in conditions of scarcity, of human organizations, traditionally called social services or social welfare systems, to meet these needs. This complex area of social life lies outside or on the fringes of the so-called free market, the mechanisms of price and tests of profitability. Though this area has some of the characteristics of the market-place, for example, all social services are allocative systems and ration demand and supply, there are many other characteristics which relate to the non-economic elements in human relations.[10]

It is implicit, in so broad a definition, that the field is not a fixed entity whose boundaries can be clearly defined. "Of one thing at least we can be certain when all else is uncertain," Titmuss concludes, "the situation in which different kinds of need arise and are recognized as 'needs' has changed and will continue to do so." As a consequence, the term "social service" is a most elastic one, ". . . its expanding frontiers, formerly enclosing little besides poor relief, sanitation and public nuisances, now embrace a multitude of heterogeneous activities."[11] Social services are now concerned with a very broad range of "states of dependency," stemming from natural vicissitudes in the life cycle, from physical and psychological disabilities, or from man-made causes such as the malfunctioning of industrial society and the maldistribution of opportunities and rewards.

There are several different ways of constructing a classification scheme for the study of the social services, depending on which dimensions are considered most relevant to the concepts which the instructor may wish to stress. At least three dimensions may be identified: the *purpose* of the service; the nature of the *activity* being performed; and the *structure* or organizational system through which the service is provided. Each of these helps. in different ways, to highlight important issues for the student's consideration. Traditional descriptive categories of the social services have divided the field into categories based on the kinds of people served (e.g., children families, aged, handicapped, etc.) or the kinds of services provided (e.g., income, medical care, counseling, rehabilitation, etc.). Recent work has strived for classification based on more analytical distinctions that will help to illuminate policy issues.

The relationship between individual and society is reflected in the social

---

[9] Titmuss, *Commitment to Welfare* (1968), p. 23.

[10] *Ibid*., p. 20.

[11] Titmuss, *Essays on* . . . (1963), pp. 39-40.

services at two levels which are sometimes difficult to distinguish from each other. At one level, the focus is on the provision of basic resources to the population in order to achieve purposes such as those that are included in any nonresidual approach. In this category, we place general education, medical care, housing, and social insurance. These are what Rein calls the "high cost services." The other level is what the British call the "personal social services," which focus more sharply on attempts to intervene on a more individualized basis in the relationship between individuals and institutions. Traditionally the profession of social work has been concerned primarily with the "personal social services." The expansion of the concepts of social work has come about through the experience that the level of personal social services is not sufficient to deal successfully with social problems unless there are adequate provisions and properly organized resources in the basic service systems. Hence, social policy is concerned with both levels.

In connection with these problems, it would be useful to examine the reports of the Seebohm Committee in Great Britain and the Task Force on Organization of Social Services in the United States.[12] Both were governmental committees which were asked to chart the future of the social services and therefore had to consider both the purpose of the services and the means of classifying them.

The Seebohm Committee, whose study ended in a recommendation for a centralized social service department at the local level, did not develop a new definition but reviewed activities which are already designated as "personal social services" within the local authorities in the United Kingdom. These cover a very wide field, including distinctively social work functions in family and child welfare as well as some aspects of the health, education, and housing fields. The functions were also subdivided, as between services rendered in the home or in the community ("fieldwork"), residential care, day care, and other services. A summary of the services included follows:

> The children's service covers preventive work, foster care, adoption, residential care, and treatment, as well as financial and material help and advice centers.
>
> Welfare refers to work with the elderly and various types of physically handicapped; special work with multiproblem families; residential care for the elderly and the handicapped; centers, clubs, and workshops; and home care services such as meals on wheels, laundry services, and sheltered housing.
>
> In the health services the coverage includes social workers in mental health and in medical social work; district nurses and occupational therapists;

---

[12] Report of the Committee on Local Authority and Allied Personal Social Services, London, H.M.S.O. Cmnd. 3703 (July, 1968); and *Services for People*, Report of the Task Force on Organization of Social Services, U.S. Department of Health, Education, and Welfare (October 15, 1968).

home help organizers and home helps; mother and baby homes; day nurseries, training centers, and infant welfare centers; and miscellaneous service such as recuperative holidays and family planning.

Education includes school nursing and school social work as well as special education of all types and youth employment services and child guidance clinics.

Housing includes not only housing welfare officers but also housing managers and housing for old and handicapped people.[13]

The United States Task Force generally included the same kinds of services within its frame of reference. It took the further step, however, of trying to conceptualize and classify the services in accordance with the objectives that they serve, as follows:

1) *Accessibility*—programs of advice, referral, liaison, and complaints which are intended to help individuals find their way to the services that they need.

2) *Treatment*—services of rehabilitation, to deal with people having problems of illness, disability, deliquency or crime.

3) *Socialization and development*—services which supplement or take the place of those customarily provided in the family for young children and old people; or by basic institutions, such as schools, the labor market, or the health system.

4) *Equalization*—services directed to people who have been excluded or discriminated against by the society, or who do not have the capacity to participate with equality of opportunity and conditions.[14]

Many of the elements touched upon in these reports and in other classification schemes are woven together by Kahn in the following comprehensive definition:

> Social services may be interpreted in an institutional context as consisting of programs made available by other than market criteria to assure a basic level of health-education-welfare provision, to enhance communal living and individual functioning, to facilitate access to services and institutions generally, and to assist those in difficulty and need.[15]

This definition catches both the specifics of health, education, and welfare provision, and the more general purposes of improving communal life. It also bridges special provisions for deprived and handicapped groups and

---

[13] Report of the Committee . . . , *op. cit.*, Appendix F, pp. 252-309.

[14] *Services for People*, *op. cit.*, pp. 9-10.

[15] Alfred J. Kahn, *Theory and Practice of Social Planning* (New York: Russell Sage Foundation, 1969), p. 179.

general provisions in specified social areas for the total population. The range of services it encompasses are categorized as follows:

Services which are available to all and used by the individual at his option (e.g., public parks).

Services available to those of a certain status (e.g., age).

Services available by professional evaluation (e.g., treatment).

It will be obvious that policy issues flow immediately from such a classification. By what criteria are different services to be placed in one or another category? What status definitions should be used? Who is to evaluate the need for treatment and by what methods? The study of boundary and classification problems as reflected in the material cited thus leads immediately to consideration of policy issues.

SOCIAL POLICY ISSUES

The field of social welfare is characterized by recurring policy issues. They are recurring issues for two reasons. One is that changing conditions bring about imbalances in the equilibrium resulting from earlier resolutions of problems. A second and perhaps more fundamental reason is that all policies involve choices which maximize some objectives at the expense of others and therefore carry within them dysfunctions which call for later correction. Most of the issues outlined below (which have been selected for their contemporary importance in social planning) pose problems of choice that are essentially dilemmas in that neither of the counterpoised goals can be chosen with complete satisfaction. A choice can therefore be made only for a particular time and set of circumstances.

1. *Social Costs of Economic and Technological Growth.* This much-neglected area is rapidly becoming a central issue of policy concern, not only for the field of social welfare, but for a number of disciplines. Questions have begun to be raised by some economists concerning the social costs of certain types of growth (through pollution, obsolescence, unemployment, etc.) and their impact on the distribution of social benefits to different segments of the population.[16]

The policy issue for the field of social welfare is to identify what Titmuss calls the "disservices" resulting from economic and technological development and how they affect different segments of the population, to participate in efforts to measure the social costs involved, to locate the responsible causal agents, to devise both compensatory and corrective measures.[17]

---

[16] For somewhat different views, see: E. J. Mishan, *The Costs of Economic Growth* (New York: Staples Press [Pelican Books], 1969); and Walter W. Heller, *New Dimensions of Political Economy* (Cambridge, Mass.: Harvard University Press, 1966).

[17] Titmuss, *Commitment to Welfare* (1968), p. 156.

2. *Income Maintenance.* A number of policy issues can be grouped under this category. One is the determination of the level of income that is to be maintained, which is related to definitions of poverty—whether in absolute or relative terms. The first premise would lead to minimum income guarantees, the second to a level of income tied to moving averages of income in the country.

However, income maintenance programs need not be based simply on the maintenance of some minimum standard, however defined. Another alternative is to relate levels of income payments, under specified condition, to past earnings, as in some forms of social insurance. Such a policy tends to maintain differentials rather than redistributing resources. Income maintenance schemes which seek both goals, as they tend to do, need to develop complex procedures for achieving some balance between the two. Involved in these considerations is also the question of incentives or disincentives to participation in the labor force and the relationship of those questions to the goal of providing more adequate income to those in the population whose earnings are lowest.

It is against questions such as these that different income maintenance proposals, such as the negative income tax, family allowances, or demogrants, need to be evaluated.

3. *Universality and Selectivity.* This is one of the most fundamental and pervasive of the basic dilemmas in social welfare policy. A universal provision is one which is available to the entire population on the basis of some universal status such as age or condition, regardless of need.

Universal provisions advance the principle of integration and avoid the segregation and stigmatization of disadvantaged sections of the population. On the other hand, they are expensive and do not contribute to redistribution and equalization. They may tend, in fact, to benefit those who have more to a greater extent than those who have less. From this point of view, policies of selectivity are more efficient in using resources primarily for the benefit of those most in need.

Attempts to escape from the dilemma would employ methods of selectivity within a universal system. This is accomplished by providing for those most in need through special benefits within a service system that is established for the entire population. An example is the use of housing subsidies instead of public housing projects, or payments for medical care instead of special free clinics limited to those without means. These measures are based on the theory that services which are available only to those who do not have their own income suffer from low quality and carry a stigma which adds to the burdens of the disadvantaged population.

The means test is a special historic case of this dilemma and has been a prominent controversial issue in social welfare history. It has become an important symbol of the negative effects of selectivity when carried to the level of individual determination of financial need as a basis for benefits or services because of the tendency of such measures to become punitive and to act as barriers to access to service.

4. *Cash and Services.* After decades in which professionals attempted to bring individualized service approaches into the administration of public assistance, the pendulum has swung toward a separation of cash maintenance payments from service. The cause is the negative experience in which service objectives have been undermined by the pressure of means-test administration and the inadequacy of financial provisions. Separation, if accompanied by depersonalized eligibility procedures, tends to emphasize assistance as a right and reduces the means-test stigma. The issue of individualization remains, however, and is not yet satisfactorily resolved even in countries that have achieved more universal income maintenance programs than those that exist in the United States.

5. *Use of the Private Market.* In a number of the definitions of social welfare cited earlier, it is stated as one of the distinguishing characteristics of the field that its functions are performed outside of the market system. This assumption is now being subjected to re-examination. As Titmuss's definition itself indicates, the welfare field is involved in the allocation of scarce resources and, therefore, does represent a type of market which may be more subject to economic analysis than has usually been thought to be the case.

Of more immediate interest, however, is a growing tendency to consider use of the private market as a channel for the provision of social services. In the United States, anti-poverty program grants have been made to private industry for job-training programs. The HEW Task Force recommended more experimentation with the use of individual benefit payments that would permit beneficiaries to obtain services in the private market rather than from government agencies.[18]

Arguments in favor of such an approach stress both individual freedom of choice (an ideological element) and efficiency. It is assumed that market mechanisms will stimulate competition and, therefore, enhance quality; it is also assumed that stigma will be removed. The counterarguments point to contrary evidence indicating that neither costs nor quality of service have necessarily been more advantageous in the private market (e.g., as in the case of private insurance to cover health and disability). There are also additional factors, such as the stake of the society in assuring coverage and utilization of some types of services and uncertainty as to whether the consumer in the private market can command enough information and power to enforce adequate standards.

---

[18] *Services for People, op. cit.*, pp. 65-66.

6. *Control Over Decisions.* The discussion of use of market mechanisms leads into some of the most controversial current policy issues which have a particular bearing on community organization and social planning. These are the questions as to who is to control the decisions on policy matters. Here we can point again to the shifting nature of social policy in relation to social change. In the United States, where liberals for many decades had supported strong federal policies against the opposition of conservatives, local community control is today a major plank in the radical platform.

Many issues of ideology, rationality, and feasibility (Rein's three approaches to policy analysis) are involved in questions of centralization and decentralization of decision-making and program execution. A number of these will be discussed later in regard to several of the practice courses. At a most fundamental level, they involve long-standing questions concerning the balance between freedom and equality—and whether equality can be achieved most securely through emphasis on central governmental planning or on maximization of individual and small group autonomy.

To help guide future community organizers and social planners, the social policy course needs to clarify the philosophical issues and to submit them to empirical testing through policy-oriented examination of historical and contemporary experience.

PROFESSIONAL INTERVENTION

Finally, we look to the social welfare-social policy sequence to provide some grounding and general orientation in the profession of social work as it relates to the field of social welfare and to the other professions that play a role in that field.

It would be well for the course to provide some background in the sociology of professions which deals with general questions such as the way that professions emerge, the nature of the professional's mandate, and issues of responsibility and accountability to clientele, sponsoring groups, the larger society. Of particular relevance to social work are issues of professionals in organizations.[19] Our conceptualization of c.o. practice as intervention at the organizational level makes the relationship between professional and organization, in both its positive and negative aspects, a central issue.

The development of social work as a profession within the context of the field of social welfare and particularly in the administration of the "personal" services as described above provides a basis for examining all of the social work methods. It is at this point in the curriculum that the

---

[19] Mark Abrahamson, *The Professional in the Organization* (Chicago: Rand McNally & Co., 1967).

concentrator in community organization will become acquainted with the nature of casework and group work intervention—the assumptions on which they rest, the problems to which they are addressed, methods employed, etc.

From the point of view of the c.o. concentration, it is necessary to deal both with the common elements in the profession and those which differentiate its several parts. An overall analysis, such as Cohen's review of the profession's position in relation to social problems, is particularly useful both in showing the relationship of the profession to the larger society and in identifying the broad value commitments which are common to all of its members.[20]

It is, however, a matter for critical examination to determine what societal role or roles the profession has in fact played both historically and on the contemporary scene, and to measure the broad ideological stance of professional bodies against actual performance. This will raise issues that are of immediate concern. To what extent is the profession in the position of contributing to social control rather than social change? What are its opportunities for furthering greater justice and equality in the society and how are these being used?

In any such examination, it becomes clear that social work, like all professions, is not monolithic and that a unifying ideology, to the extent that it exists, rests on very broad value positions which are subject to many variations in interpretation, some of which may indeed be in conflict with one another. The lack of a common position in the profession on income maintenance proposals is one specific indication of the range of differences that exists; the differences are not only technical but involve value issues as well, which is generally the case in choices of social policy.

General issues concerning the relationship of professions to ideologies and political movements are being contested in the wider social arena today and satisfactory answers are not available. The curriculum should provide opportunities for persistent analytical probing in an effort to achieve both greater clarification of the issues, and the development of the student's own individual professional identity and self-confidence. The links between professional competence and ideological positions are a central concern, particularly for practitioners in community organization and social planning whose very practice will put them almost invariably within a field of conflicting value positions. Such a practitioner is frequently identified both with the value of the profession and with the social goals of the organization, agency, or social movement in which he is functioning as a professional. The present assumption, either implicit or explicit, is that such commitments are at least compatible over a wide

---

[20] Nathan E. Cohen (ed.), *Social Work and Social Problems* (New York: National Association of Social Workers, 1964).

area of the field—that is, that a properly committed professional can serve with integrity under a variety of auspices which have different views on many social issues. Much more needs to be said, however, about just what the boundaries of these interrelated commitments are and at what point they become incompatible.

It is also important for the concentrator in community organization and social planning to obtain some orientation toward other professionals with whom he will be working in inter-disciplinary settings that are particularly characteristic of his area of practice. The discussion in this chapter has pointed to one facet of that orientation, which is the need to obtain a grounding in the special concerns, responsibilities, and areas of competence which define his contribution to an interdisciplinary effort. That experience lies in the social welfare–social policy area and will be detailed further in the outlines of the practice courses. It should be stressed again at this point, however, that unsettled and evolving definitions of social welfare mean that there is a growing field where no profession has a clear or exclusive claim and where many are seeking to define their contribution. As far as the community organization concentrator is concerned, a key goal of this section of the curriculum is to provide him with the necessary background to participate knowledgeably and creatively in those explorations.

PART III

CURRICULUM CONTENT: PRACTICE AREAS

Introduction

THE PRACTICE COURSES which will be discussed in this part of the report focus on the practitioner in community organization and social planning. Unlike the foundation courses, these courses deal directly with the content of the practitioner's responsibilities, roles, and tasks. However, they are not limited to the teaching of methods. Their objective is to integrate knowledge, methodology, and skill in dealing with substantive social problems. The courses therefore include a review of the contexts in which the practice of community organization and social planning takes place, the typical problems and issues that are faced in practice, and the solutions available to the practitioner. These are elements of knowledge on the basis of which the practitioner makes his choice of behaviors. Skill is the ability to use such knowledge effectively in carrying out actions which are deliberately designed to achieve practice goals.

The discussion of practice courses here is in the nature of a summary and should be supplemented by reference to the companion volumes produced by the Curriculum Project. The textbook, *Community Organization and Social Planning* by Arnold Gurin and Robert Perlman, provides the framework for the courses. *A New Look at Field Instruction: Education for Application of Practice Skills in Community Organization and Social Planning*, by Jack Rothman and Wyatt C. Jones, offers detailed illustrations of the ways in which classroom teaching and field experiences can be integrated. The casebook, *Community Organizers and Social Planners* by Joan Levin Ecklein and Armand Lauffer, provides additional teaching material bearing on many of the methodological issues to be covered in the courses.

In line with the general position that has been taken in this report, the suggested practice courses are not designed as definitive blueprints. They are presented with two purposes in mind. One is to identify the elements of content in the practice of community organization and social planning which the Project staff considers to be essential. The second purpose is to demonstrate how the different elements might be combined into a coherent format for teaching. Our recommendations are more definitive in the first area than in the second. Provided that the basic elements are included, there can and should be wide experimentation in the use of different types of formats. Some of the possible variations—but by no means all of them—will be indicated in the course of the discussion.

The material on practice courses will be presented in sections, as follows:

1. *Core courses* (Chapters 6, 7, and 8). These are designed to provide a broad introduction to the entire field of community organization and social planning, including its settings, methodologies, and practitioner behaviors. An initial survey course is designed to deal with the contexts in which practice takes place and with the typical issues that arise in each of them. The survey is followed by two methods courses which focus respectively on organizing and planning and involve training for the acquisition of necessary practice skills. Associated with these courses are various laboratory and field experiences described in detail in the Rothman-Jones volume.
2. *Specialized courses* (Chapter 9). These provide more intensive exploration of specific types of practice and more direct training in methodology and application skills.
3. *Practicum* (Chapter 10). This is designed to provide intensive experience in carrying out community organization and social planning processes within a specialized area.

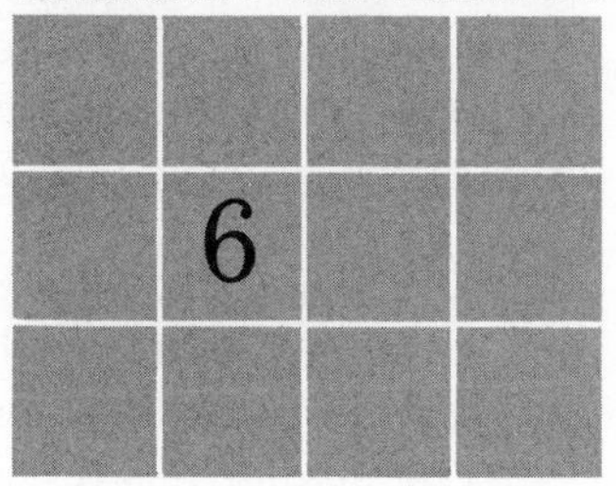

Introductory Survey

THE SOCIETAL CONTEXT OF PRACTICE

Professional practice in community organization and social planning represents one form of intervention in dealing with social problems. Issues regarding the relationship of professional activity to other mechanisms of social change, such as citizen action, social movements, and governmental intervention are raised at this point but no attempt is made to resolve them. The point is made, however, that it is one of the basic tasks of the practitioner to identify himself within the broader social context in which his effort is undertaken and to be knowledgeable concerning the various forces that are at work in a process of change. Material on social problems and social change which was included in the section on foundation courses is reviewed here and focused in relation to the responsibilities of practice.

CONCEPTUALIZATIONS OF PRACTICE

The companion textbook to this volume contains a critical review of the theoretical literature in community organization, with particular reference to suggested "models" of practice. These may be briefly summarized as the "integration" model of Ross, which placed the emphasis upon the enabling role of the practitioner in helping people to identify their needs and to develop methods of meeting them; the "planned change" model of Lippitt *et al.*, which conceptualized the community as a "client" whose behavior is subject to change through interpersonal influence; the "planning" model of Morris and Binstock, which views the practitioner as an expert in recommending appropriate definitions of the problem to be tackled and the methods best calculated to deal with it; and the "social action" models of Grosser, Haggstrom, and other writers, in which it is the practitioner's role to work with disadvantaged groups in order to achieve basic changes in the distribution of power and resources.[1]

The purpose of this review is to make the student aware of the many aspects of practice and to indicate that no single model is adequate to cover all situations that arise. The student will therefore be invited to use the literature heuristically as a source of insight into the nature of practice but to leave open issues of definition and conceptualization until there has been an opportunity to gain a greater exposure to the specifics of practice itself.

SUGGESTED FRAMEWORK

The general framework set forth in the textbook is presented as a way of ordering the material to be covered in the survey of practice. The framework is multi-dimensional and essentially descriptive rather than typological and analytical. It has three major components:

1. A division of the field of practice by structure and function into three major contexts: voluntary associations, direct service agencies, and planning and allocating organizations.
2. A problem-solving model of the typical steps in practice including the following: (1) defining the problem, (2) establishing structural and communication links for consideration of the problem, (3) studying alternative solutions and adopting a policy, (4) developing and implementing a program plan, and (5) monitoring and receiving feedback.
3. A division of practitioner tasks into "analytical" and "interactional" elements, both of which are considered essential to practice. The analytical elements refer to the rational processes in which the practitioner engages in order to understand the problem with which he is dealing and to choose a line of action. The interactional elements refer to the actual implement-

---

[1] Murray G. Ross and B. W. Lappin, *Community Organization: Theory, Principles, and Practice*, second edition (New York: Harper and Row, 1967); Ronald Lippitt, Jeanne Watson, and Bruce Westley, *Dynamics of Planned Change* (New York: Harcourt, Brace and World, 1958); Robert Morris and Robert Binstock, *Feasible Planning for Social Change* (New York: Columbia University Press, 1966); Charles F. Grosser, "Community Development Programs Serving the Urban Poor," *Social Work*, Vol. 10, No. 3 (July, 1965), pp. 15-21; Warren Haggstrom, "Can the Poor Transform the World?" in Irwin Deutscher and Elizabeth Thompson, (eds.), *Among the People: Encounters with the Poor* (New York: Basic Books, 1968); and John Erlich, "Organizing the Poor," *Bibliography in Poverty and Human Resources Abstracts*, Vol. 1, No. 6 (1966).

ing moves that he makes in order to carry out the plan that he has chosen.

The survey will be built primarily around the organizational contexts, since experience indicates that these seem to have a more powerful impact on the nature of practice than any of the others. They therefore provide a useful device for ordering a large volume of specific material.

The framework need not be elaborated extensively at this point but can be explicated as the survey proceeds to detailed examination of all the components in the scheme. As the survey course unfolds, there will be opportunity to concretize various aspects of the framework. It would be desirable even in this initial presentation, however, to avoid excessive formalism and abstraction by the use of illustrative material. Some of this may be found in the Ecklein-Lauffer casebook. Other brief illustrations can be drawn selectively from recent literature in community organization and social planning.[2]

VOLUNTARY ASSOCIATIONS

The term "voluntary associations" is used broadly to cover a wide range of activities in which people engage in order to achieve specified ends. It includes both *ad hoc* informal groups and formally structured organizations. The most salient feature of practice with voluntary associations is that the practitioner is engaged directly with a population that is being served. In that respect it differs from the other two contexts (direct service agencies and planning and allocating organizations) in which the central tasks involve relationships within or between organizations. Most of our thinking concerning direct practice with populations has been influenced by experience in community development work in developing countries or in the organization of low-income urban neighborhoods, primarily in the United States. The neighborhood work shares many of the community development concepts, though frequently combining them with a militant social action ideology and strategy. In the survey course, special attention should be given to the characteristics of practice with groups subject to the problems of low income and other social deprivations. The survey should also attempt to identify a number of recurring issues which arise in work with all types of voluntary associations.

The following are some of the important dimensions in which voluntary associations vary:

---

[2] See especially: John Turner, (ed.), *Neighborhood Organization for Community Action* (New York: National Association of Social Workers, 1968); Alfred J. Kahn, *Theory and Practice of Social Planning* (New York: Russell Sage Foundation, 1969) and *Studies in Social Policy and Planning* (New York: Russell Sage Foundation, 1969); Ralph M. Kramer and Harry Specht, *Readings in Community Organization Practice* (Englewood Cliffs, N.J.: Prentice-Hall, Inc., 1969); and George A. Brager and Francis C. Purcell, (eds.) *Community Action Against Poverty: Readings from the Mobilization Experience* (New Haven, Conn.: College and University Press, 1967).

Class and ethnic factors. Voluntary associations may be based on a common interest or on a common status such as race, ethnicity, religion, or class (or some combination of these). Distinctive cultural factors related to the status determine the purposes of the association and the character of its activities and comprise some of the specific knowledge that the practitioner must master.

Ideology. Associations have some ideological orientation, whether implicit or explicit, which determines their stance in relation to other institutions in the community. Some are explicitly ideological either in defense of or in opposition to the status quo. Most are less explicitly ideological but may have value judgments on more limited and specific issues. Ideologies are sometimes linked to class or ethnic identities, but not necessarily so.

Purpose and functions. These vary on a number of dimensions. One is the target of the effort—whether to serve members of the association themselves or to perform a service for others. Another is the nature of the activity—whether to conduct programs and services or to advance an interest or cause.

Autonomy. Associations may be self-appointed and independent or sponsored by another organization; if the latter, the extent of outside control is an important consideration.

Scope. Associations may limit their activities to one locality or extend them to wider geographical areas; they also vary as to whether it is part of a wider movement or simply a local movement.

Elements of practice

It is a central aspect of the practitioner's task to identify variables such as those outlined above and to calculate their implications for the setting of goals and selection of strategies. The first step in this process is an analysis of the "relevant" community—a more specific and limited notion of community than the total population of an area, and one which calls for specifying the basis on which segments of a population are being organized.

In the Rothman-Jones companion volume, there is an outline for a student field experience in making a study of the "community system context" in which an organization operates.[3] This calls for an examination of the characteristics of the population to which the organizational effort is directed and an inventory of the problems found in the area; it also calls for an estimate of the potential resources for dealing with the problem. It will thus provide the student with an opportunity to identify the segments of the community which are relevant to various purposes. If an

[3] Jack Rothman and Wyatt Jones, *A New Look at Field Instruction: Education for Application of Practice Skills in Community Organization and Social Planning* (New York: Association Press, 1970).

effort is being made to build a neighborhood-based association, it is necessary to determine the characteristics of the neighborhood and its problem situations, both as measured through "objective" indices and as perceived by the people of the neighborhood. On the other hand, an organizational effort need not be geographically bound at all but may instead be based on a particular status or a common interest. In this case the analysis would attempt to define the character of this common interest and the present and potential extent of its relevance to various members within a given population.

Frequently the practitioner finds himself in an undefined situation where it becomes his initial responsibility to identify the "relevant community" on the basis of his own estimate of the needs of the situation and of the potentialities for launching an organizational effort. The tasks involved in this process are not solely analytical but include a combination of what the framework has described as "analytical" and "interactional" components. Actually, the initial phase of an organizing effort in an unstructural situation is an important aspect of c.o. practice that merits special attention both in class and in laboratory experiences. The survey course can provide a beginning exposure to such work, but further experience is to be obtained through specialized courses and in the practicum at a later point in the student's education.

In working with voluntary associations in low-income areas, two broad approaches to practice can be identified. One might be termed a "developmental" approach in which the emphasis is on building a greater capacity on the part of the deprived population to deal with its problems, and the other is a "social action" approach in which the focus is on efforts by the deprived population to change the policies of organizations which affect power relationships and the distribution of resources. Both the literature and the student's own experience in the laboratory will make it clear that these approaches are not mutually exclusive but that they co-exist within many programs that are conducted among low-income populations. The differences are matters of emphasis, determined partly by ideology and partly by situational factors.

Voluntary associations, whether middle-class or lower-class, fulfill multiple functions. In addition to the manifest goals and activities which the association pursues, it also performs less explicit functions which provide satisfaction to the participants and help to keep them affiliated. One of the essential elements in practice is the responsibility of the practitioner to help the association maintain its focus on its purposes and functions so that the tasks which it has undertaken may be performed effectively. On the other hand, the maintenance needs of the association must also be met if it is to survive and fulfill its functions.

In order to avoid goal displacement, the practitioner needs to focus both on the clarification of goals and the selection of strategies that are consonant with them. Goals are determined by a combination of objective analysis and value choices. Voluntary associations that seek changes in a community situation generally have one or more of the following objectives: (1) to achieve better connections between people and services; (2) to organize new services; and (3) to achieve long-range institutional changes. Each of these objectives calls for somewhat different strategies.

The relationship between organization and services constitutes a recurring practice issue, particularly in work with low-income populations. It has been found, for example, that organizations whose basic purpose is to develop a social movement that will engage in social action may have their goals displaced by responding to calls for help in areas of individual need.[4] On the other hand, the development of services can help to build a social movement, provided that effort is directed beyond self-help activities to larger goals that call for institutional change.[5]

One of the most general issues to be explored in the section of the survey which deals with voluntary associations is the relationship of such efforts to larger community and societal systems. Even the most limited type of association represents the expression of an interest or need that has connections with other segments of the community and society. Isolated *ad hoc* actions which do not have such links with larger social systems tend to disappear after a short period and to leave their participants with a sense of frustration and lack of accomplishment.

Sponsors of voluntary associations who focus on a specific and immediate objective may not be fully aware of the interdependence between their effort and other systems. It is part of the responsibility of the practitioner to have this larger view and to include those connections explicitly in his analysis of the organizational situation and his evaluation of goals and strategies. In planning actions to be taken, he attempts to foresee the consequences of such actions both immediately and over a long-range period, taking into account both the consequences within the association itself and those in the larger system of networks with which the association is involved.

The identification of a relevant community and the selection of objectives and strategies call for an interplay between the practitioner and the population that he is trying to serve. Even though it is recognized that the practitioner enters such a situation with his own biases and orientations toward what needs to be and can be done, he must adapt his prior views to what he discovers in the process of his interaction with the people being served. The personality and ability of the practitioner are important variables which cannot be controlled and which cannot be taken fully into account in making a rational analysis of alternative choices and their

[4] Robert Perlman and David Jones, *Neighborhood Service Centers* (Washington, D.C.: U.S. Government Printing Office, 1967).

[5] Turner, *op. cit.*

potential consequences. The education of the practitioner should include, however, opportunities for him to gain some insight into his own methods of operation and areas of strengths and weaknesses as elements to be evaluated in choosing a course of action.

DIRECT SERVICE AGENCIES

The second context of practice is that of an agency which has a responsibility to meet the needs of a specified target population through the provision of direct services. Like voluntary associations, service agencies vary widely in regard to specific goals, programs, and other dimensions. They do, however, have a number of common characteristics. The direct service agency is a *formal* organization (which the voluntary association may or may not be) which faces two ways—toward the population to whom it is responsible and to the institutional network from which it draws its mandate and resources to provide the services needed. Much of the discussion within this section of the survey can be based on elaboration of these two essential characteristics of the service agency.

The perspective from which a service agency views its client population is different from the perspective of the voluntary association. In the case of the latter, the focus is on the needs and aspirations of the population, and service issues are approached in terms of the association's more general goals for the population. In the case of the service agency, the responsibility to the population is more specifically defined. The practitioner must study not only the population and its needs but also must develop a careful analysis of the nature of the organization through which the service is being rendered.

The laboratory-observatory exercises described in the Rothman-Jones volume suggest ways of analyzing the organizational structure of the service agency, including its governing body, staff, and sponsorship within the community. The exercises are designed to help the student identify the orientations which different elements within the organization have toward the responsibilities that they are expected to assume. Drawing upon both organizational studies and their own analysis, students will be expected to acquire an understanding of recurring problems in service agencies, such as the impact on organizational goals of competing pressures from different levels of an organization (staff, administration, and governing body or sponsors).

The analysis should be addressed to questions such as whose values and preferences are being served in the decisions concerning allocation of resources and the selection of priorities among different services, who the "public" is to whom the agency is or should be responsible, and how this public expresses its views and exercises control over the decisions of the agency.

Students should be provided with an opportunity to compare agency-clientele relationships in situations where there are class differences with others where such differences do not exist, in order to determine the extent to which unsatisfactory relations between agencies and clients are related to class differences or to more general factors in the functioning of service bureaucracies.

A central problem that faces the practitioner in a service agency is his need to function within the framework of the organization and yet to be an agent of change in attempting to meet the needs of people more effectively. This means that the practitioner must operate within a broader frame of reference than that furnished to him by the organization at any particular moment. In effect, he must be a critic of the organization's current assumptions and behaviors and therefore must be able to draw upon other possible assumptions and criteria which present alternatives to the current situation. He is expected to be aware of the constraints in the situation but also to introduce additional expert knowledge pointing to possible alternatives to present policies and programs.

As indicated earlier, the practitioner in the direct service agency faces two ways—toward the population being served and toward the wider community from which resources need to be derived in order to carry out the service function. It is his responsibility to play an active role in obtaining more adequate resources and the better utilization of such resources in meeting the needs for which he is responsible.

Three major functions are identified in this area:

1. *Mobilization of support.* The practitioner is responsible for the maintenance of lines of communication both within the organization and between the organization and the community which provide regularized means for making known the scope and character of the needs which have to be served. This calls not only for the use of general media of communication promotion, etc., but the building of relationships with relevant segments of the community that can contribute to meeting those needs.

2. *Exchange of resources.* A direct service agency is part of a network of organizations which are interdependent in various ways. It is part of the practitioner's responsibility to build both short-term and long-range relationships with other organizations, depending on the specific needs of the service for which he is responsible. Some of the general components of such interdependencies and exchange systems have been described in the literature on inter-organizational relationships.[6]

---

[6] Sol Levine and Paul E. White, "Exchange as a Conceptual Framework for the Study of Interorganizational Relationships," *Administrative Science Quarterly*, Vol. V, No. 4 (March, 1961); Eugene Litwak and Lydia Hylton, "Interorganizational Analysis: A Hypothesis on Coordinating Agencies," *Administrative Science Quarterly*, Vol. VI, No. 4 (March, 1962); and Violet M. Sieder, "Community Organization in the Direct Service Agency," *Social Welfare Forum, 1962* (New York: Columbia University Press, 1962).

3. *Changes in resources.* Considerable emphasis should be placed on the responsibility of the direct service agency to be an active agent in the creation of additional resources rather than limiting itself to the narrow task of promoting its needs and obtaining support from the existing pool of available resources. This calls for an ongoing evaluation of needs, for experimentation by the agency itself in undertaking new projects for which existing resources are not available, and for participation in wider inter-organizational networks that undertake broader efforts to increase resources.

PLANNING AND ALLOCATING ORGANIZATIONS

This third context of practice covers a wide field. The kinds of boundary issues which were discussed in the foundation courses on social welfare and social policy come into focus in attempting to "map" the scope of planning and allocating organizations. Several different levels may be identified as follows:

1. "Sectoral" planning within a particular field of service or problem area, such as aging, income maintenance, income security, family welfare, or juvenile delinquency.
2. Social welfare planning across a number of problem or program sectors, in order to achieve better integration and coordination of a number of welfare services.
3. Planning within the "social sector," including not only the services generally identified as belonging in the welfare field but also health and educational services as they impinge on one another in meeting social needs.
4. Comprehensive planning in which the "social sector" is related to both physical planning and economic planning with a view toward examining the impact of all these different sectors on social problems and social needs.

In addition to these categories dealing with the *scope* of social planning, two other dimensions have a major impact upon the character of practice.

1. Geographical—that is, whether the planning effort is limited to the local level (and whether it is bound to a neighborhood or other small locality, as against an effort which is community-wide within a city or metropolitan area); state or regional; or national.
2. Whether the effort is undertaken under the auspices of governmental or nongovernmental bodies.

There are a number of common elements which characterize practice in all planning settings and which distinguish it from practice in the other contexts (i.e., voluntary associations and direct service agencies):

1. Just as the context of voluntary associations has at its center the engagement of the practitioner in direct relationship with a population, and the practice in direct service agencies gravitates around the functions of a single organization, the distinctive feature of the planning and allocating organization is that it is the center of a system of interorganizational relationships. This means that decision-making and policy formation are proces-

ses which are distributed through a number of organizational structures, each of which has some degree of independence in determining its course of action.

2. Because of this situation, there are many constraints on the ability of a planning organization to reach decisions and to implement decisions even after they have been adopted.

3. It follows that structural arrangements and the distribution of authority within such structures are key elements in the establishment of interorganizational planning organizations. The test of the effectiveness of a structure is the ability to develop a view of the problem and a definition of the task to be performed, to formulate policies and plans, and to secure the implementation of such plans through the appropriate organizational systems.

4. Planning and allocating organizations are concerned in one way or another with the issues of coordination, allocation of resources, and innovation. In both coordination and allocation, there is an implication that the current distribution of functional responsibilities is accepted as given, and that the task is to achieve better implementation through proper use of resources and effective complementary working relationships. Innovation, on the other hand, is a process initiated by a question as to whether the existing definitions and assumptions are valid.

There seems to be some tension between these two types of goals and it may be that they require different structural arrangements as well as the use of different techniques for problem identification and the pursuit of action programs. Some beginning attempts have been made to establish empirical relationships between organizational functions and/or structures and strategies of action such as consensus or conflict.[7] Such variables need to be related more systematically to other sources of variation in community characteristics.

The geographical and governmental dimensions listed above play an important part in determining the characteristics of practice. The problem of decision-making and authority is different within a governmental body than it is in a voluntary system. Similarly, the "relevant" framework for planning will depend both on the scope of planning being considered and its geographical location. In all cases there are specific sets of relationships which proceed along both horizontal and vertical lines, all of which need to be taken into consideration in the development of the planning task. Ideological orientations, class interests, and political cross currents play an important role in the context of planning and allocating organizations as they do in the other two contexts of practice. Most typically, the planning and allocating organization provides an area in which contending forces meet one another either for conflict or cooperation or some combination of both modes of relationship.

---

[7] See, for example: Martin Rein and Robert Morris, "Goals, Structures, and Strategies for Community Change," *Social Work Practice* (New York: Columbia University Press, 1962); and Roland L. Warren, *Types of Purposive Social Change at the Community Level*, Brandeis Paper No. 11 (Waltham, Mass.: The Florence Heller Graduate School for Advanced Studies in Social Welfare, Brandeis University).

A planning and allocating organization which places the stress on innovation is itself a mechanism of change. Its problem is to consider the resistances it must overcome as well as the resources it can tap in order to achieve such change. This is the stance that has been described by Morris and Binstock as "feasible planning" which involves a careful examination and weighing of the interests, commitments, and resources of the relevant parties in a systematic manner.[8]

A planning and allocating organization may, however, be concerned primarily with coordinating and allocating resources, in which case it becomes a mechanism for resolving conflicts among contending forces into working relationships. This also calls for a careful examination and weighing of interests, commitments, and resources of the relevant parties, but the process and strategies might be very different. The emphasis in this case would be much more heavily on the definition of the task and the location of a goal which represents areas of common interest in dealing with a problem. In the innovating approach, the focus is on the implementation of a goal through the exertion of influence by the planner upon the policies of target organizations.

Against the backdrop of this charting of the field of planning and allocating organizations and the identification of the major kinds of problems that arise in practice, it will then be possible to deal more specifically with the role of the practitioner himself. As indicated in the framework outlined earlier, practice is viewed as a problem-solving process which involves both analytical and interactional tasks.

An over-simplified sketch of the problem-solving process would be formulated as follows:

1. The examination and joint consideration of values and preferences in order to agree upon a choice of objectives.
2. The development of an appropriate structure to obtain the necessary mandate and legitimacy for engaging in planning with a view toward maximizing the effectiveness of that planning.
3. Rational processes of examining and evaluating needs through the steps of policy formulation, programming, evaluation, and feedback.
4. Systematic evaluation of consideration of feasibility to be interwoven with the process outlined under point 3.

This outline, like the overall framework of the Curriculum Project, merges into a single scheme of elements which have sometimes been separated under such titles as "community organization" and "social planning." Both analytical and interactional skills are required in order to conduct a process of problem identification and problem-solving. The practitioner engages in analysis in order to define the interorganizational network that is relevant to the planning task. However, this would not be sufficient to accomplish the steps in the process unless the practitioner

[8] Morris and Binstock, *op. cit.*

is himself able to generate channels of communication and mutual exploration among the people involved.

Evaluation of needs calls primarily for analytical skills. The practitioner should be as expert as possible in bringing forward bodies of data that help to measure the extent and characteristics of problems and that help to pose alternative policies and programs. In program implementation, both analytical and interactional tasks are essential. Many possible strategies, involving the use of resources of funds, manpower, and prestige through techniques of education, persuasion, contest, and conflict need to be considered analytically on the basis of their potential effectiveness. They must, however, be implemented skillfully by the practitioner in conjunction with the people carrying the responsibility for the action.

At this point, as elsewhere in the course, it should be made clear that the problem-solving model being suggested does not proceed in a linear direction but that the various elements continue to react upon one another in a spiral-like fashion; also, the practitioner may be entering a situation at any point in this scheme. Thus, a project might very well start with an expert evaluation of needs rather than with an examination of values and preferences. The general point is that the planner is inevitably involved not only in the execution of a goal but also in the process of defining and redefining the objectives of the planning enterprise. This requires not only analysis but also interaction with the sponsors of the project and with the target organization to which the effort is directed.

Practitioners will inevitably differ in their native abilities and interests. Not all will be equally competent in all types of analytical and interactional processes. Specialization within portions of the field is to be anticipated. The foregoing discussion is meant to highlight the connections between interactional and analytical tasks, regardless of whether they are performed in any given instance by the same practitioner or divided among several. Within the curriculum each student is exposed to both types of processes and to their interrelated character.

The emphasis of the survey course is on understanding the scope and variations of community organization and social planning rather than on the acquisition of specific skills. It follows, therefore, that the laboratory experiences which are an integral part of this course rely more heavily on observation than on the performance of specific tasks. There should, however, be within the course an initial exposure and some beginning experience in the performance of a number of tasks in such basic areas as interviewing, obtaining information both from people and through documentary sources, some involvement in organizational efforts in different contexts of practice and an initial exposure to some of the techniques that enter into the processes of planning and allocating functions. A number of ways of accomplishing these objectives have been outlined in the Rothman-Jones volume.

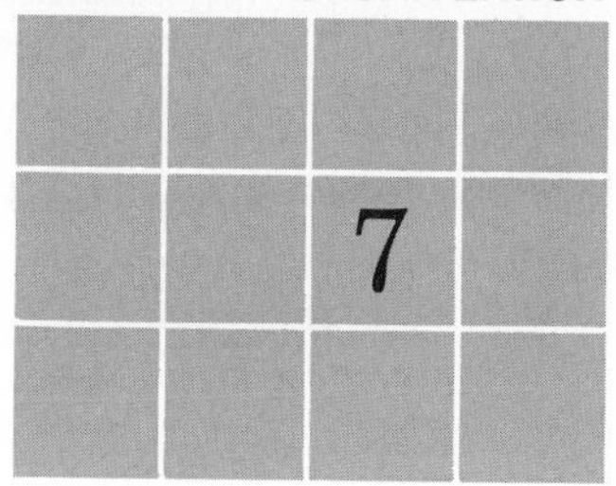

Methods of Organizing

THE BACKGROUND FOR AN UNDERSTANDING of the problems and issues to which practitioner activity is directed will have been supplied in the survey course. The course in methods of organizing attempts to define the typical and recurring methods which practitioners use in performing organizing tasks across a variety of settings and practice contexts; and to provide beginning training in the skills required to perform such tasks. While the focus in the methods course is upon tasks and skills, these must always be referred back to the purposes that they are designed to serve.

A series of skill units, with suggestions as to learning experiences which would help the student to acquire them, have been outlined in the companion volume by Rothman and Jones.[1] They are not necessarily exhaustive, but they do point to major types of recurring activities which constitute a large part of the practitioner's work. In order to help establish the interrelationship of these skills (none of which is in reality a completely discrete operation), they have been grouped as shown below into a few clusters that represent major segments of practice which can be linked to the discussion of problems and issues outlined in the survey course.

[1] Jack Rothman and Wyatt Jones, *A New Look at Field Instruction: Education for Application of Practice Skills in Community Organization* (New York: Association Press, 1970).

Organizational Process
- Initial organizing
- Participation
- Committee technology
- Leadership development and training
- Training and supervision of indigenous professionals

Design and Implementation of Strategies
- Coalitions and coalition formation
- Bargaining
- Advocate role and conflict
- Broker role
- Power structure and the establishment

General Interactional Skills
- Interviewing
- Interpersonal influence and use of self
- Group discussion and enabling

ORGANIZATIONAL PROCESS

A major objective of this methods course is to help the student understand and experience the interrelatedness of different actions within a continuous organizing process and to deal with at least some of the demands that tend to arise at different stages in such a process. Organizing may be divided into "initial" and "ongoing" phases. Two of the proposed skill units ("initial organizing" and "participation") apply particularly to the initial phase.

INITIAL PHASES

A number of analytical questions need to be answered as background for any organizing effort. The starting point is a conception of the purpose that is to be served, guided by an analysis of the problem situation or condition that is to be affected, and by whatever theories and data are relevant to the definition of a goal. Such a conception is either provided to the practitioner by the sponsorship to which he is responsible or, as is more often the case, he is given only a rather general and loose formulation of the purpose or goal which it then becomes his responsibility to specify more concretely. The initial organizing process therefore may be viewed as an exploratory effort in which the answers to a number of the basic analytical questions are arrived at gradually through a conscious process of trial and error guided by preliminary assumptions and hypotheses.

Such exploration is required in order to identify the population or constituency which is to be involved in the organizational effort. A general definition of the "target" population may be available, but the practitioner will usually find it necessary to give this definition greater specification or perhaps to modify it substantially. The trial-and-error methods of initial organization will help to clarify what kind of constitutency is appropriate to the goal (as the goal becomes clearer) and also on what basis people are to be approached—the appeals are being made to what motivations and those being organized will have what interests served by the organizational venture.[2]

Within the general framework of the organizational task that has been identified, people are approached who are presumed to have a potential interest in the venture as a basis for motivation to become part of it. Part of the practitioner's skill is to make such expectations specific. He is not simply observing and testing motivation and interest in the organizational goals but is an active agent in attempting to build participation along the lines that he has set for himself. An element of skill is involved not only in judging correctly the potential base for participation in an organizational effort but also in helping the potential participants to recognize the common interest that they might have in such an organizational effort.

The practitioner makes a tentative judgment as to what individual or group of individuals should be approached first to initiate an organizational effort. Depending on the situation and the objective, this may be an established leader or it may be an individual or individuals previously unknown who are uncovered by the practitioner himself as he explores the interest of potential people. The initial organizing process involves moving from these early recruits along available networks of informal or formal relationships in the gradual expansion of the organizing effort.[3] The skill of the practitioner lies in being able to identify these networks and the motivations that will encourage participation. He must also possess personal qualities of leadership that will help to stimulate others to make the necessary efforts. That ability may be essentially innate and difficult to transmit through training. The educational process, however, should be directed toward helping practitioners who do have native ability to make their actions more deliberate and explicit. Training is also designed to equip the practitioner with self-correcting mechanisms so that, if his initial judgments or "hunches" turn out to be faulty, he will recognize his errors and be able to find alternative ways to proceed.

---

[2] A good discussion of some of the criteria for making such selections will be found in Peter H. Rossi, "Theory, Research and Practice in Community Organization," in Charles P. Adrian, (ed.), *Social Science and Community Action* (East Lansing, Mich.: Michigan State University, 1960).

[3] For a model of an organizing process which begins with an "initiating set," see: Christopher Sower *et al.*, *Community Involvement* (Glencoe, Ill.: Free Press, 1957).

ONGOING ORGANIZATION

The ongoing, continuing phases of an organizational process are in many ways more complicated than the initial organizational steps. It is frequently more difficult to sustain continuing interest and involvement than it is to achieve an initial success in the first steps of organization. Part of the ability to sustain an organizational process is dependent on the soundness of initial judgments in selecting the people to be organized and in setting up a structure for their interaction. There are also actions which could be taken as the process continues in order to sustain the organizational effort.

One of the first methodological issues that arises immediately after the initial work of recruitment has been accomplished (or at least begun) is the development of an organizational structure. There are two functions which structure is expected to serve. One is to create channels of interaction which make it possible for actors to influence one another. Structure also provides the medium for decision-making and task accomplishment. On the other hand, organizational studies tell us that structures can impede effective communication and task achievement. The skill of the practitioner lies in being able to analyze the strengths and weaknesses of various types of structural arrangements, and the ability to develop corrective mechanisms through suggesting alternatives to decision-makers and to argue their efficacy on the basis of logic and demonstration.

More specifically, decisions must be made as to the membership base—how large it should be, who should be eligible, and what powers should reside in the membership as a whole as compared with the smaller bodies to which it delegates its authority. Difficult problems are involved in weighing the assets and liabilities of a broad democratic base (which has the strength of participation but may interfere with rapid and effective task achievement) against a more tightly controlled operation by a small and more homogeneous group. Value preferences and commitments enter into such choices and may in some instances have a determining effect. It is the responsibility of the practitioner, however, to make available expert judgments based not only on values but also on rational evaluations of gains and losses related to the potential consequences of different choices of structure as they might affect the results to be achieved.

Not to be minimized in this process is the play of personalities within organizations. Successes and failures of organizations may often depend upon the influence of a single dominant personality at a particular time. Such influences are not entirely predictable and often not controllable, yet they are capable of overbalancing plans that are based on more rational criteria. Skill in the handling of interpersonal relations is an essential part of the practitioner's equipment. This involves conscious use of his own personality and abilities in his interactions with others engaged in an organizational effort. It also means that he must have an understanding of the dynamics of the interpersonal relationships which exist among people with whom he is working and an appreciation of the influence of such factors upon the organizational process. On the intervention side, he should also have skill in being able to find organizational means for dealing with those interpersonal relationships that may be interfering with the effective movement of an organizational process. Some of the techniques of sensitivity training can be incorporated into the methods course to help achieve this kind of understanding and skill in the area of interpersonal relationships.

The skill units in the Rothman-Jones volume which bear on ongoing phases of organizing are "committee technology," "leadership training," and "supervision of indigenous professionals."[4]

The management of an on-going organizational effort may be conceptualized as a problem-solving process designed to help the organization maximize its chances for successful achievement of its purpose. The central task is operationalized through the program of the organization. Programming calls for defining specific tasks that are tied together in a deliberate order and the maintenance of a timetable which assures that they are phased properly. It also involves working out effective divisions of labor so that necessary pieces of the total job are distributed among the participants in the effort. The structural unit for such activity is the "committee" in one form or another; therefore, the basic elements of "committee technology" must be mastered by the practitioner. Included here are such matters as the formulation of assignments to committees, the selection of appropriate personnel to man them, the preparation of schedules of meetings that are phased into stages of the action, and communication back and forth among committees, the sponsoring groups, and the larger constituencies to whom they are responsible.

The practitioner is always concerned simultaneously with the content of the work to be performed and with the personnel who are involved in the organizational process and on whom the performance of the task depends. Leadership training is a basic aspect of his responsibility. He therefore needs to acquire skills in supervision and teaching which will be used in dealing with staff (both professional and nonprofessional) and volunteers at policy-making and operational levels in the organization.

Decisions made at the initiation of the process concerning the basis for recruitment of participants and their distribution within the organizational structure are subject to review and modification as the process develops. Changes in leadership come about through retraining, replacement, or removal. Diagnostic judgments are to be expected from the practitioner as to when and how to make changes in personnel. He also needs to be

[4] Rothman and Jones, *op. cit.*

able to build mechanisms into the organizational structure that will facilitate effective use of personnel.

DESIGN AND IMPLEMENTATION OF STRATEGIES

At the heart of the methodology of organizing is the choice and implementation of strategies. Building upon the survey course, where strategies were discussed on the basis of the purposes to be served and the organizational issues with which it is necessary to deal, the methods course focuses on the acquisition of skills that are involved in employing strategies properly.

The Rothman-Jones volume outlines a number of exercises, simulations, and field experiences that are related to several alternative strategies which play a major role in community practice. The "broker" strategy emphasizes linking clients and resources. An "advocate" strategy calls for mobilization and exertion of pressure in order to further a particular interest or cause. The use of conflict as an element in the exertion of such pressure is included. "Bargaining" and "coalition" are both strategies based on the development of exchange relationships with other individuals and groups whose resources are needed in order to achieve the purpose in view. They call primarily for skills in negotiation.

In addition to helping students acquire skills in the use of each of these strategies, it is the purpose of the methods course to foster flexibility in using the different strategies appropriately under different circumstances. This second purpose can be accomplished first by covering a range of strategies within the same course. Also, if there is a wide battery of learning experiences available which includes both classroom exercises and field experiences, the student can be helped to shift gears fairly rapidly through a variety of situations which call for differing approaches. Continuous references should be made to propositions available in theoretical and research literature concerning types of strategies and the condition under which they should be used.[5] The methods course provides an opportunity to test such propositions operationally.

Strategy most often involves an attempt to influence some external individual or body in order to achieve a goal of the organizational effort. A methodology for such strategic planning has been described in detail

---

[5] See, for example: Paul Davidoff, "Advocacy and Pluralism in Planning," *Journal of the American Institute of Planners,* Vol. 31, No. 4 (November, 1965), pp. 331-38; Martin Rein and Robert Morris, "Goals, Structures and Strategies for Community Change," *Social Work Practice* (New York: Columbia University Press, 1962); Jack Rothman, "An Analysis of Goals and Roles in Community Organization Practice," *Social Work,* Vol. 9, No. 2 (April, 1964), pp. 24-31; Harry Specht, "Disruptive Tactics," *Social Work,* Vol. 14, No. 2 (April, 1969), pp. 5-15; and Roland L. Warren and Herbert Hyman, "Purposive Community Change in Consensus and Dissensus Situations," *Community Mental Health Journal,* Vol. II, No. 4 (Winter, 1966).

by Morris and Binstock.[6] The Rothman-Jones volume deals with some of the same elements in the proposed skill unit labelled "Power Structure and the Establishment." Training would include the use of established methods to locate the nature of the power structure in a particular situation and also for the selection of strategy to influence this power structure. Power structure is dealt with in this context not as a general sociological phenomenon but much more specifically in relation to the nature and purposes of the organizing effort that is being pursued. The sociological literature is useful in describing the nature of power structures in communities and the different approaches which can be used in identifying the patterns of influence which maintain it and which govern its operations. However, the purpose is to select a strategy of cooperation and/or conflict with elements of the power structure that will help to achieve the goals of the organizational effort.

GENERAL SKILLS

Over and above the kinds of specific methodological skills that have been outlined up to this point, the methods courses are to include training in a number of general skill areas which are necessary for the practitioner and which are employed in a variety of contexts rather than being tied to specific elements of practice.

Generally speaking, these are skills in the broad area of communication. The practitioner should have facility in communicating both orally and in writing, and should be able to use such communications as conscious tools in furthering the organizational processes that have been outlined above. Basic to this is the practitioner's disciplined use of his own personality and influence in forming relationships and guiding them toward the achievement of a desired outcome.

A number of communication skills can be isolated and treated as somewhat discrete elements for training purposes, although they are useful only to the extent that they are integrated into a purposeful process of analysis and action. One of the most fundamental skills is interviewing, in which the practitioner engages constantly in the course of his organizing activity. Attention should be paid to both formal and informal interviews and to the different purposes for which interviews are conducted, such as obtaining information, transmitting information, or mutual exploration of ideas, proposals, and alternatives around organizational issues.

Equally prevalent is the use of group discussion as a channel for communication and decision-making. Skill in the leadership of group discussion involves both direct and indirect techniques. Partly, the skill called for is knowledge of the issues under discussion, ability to contribute to

[6] Robert Morris and Robert Binstock, *Feasible Planning for Social Change* (New York: Columbia University Press, 1966).

their clarification in an expert manner, and guidance of the *content* of the discussion toward effective decision-making. The other side is skill in guiding the *process* of the discussion so that the contributions which are needed from the various participants have an opportunity to be made effectively. That aspect is what is generally termed the "enabling" role, and the practitioner needs to acquire enabling skills both in the leadership of group discussions and in other types of communication in the organizing process.

Finally, this category includes formal communications, such as reports, proposals, position statements, etc., which need to be conveyed both within the organization and between the organization and its external environment. Skill involves the ability to choose the proper form of communication for the purpose at hand, to use the communication mode effectively in making the desired impact, and to enable and train others to use the communication channels effectively.

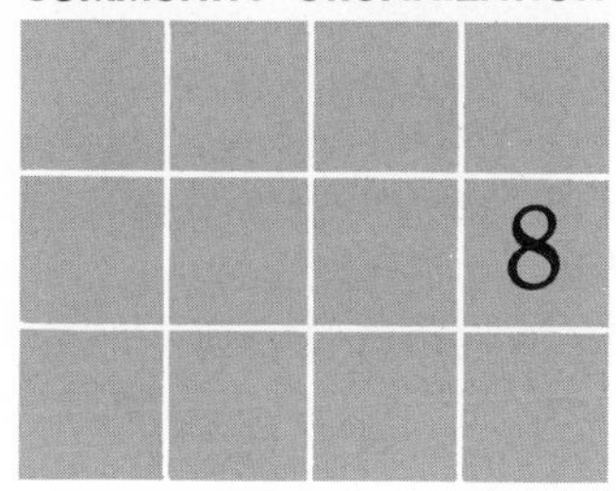

Methods of Planning

ALTHOUGH SUBJECT MATTER is divided between the two methods courses for purpose of feasibility in arranging curriculum content, there is no sharp line between "organizing" and "planning." In a general way, it may be said that planning deals with the content of problems, policies, and programs, whereas organizing is concerned with actors and their relationships in dealing with the problems. In the casebook produced by the Curriculum Project, where cases are divided into these two major categories, the following formulation is used:

> Planners concern themselves with the modification, elimination, or creation of policies, programs, or resources in the service systems.
>
> Organizers direct their activities toward modifying the behavior of people in their roles as citizens, consumers, clients, members of organizations, or functionaries.[1]

As in the case of the course on methods of organizing, reference will be made to the exercise and field experiences proposed in the Rothman-Jones volume.[2] The relevant skill units for this course are organized into two clusters.

---

[1] Joan Ecklein and Armand Lauffer, *Community Organizers and Social Planners: A Casebook* (New York: John Wiley & Sons, Inc., 1970).

[2] Jack Rothman and Wyatt Jones, *A New Look at Field Instruction: Education for Application of Practice Skills in Community Organization* (New York: Association Press, 1970).

Design

Fact-finding and social survey techniques
Policy analysis
Program development
Decision-making
Political process
Legislative process
Governmental process and structure

Implementation

Administrative role and function
Fund raising and proposal writing
Consultation
Staff development and supervision
Promotional-education-public relations techniques

It is one of the premises of these curriculum recommendations that organizing and planning are interrelated aspects of practice which must be employed in close conjuction with each other. Elements of skill training that are included under organizing must therefore be drawn upon for the planning course, and vice versa. Thus, for example, at certain points in the discussion of the implementation of plans it will be necessary to refer back to an item such as "committee technology," which was listed in the organizing skills group. On the other hand, data gathering and analysis are also part of the organizing task.

The division between "design" and "implementation" in the listing of clusters of planning skills is equally imprecise and involves similiar overlapping. Design and implementation are two phases of a planning process which flow into each other and also feed back from one to the other. A number of the skill units are applicable or can be applicable to both. Thus, the units concerned with political and legislative intervention enter into the design stage as possible strategies to be selected in mapping the planning project and are also implementing mechanisms to carry out the plan.

The groupings of the skill units therefore point to their *major* role within a planning process, but not an exclusive role. In broad terms, the skill units clustered under "design" are most relevant for problem identification and policy formulation, whereas those under "implementation" are more related to those aspects of the planning process that involve programming, implementation, evaluation, and feedback.

CONCEPTS OF PLANNING

While concepts and definitions of planning differ, all imply some form of relationship between means and ends. Planning is behavior directed toward a goal. It is a rational process. Within such an approach there are variations in detail and emphasis. Some stress only the implementing aspects, assuming the goal as given. Others include in planning the process of determining the goal as well as devising and/or implementing the means to carry it out. Those who include goal determination place planning in a larger framework—as a process designed to solve social problems or to promote social development. Such views are still encompassed within a rational model.

There is, however, a view of planning which breaks away from the rational model altogether and substitutes a process approach. Instead of specifying a goal and attempting to affect actions in such a way as to realize the goal, planning, in this view, establishes processes of interaction out of which both goals and methods of achieving them will be generated.

There are echoes here of the discussion in sociology of the "rational system" vs. the "natural system."[3] Within the planning field, the notions of "incremental planning" have been posed as alternatives to the rational model. Webber, in reviewing the newer conceptions of planning that point the way for the furture, combines concepts based on ecology, program planning, and development to emphasize an open-system approach, based on adaptive, self-regulating mechanisms. He finds that planning today is viewed not as a straightforward march toward an end-state but as an ongoing enterprise which merges "intelligence and purpose into evolutionary processes."[4]

Upon close examination it appears that the revisions of the rational model are somewhat less definitive than they seem to be on the surface. Purposes and goals are still involved in the process. However, the means-ends relationship is described in more complex and subtle terms. It is not to be viewed as a simple linear relationship but as an interacting chain in which both ends and means are subject to continuous redefinition and correction in the light of experience. Ends, in this light, are not merely the broad global social goals which may motivate a project. They are also the more limited, more operational goals which are defined and redefined progressively within an evolutionary process.

Another element in the challenge to overly rationalistic conceptions of planning relates to the scope of control that is claimed for a central planning process. The weight of evidence in theory, research, and practice indicates the severe limitations in the ability of any central planning body to control complex social processes in clear and economical relationships

---

[3] Alvin Gouldner, "Organizational Analysis," in Leonard S. Kogan, (ed.), *Social Science Theory and Social Work Research* (New York: National Association of Social Workers, 1960).

[4] Melvin M. Webber, "Systems Planning for Social Policy," in Ralph M. Kramer and Harry Specht, (eds.), *Readings in Community Organization Practice* (Englewood Cliffs, N.J.: Prentice-Hall, Inc., 1969), p. 418.

to a predetermined goal. That is the meaning of planning against which Webber argues in saying that "Comprehensive planning is not equivalent to either centralized control or coordination. Its output is *improved coherence* among components. . . . It calls for a process of looking outward from one's own focus of activity in search of relations to other activities and in an attempt to fit the one to others" (emphasis in original).[5]

Given these appropriate and reasonable modifications in the rational model, planning continues to represent a rational process in which an attempt is made to choose and implement lines of action that will help to achieve certain desired outcomes. The expectations need to be stated in some form although they can and should be subject to revision on the basis of continuous monitoring, feedback, and evaluation.

The problem-solving framework that was outlined in the survey course (Chapter 6) together with the model used by Kahn in his recent work on social planning provide a useful framework for the course in planning methods.[6] Four major elements—problem identification, policy formulation, program development, and evaluation and feedback—will be used as pegs to which specific skills units will be attached.

PROBLEM IDENTIFICATION

At the risk of oversimplification, the methodology of planning may be characterized as the effective utilization of data in relation to decision-making. Since the data available in areas of social problems are generally not adequate to answer the questions being posed, the methodology must include ways of creating data as well as using that which already exists. It must also incorporate techniques for facilitating the decision-making process in the absence of adequate data. The issue which arises at the point of problem identification is whether to accept an existing formulation as provided by an existing service, organization, profession, or interest group or to define the problem in more "objective" terms, based on a body of data which will somehow describe the condition more adequately and therefore (presumably) provide a better guide to the appropriate interventions. Although the planner is frequently enmeshed from the outset in a variety of prejudgments and constraints that stem from the auspices under which he is operating and various other factors, the theoretical model is nevertheless useful in defining some of the tasks that need to be performed, for the planning process necessarily rests on an appraisal of the situation that is to be affected. The exercise of appraising the problem with

---

5 *Ibid.*, p. 424.

6 Alfred J. Kahn, *Theory and Practice of Social Planning* (New York: Russell Sage Foundation, 1969).

as much freedom from predefinition as possible provides an opportunity to consider a range of alternatives in addition to those that may already exist in the situation as viewpoints of relevant actors.

Another initial issue is the question of boundaries. On the one hand, the planner seeks to understand the problem in its broadest dimensions in order to consider all of the factors that may be relevant to his work in the later stages of policy and program development and implementation. The kind of information that is brought into view and the way it is organized have an important effect on subsequent decisions. "A knowledge-organizing scheme," writes Kahn, "is in a sense also planning framework."[7] On this basis, he calls for "a systematic review and appraisal of relevant research in an applied field."[8] General sources of data, such as census studies, trend studies, statistical series, and breakdowns of aggregate data which pinpoint the characteristics of particular subgroups and geographic areas, are all important check-points in the first approaches to a problem.

The other side of the picture is that data cannot be used effectively unless they are gathered in relationship to some focus or question that has been adopted as a basis for pursuing knowledge. To quote Kahn again,

> Planning without adequate investigation of relevant realities, relevant social facts, is utopian thinking or travelling blind. Planning that assembles volumes of data without imposing criteria of relevance and priority in the appraisal is useless ritual.[9]

The essential skill to be learned by the practitioner is the appropriate use of research techniques to advance the planning process.

One approach to this issue is to explore in some depth the concept of "need" as a framework for social planning and to pursue some of the issues involved in operationalizing "need." A number of writers have dealt with this question.[10] It is also very much involved in the attempt to construct social indicators to measure the "state of the nation" in regard to certain concepts of social well-being—a notion which has not yet been clarified in any satisfactory way.

Approaches to the measurement of needs are therefore an important section of subject matter to be included in the course. Older forms of "needs" studies in local communities were based primarily on studies of

---

[7] *Ibid.*, p. 79.

[8] *Ibid.*

[9] *Ibid.*, p. 71.

[10] See: Genevieve W. Carter, "Measurement of Need," Norman A. Polansky, (ed.), *Social Work Research* (Chicago: Chicago University Press, 1960); and Robert Morris, "Social Planning," in Harry S. Maas, (ed.), *Five Fields of Social Service: Reviews of Research* (New York: National Association of Social Workers, 1966).

agency data. Recent studies have made it clear that only a fraction of the people who might be eligible for services actually become clients, so that measurements of need based on agency clientele are inevitably an understatement of need even as defined by the agency itself.[11] Because of this, it is necessary to seek broader measures within the population. The techniques of survey research based on samplings of populations have to be employed in order to approach greater adequacy in the measurement of need.

However, this is but one—and, in a sense, the simplest—of the issues involved in determining need. The major questions are not technical or procedural, as is the differentiation between need in a population and need as measured by agency clientele. The most difficult problems are conceptual, because there is no single or precise meaning to the term "needs." One issue is whether the concept is to be defined by "objective" criteria—that is, by standards external to the motivation or behavior of the "needy" person, or by a person's own view of his condition and requirements. Another problem is that needs are not static but develop in relation to changes in the environment. Not the least among these is the availability within the community of resources to meet "needs." It has been demonstrated repeatedly that the establishment of a service in a community will bring to light users of the service who were not previously identified as in need, because there was no such facility to which they were able to turn. More fundamentally, the creation of the services actually defines needs by offering service to certain categories of people and conditions.

The practitioner is called upon to use a variety of approaches in developing data for planning purposes. Neither needs nor goals are established by single acts which then settle the issues for the duration of a project. On the contrary, in regard both to needs and goals, there is an ongoing process of interaction which moves from first approximations to more precise definition. In that process, concepts of need and goal are in constant interaction and affect each other. Kahn's term for this is the "needs/task concept—a concept to guide the planning in which needs and task are shaped together, each affecting and modifying the other."[12]

The tasks of gathering and utilizing data for problem identification should be looked upon as involving a series of approximations which follow a rough logical order, although that is not necessarily the chronological order in which they are performed.

Information available through general sources, such as census reports and special studies, provides some guidelines to the parameters of a problem or condition, with indications also of variation among subgroups that may be of particular interest to the project and variations over time.

---

[11] For a review of relevant studies, see: Morris, *op. cit.*

[12] *Kahn*, op. cit., p. 63.

Previous research on the problem, including published scholarly literature as well as the investigations performed by governmental and voluntary agencies, are other sources of information. The volume of such research, especially in the past decade, has multiplied substantially because many programs have required the collection of data on various social problems and needs as a condition for federal grants to local communities. The review and critical analysis of examples of such studies, which are now available in most states and urban communities, provide a useful exercise in this area.

Relevant to this discussion is the more general work that has been taking place in an attempt to develop social indicators. It is useful to include in the course an introduction to the concepts and problems of developing social indicators at this point because both the aspirations and the limitations in those efforts help to clarify the operational problems facing the planner in his quest for and use of data.

SOCIAL INDICATORS

The search for "social indicators" is an attempt to capture in some few quantitative measures a reflection of the state of "social health" of the population. The general idea is an attractive one, and the success of establishing such measures in the economic area has given impetus to a number of efforts in the United States and elsewhere to achieve social indicators. A rapidly growing literature on the subject reveals the difficulties and limitations of the enterprise while reaffirming the desirability of continuing the effort.[13]

Two properties of social indicators that would be useful in planning would be (1) that they measure accurately a problem or condition that is amenable to intervention, and (2) that the components of the condition or problem can be isolated so that the intervention can be directed to the proper target. A third property, implied in the first two, is that the measurements can be taken at different periods of time in a comparable manner so that it becomes possible to judge whether the problem is growing or diminishing in volume.

Difficulties that are probably not solvable in any fundamental sense at the present time arise in attempting to define the social values that are to be measured. There is certainly no single dimension nor even very few dimensions taken together which could be agreed upon as representing the quality of social life in any overall sense. What is more feasible, how-

---

[13] See, for example: Raymond E. Bauer, (ed.), *Social Indicators* (Cambridge, Mass.: The Massachusetts Institute of Technology Press, 1966); E. B. Sheldon and W. E. Moore, (eds.), *Indicators of Social Change: Concepts and Measurements* (New York: Russell Sage Foundation, 1968); and U.S. Dept. of Health, Education, and Welfare, *Toward a Social Report* (Washington, D.C.: U.S. Government Printing Office, January, 1969).

ever, is the development of series of measures in a number of different fields, within each of which there may be more limited working agreements on the usefulness of given measures.

One of the most recent efforts in this direction was conducted by a special group in the United States for a three-year period. A report produced by this group outlines measurement possibilities in a few fields, as follows:

> *Health*—healthy life is defined as life expectancy free of bed disability or institutionalization; also measures of use of preventive and curative medical care.
> *Social mobility*—intergenerational differences in occupational status (related to education).
> *Physical environment*—measures of air and water pollution; housing adequacy measured by structural soundness and degree of crowding.
> *Income and poverty*—measures of both absolute income and income distribution.
> *Public order and safety*—measures volume of crime and victims of crimes by age, sex, race, and income.
> *Learning, science, and art*—achievement test scores, amount of education, volume of activity, and resources expended on science and arts.
> *Participation and alienation*—the report says that in regard to the functioning of social institutions, the authors "can do little more than to ask the right questions." Measures are needed of intergroup tolerance, civil rights, family functioning, participation in neighborhood and community life, and the like.[14]

Summarizing the state of affairs concerning the availability of the kind of information needed for decision-making, the report states:

> Only a small fraction of the existing statistics tell us anything about social conditions, and those that do often point in different directions. Sometimes they do not add up to any meaningful conclusion and thus are not very useful either to the policy-maker or the concerned citizen. The Government normally does not publish statistics on whether or not children are learning more than they used to, or on whether social mobility is increasing or decreasing. It does publish statistics on life expectancy and the incidence of disability due to ill health, but some diseases are becoming more common and others less common, and no summary measure indicating whether we could expect more healthy life has been available.[15]

One of the problems in constructing social indicators is the difficulty of finding a common measure that could unify the diverse components of social life into a meaningful aggregation. This is the function performed by relative prices as the common measure for aggregating very diverse economic activities into national income and product accounts. A system of

---

[14] Department of Health, Education, and Welfare, *op. cit.*

[15] *Ibid.*, p. 95.

accounts requires both aggregation and disaggregation so that the sources of change or lack of change may be identified.

In the field of social indicators, aggregation can be achieved in specific and limited areas only, of which the above are illustrative. Further work is indicated, with complex problems to be solved in regard to the weighing of different social phenomena so that they can be compared (e.g., amount of crime, related to seriousness of each type; or amount of voluntary activity in relation to degree of satisfaction obtained). Many of the crucial questions are quantifiable only as aggregations of people's judgments. Therefore the use of diverse research approaches is necessary, including techniques such as survey research which will tap people's opinions and attitudes.

The other major problem is that the indicators, even if available, do not in themselves point either to the causes of the condition that they measure or to the results of efforts undertaken to correct undesirable conditions. The report concludes:

> Though an impressive set of social indicators could be developed at modest cost in the near-term future, a complete set of policy accounts is a utopian goal at present. This does not mean that work on a more integrative set of statistics should be postponed. These accounts will never be available unless we start thinking about the statistics we need for rational decision making now, even if this only entails marginal changes in the statistics we already have. . . . Only a systematic approach based on the informational requirements of public policy will do.[16]

PLANNING STUDIES AND SELF-SURVEYS

As the foregoing discussion indicates, there is as yet little available in the form of general indicators or bodies of data which are directly relevant to planning, and much of the work of data collection needs to be done within the planning process itself. While data available through general sources can provide a framework and starting point for the planning process, the more specific questions which begin to arise almost immediately can be pursued only through additional investigations tailored to the purposes at hand.

A variety of research approaches and techniques come into play at this point. A number of these are included in the proposals for skills training advanced by Rothman and Jones.[17] These are mostly in the area of survey research. Tools of interviewing, design, questionnaire construction, coding, processing, and interpretation of data which presumably will have been covered in research foundation courses come into play at this point within

[16] *Ibid.*, p. 101.

[17] Rothman and Jones, *op. cit.*

the context of a planning purpose. The key element, therefore, is study design—a clarification of what specific aspects of survey research (or some alternative methodology) will assist in the planning project.

Survey research is an important tool precisely for the reasons that have been outlined above—namely, the gaps in available measures on important questions that need to be answered. Just as "need" is defined in terms both of "objective" conditions and people's perceptions, so are all issues in the planning process subject to opinion, evaluation, etc. Therefore, it is necessary to tap the perceptions, attitudes, and opinions of actors as the planning proceeds. Actors include participants of various types—constituents, sponsors, clients, and members of the general public.

In addition to information on the conditions and views of people in a problem situation, the planner needs to undertake community and organizational analysis along the lines of what Kahn calls "inventories," that is, estimates of available resources, manpower, and knowledge.[18] It is the kind of data that has been included in "needs-resources" studies conducted in many local communities under the auspices of local welfare planning bodies. Sophisticated analysis would call for examination not only of existing resources but of community structure, patterns of relationship, leadership, and potentials for action within a community situation. At the organizational level, issues of concern are goals, relationships, commitments, and constraints that can affect the role of the organization in the planning process. Self-studies or action research are methods designed to link factual research with the identification of value choices and expression of preferences. In such methods, an intimate connection is established between the research process and the development of the action project. Those responsible for the action are also the ones who determine what study is to be undertaken and, in the process of conducting such a study, have an opportunity to think through the questions they are trying to answer and the use they will make of the data obtained. It is claimed for self-study approaches that they are useful in educating people concerning problems and in motivating them to become involved actively in contributing to desired objectives.

Whether or not a self-study does in fact have such effects, and whether it is the best method either for those purposes or for obtaining needed data, are matters that need to be evaluated in relation to specific situations. The self-study is one approach that both organizers and planners have available in their repertoire.

POLICY ANALYSIS—GENERAL ISSUES

Planning, as developed in this course, is to be understood as a complex and dynamic process in which specifications of ends and means interact

---

[18] Kahn, *op. cit.*, pp. 83-88.

continuously. Policy formation represents one stage in that process. It takes its point of departure from general statements of goals and values and leads into more specific program measures. It is an operational statement of a goal or goals. Some of the essential properties of a policy are: continuity over time (although subject of course to change), institutionalization in the form of law or regulation or statement of principle, and, most importantly, provision of an explicit guide to future actions.

Because policy involves both ends and means, it cannot be viewed entirely as a technical implementing function. Policy formation is a process of making choices, as indeed is all of planning. The choices at the level of policy are, however, at least in large measure, choices of "values" in the sense that they determine the purposes that are to be served and the benefits to be sought. They involve, at least implicitly, a judgment as to desirable social outcomes. A methodology of policy analysis is therefore a technique for making choices clear and explicit and for using data in order to achieve that purpose. The course offers the student a framework of the elements that go into the process of policy formation; in a sense, a checklist for the types of choices that will have to be made.

The literature in the field of social policy is concerned primarily with the substantive issues of social welfare, and there is little on the methodology of social policy analysis. The discussion in this section draws primarily from Kahn, from a paper prepared for the Curriculum Project by Martin Rein, and from several course outlines now in use.

Kahn views policies as "standing plans."[19] They are general guides to further decision-making. Wickenden uses the same notion in referring to social policy as:

> . . . a settled course of governmental or group action and viewpoint, typically incorporated in an institutional mechanism such as law, regulation, program, or statement of priniciples which in turn governs future decisions in the same area.[20]

Rein argues for a critical approach that will challenge all assumptions and reveal the value premises inherent in what are ostensibly technical proposals; he also argues for a careful delineation of costs of choices made and choices foregone. He suggests that policy analysis needs to take account simultaneously of three different frameworks that have been used: ideology, feasibility, and rationality. Questions are to be explored in relation to all three criteria.[21]

---

[19] *Ibid.*, p. 130.

[20] From mimeographed notes prepared by Elizabeth Wickenden for use in a course in Urban Planning at Hunter College, New York, N.Y.

[21] Martin Rein, "Social Planning: Welfare Planning," in *International Encyclopedia of the Social Sciences* (New York: The Macmillan Company and Free Press, 1968), pp. 142-154.

Discussion of policy choices poses the question of the role of the planner as an agent in the process of choosing and therefore the issue of values. Dyckman argues that the planner "must have a theory of long-run client interests" in order to help shape goals, since these will not be given to him as a "set of well-ordered preference functions."[22] The planner is an instrumentality for the creation of aspirations and demands, not only for identifying them. Davidoff agrees, stressing the role of planner as advocate.[23] On the other hand, Reiner's conception stresses the planner's role as analyst of alternatives and their consequences, with the implication that the planner presents choices rather than makes them.[24] Webber does not deal directly with this issue, but presents a developmental view of planning in which the emphasis is on processes of interaction, mutual adaptation, and continuous analysis.[25]

The course should provide opportunities for the students to test these and other formulations for their efficacy in different kinds of situations. The instructor will have his own views, both theoretical and ideological, which should be considered along with others. In addition, it is his function to keep central issues in focus, so that it is clear what the debate is about. The basic question posed in the different views of the planner's role is what responsibility he should assume for setting goals. The planner may operate in one of two ways or, more frequently, in some combination of two ways. One is to operate as an expert on what Dyckman calls "client interests."[26] The other is to operate as an expert analyst of the options available and their possible consequences. In either case, he must have substantive expertness in the problems and potential remedies in a specific field of social needs, provision, and processes.

There are undoubtedly some criteria that can be used to make the choice as to the "mix" between advocating a specific course and outlining the available options. These might include such factors as the state of knowledge concerning causes and solutions of social problems, the sponsorship and organizational context of the planner's operation, and the degree of agreement or disagreement concerning values on the part of the groups with whom the planner is working. Too little is known as yet to permit systematic formulations of such guides. Ideology and judgment

---

[22] John W. Dyckman, "Societal Goals and Planned Societies," in H. Wentworth Eldredge, (ed.), *Taming Megalopolis,* Vol. I (Garden City, N.Y.: Anchor Books, Doubleday & Co., 1967), p. 258.

[23] Paul Davidoff, "Advocacy and Pluralism in Planning," *Journal of the American Institute of Planners,* Vol. 31, No. 4 (November, 1965), pp. 331-38.

[24] Thomas A. Reiner, "The Planner as Value Technician: Two Classes of Utopian Constructs and Their Impacts on Planning," in H. Wentworth Eldredge, (ed.), *Taming Megalopolis,* Vol. I (Garden City, N.Y.: Anchor Books, Doubleday & Co., 1967).

[25] *Webber, op cit.*

[26] Dyckman, *op. cit.*

together will have to determine these choices for the present, with the hope that accumulated experience and research can provide more assistance over a period of time.

ELEMENTS IN POLICY ANALYSIS

Paraphrasing several approaches that have been referred to in the previous section, a number of major elements in the methodology of policy analysis are outlined below. The course, using such "skills laboratory" aids as suggested in the Rothman-Jones volume, should provide students with an opportunity for acquiring skill in dealing with these elements of policy analysis.

1. *Ends-means analysis.* Looking at ends and means as a chain of interaction, analysis aims both at distinguishing between them (at any given point) and showing their interrelationships. This calls both for revealing value assumptions that may be hidden behind instrumental proposals and for questioning whether ideological statements propounded as goals are actually being made in support of instrumental technologies. An example of the former would be a proposal for a work relief program; of the latter, a call for additional professional services of a given type.

It is recognized that ends and means are subject to varying definitions and that such variations may involve questions of value; it is also recognized that ends and means vary over time. It is the function of policy analysis to identify these variations and to establish the alternative relationships between ends and means that are possible within a given situation.

2. *System analysis.*[27] The term is used here in a loose nontechnical sense, although attempts are being made to apply more formal systems analysis techniques to problems of social planning, and it is to be expected that further work will be done in that direction. By system analysis we mean specification of the structures and relationships which the planning project might affect—what target group or groups, what spread of problems and conditions, what elements of social structure, what organizational fields, and the like.

Alternatives are present here as they are in the selection of ends and means. Considerations of value, rationality, and feasibility are involved in the choice among specifications of system boundaries, as they are in the delineation of goals.

3. *Benefits analysis.* Different policy choices will, it is assumed, result in different benefits. Differences in the types and amounts of benefits and in the degree to which different individuals and groups do or do not benefit are to be traced in relation to different policy alternatives. Costs, insofar as they can be anticipated, are part of benefits analysis, particularly

---

[27] Webber, *op. cit.*

in the quite usual event that benefits to some groups involve expenses for others.

4. *Resources analysis.* A first approximation of the possibilities and constraints that will affect alternative policy approaches. Resources include not only funds but manpower and knowledge, as well as sanction and authority.

5. *Policy strategy.* The result of all of the choices outlined above is the selection, among alternatives, of a broad policy strategy, which incorporates decisions as to the level of intervention and the target or targets of the effort, taking into account (subject to testing and correction by experience) both the benefits to be anticipated and the resources available.

PROGRAM DEVELOPMENT

Planning that limits itself only to policy analysis is incomplete from the point of view of practice. It is here that one of the distinctions can be made between academic and practice orientations. The former appropriately may stop with analysis, identifying values, choices and consequences, and developing theoretical frameworks for their evaluation. The practitioner needs to incorporate all of that into an action situation, which means building a program to operationalize the choices made.

Programming involves the detailed spelling out of implementing actions to carry out broad policies related to a goal. It is essentially a logistical type of activity, guided by considerations of effectiveness and efficiency in seeking a result.

Like any logistical enterprise, programming involves the mobilization of resources and their delivery to where they are needed. The following would seem to be the major elements to be considered:

1. *Content of the jobs*—what are the specifics that need to be done—what kinds of activities, programs, services; in what sequence and what quantities; and through what physical arrangements.

2. *Resources*—what is required to do the various pieces of work—capital facilities, manpower of what qualifications, and funds. Where those resources are now located, who controls them, how they can be mobilized.

3. *Feasibility*—availability or non-availability of resources; changes needed in order to achieve the objectives, in policies, distribution of resources, creation of new resources, etc.; existence of acceptance or resistance; strategies for achieving necessary changes (conflict, negotiation, bargaining, etc.).

The following exercises proposed in the Rothman-Jones volume are relevant to program implementation:

Decision-making—this element lies in between design and implementation of program. It involves choices of strategy as well as the initiation of feasibility planning to deal with resistance.

Political, legislative, and govermental process—techniques for following one major direction in the implementation of goals—namely, through the public sector. Skills range from drafting the content of public measures to the organization of channels of influence to bring about the desired results.

Administration and consultation—specific details of implementation, through staff organization and supervision, internal reporting and evaluation, maintenance of external relationships, managing relationships among governing body, community, and administrative and staff structure; construction of budgets and reports.

Staff development and supervision and *fund-raising and promotion*—elaborations of administrative processes in specific areas that call for major attention in implementing programs.[28]

PROGRAM PLANNING BUDGETING SYSTEMS (PPBS) AND COST BENEFIT ANALYSIS[29]

A special section is being devoted to a discussion of PPBS because it is a major factor in the recent attempts to develop more systematic tools for planning.

Although a mystique has grown up around PPBS because of its apparent effectiveness in the work of the Defense Department and its subsequent extension in the Johnson administration to the rest of the government, at this stage of application to the social sector it is much more of a common sense approach than a complex technology. Basically, it is a system for thinking about objectives and means-end relationships in regard to both results (benefits) and costs. It grew out of earlier developments in budgeting procedures ("performance" budgeting) in which costs were presented in relation to outputs (products or services) rather than inputs (costs of capital, labor, etc.). This made it possible to begin to analyze costs in relation to results achieved. PPBS extends this budgeting principle to the planning function. It attempts to use cost analysis not only to evaluate a result but also to help choose a course of action among proposed alternatives. One of its important features is that it cuts across existing administrative structures, such as departments or agencies, in order to bring together for analysis activities that serve related functions.

The following is a schematic view of the major elements in PPBS:

Objectives—specification of what product is being sought, for whom, to serve what need. Simply to state the product (e.g., counseling interviews) is not adequate. An objective would be the purpose of the counseling (e.g., improved earning for specified types of people, or certain types of behavioral changes).

---

[28] Rothman and Jones, *op. cit.*

[29] This section is based primarily on the Symposium on PPBS in *Public Administration Review*, Vol. XXVI, No. 4 (December, 1966), pp. 243-310.

Programs—activities linked to specified objectives. These are not administrative functions (e.g., personnel management) or specific skills (e.g., X-ray examinations). Rather, they are combinations of activities that are related to an overall objective. An example would be a cancer prevention program, which would include X-ray examinations as well as many other activities such as publicity, community organization, other types of examination, research, etc.

Outputs—important products of activities, which are indicators of the achievement of the objective. An output is an end product of a program. The key word here is *end* product. What is considered *end* and what *means* is a matter of definition, but it is precisely this kind of specification which is one of the purposes of PPBS.

Progress measurements—degree of achievement of specified end products, including both amounts and distribution, and their delivery (or distribution) in accordance with plans.

Inputs—manpower, facilities, equipment, materials, etc., applied to the program. Outputs of one program may represent inputs for another program. When translated into money, inputs are synonymous with costs.

The key to the use of these elements is the concept of "alternatives." The weighing of alternatives occurs at two points. First, there is the problem of choosing among *program* alternatives where the question is what program is best-suited to achieve the stipulated objective. The second point is in the selection of alternative ways to implement the program, which means choosing the amounts and mixes of *inputs* that will maximize efficiency in the achievement of output targets. The first issue is at the level of policy, while the second is operational.

Cost-benefit analysis refers to techniques of measurement which assist in the choice of alternatives and in the evaluation of progress. Cost-benefit techniques are applicable both to outputs and inputs, at the point of choosing among alternatives or evaluating results.

ISSUES AND LIMITATIONS

Kahn points out that the crucial question in PPBS is the determination of the program unit.

> Identification of programs is a process of delineating major categories so as to capture major objectives and goals, doing so in a fashion which makes sense to policy-makers and administrators; utilizing units which lend themselves to consideration of alternatives; while still seeking categories across traditional bureau or unit or departmental lines to sharpen the choices available.[30]

Further, because policy objectives are not always clearly delineated but are subject to progressive clarification, it is desirable to use more than one principle of program categorization. Kahn suggests "the utility of classifica-

[30] Kahn, *op. cit.*, p. 248.

tion by two or three principles in a PPBS undertaking to maximize results."[31] Thus, in social services, programs could be developed by population characteristics (age or socio-economic groups), program objectives (entrance into labor market, advancement within labor market, maintenance outside labor market, etc.), or type of intervention (income maintenance, personal service). Depending upon what is seen as the central objective, one of these classifications may be the basis for major categories, with another used for sub-categories (e.g., classification by age groups, within each of which there is further sub-categorization in terms of labor market participation).

Whatever decision is reached, the programming and administration that follow from it need to be consistent. There is a chain from program budgeting to cost-effectiveness analysis, evaluation, and feedback. A whole series of administrative arrangements are required in order to maintain this chain. Both the service reporting system and the accounting system need to be set up in such a way that information can be obtained in a form which will fit the PPBS categories and make it possible to evaluate the results of the policy and program decisions adopted. There is equal need for communication and decision-making procedures within the administrative process that will facilitate the combinations of activities implied in the program definitions adopted for PPBS purposes.

Thus, for example, if a PPBS projection is based on the objectives of maximizing the upgrading of the economic status of heads of large families, then there has to be some way of coordinating educational, training, and employment placement activities related to that objective and to that group. If these activities are separated by rigid departmental lines, the central objective may become submerged in the priority concerns of each individual department, which are not necessarily determined by the central program objective but by segmented interests.

The difficulties and limitations of PPBS are both conceptual and technical. Conceptually, it is extremely difficult to formulate objectives in the rigorous manner that PPBS requires. Goal statements in the field of social issues tend to be global value positions and therefore, for the most part, non-operational. The attempt to translate global statements into operational objectives raises a host of problems as to who is to gain and who is to lose what and how much, and whose value choices are to be dominant in any given situation.

At least equally difficult is the task of defining a benefit. This problem is in part an aspect of the first—that is, the difficulty of operationalizing objectives—since benefits are, in effect, objectives achieved. An additional problem is the difficulty of finding a suitable way of measuring benefits so that they can be compared. In order to make comparisons, both benefits

[31] *Ibid.*

and costs are stated in money terms, but translating into monetary terms benefits such as increased participation of poor people in decision-making in neighborhood programs or even the benefits derived from increased tenure in school is not a simple problem. Additional research which establishes relationships among variables in terms of inputs and outputs will help, but the data now available in this form are very limited. Finally, comparison of benefits across different fields—health and education, for example—compounds all of the difficulties both of value choice and measurement.

Because of this, there is wide agreement that the techniques of PPBS and cost-benefit analysis are most applicable at least for the present to situations in which there is consensus both as to objectives and as to the criteria that will be used to evaluate the achievement of those objectives. Under such conditions, PPBS techniques can help to determine a choice among alternative methods for achieving the desired result.[32]

Even so narrow an objective, however, would, if implemented, bring a greater measure of rationality into social planning than exists at the present time. Even more primitively, it would correct one of the major difficulties of the present, which is the lack of adequate service data organized in such a way as to help in the planning process. Elementary information concerning the characteristics of people receiving different types of community services and the factors that account for either their receiving or not receiving service are generally not available under present conditions. The student, in attempting to develop PPBS approaches, will learn what changes are required in existing procedures in order to make such planning possible.

Despite all the limitations that have been outlined, the course can profitably draw upon some work that has already been done in the application of PPBS to the social field. One very useful example is a study by the U.S. Department of Health, Education, and Welfare of five disease control programs.[33] After considering a number of possibilities, the study chose as its outcome criterion the reduction in number of deaths resulting from each of the diseases, and the chief measurement device was the cost per death averted. A detailed study of the rationale for selection of such measures, other ways of approaching the same problem that might be possible, and experimentation with application of similar techniques to other problems would constitute a useful exercise in the course. In that process, the student would become familiar with some of the details of cost-benefit analysis, such as pricing techniques, use of different time

[32] William Gorham, "Notes of a Practitioner," *The Public Interest*, No. 8 (Summer, 1967).

[33] Elizabeth B. Drew, "HEW Grapples with PPBS," *The Public Interest*, No. 8 (Summer, 1967), pp. 9-29.

periods, measurement of the costs of side effects, or the costs of foregoing alternative uses of the resources employed.

In summarizing the issues involved in the use of quantitative approaches to planning (PPBS and cost-benefit analysis), Kahn states the general problem of all planning:

> . . . it represents an attempt to introduce rationality into a world of interest groups, bureaucratic rigidities, informal organization, politics, and many uncertainties. If the planner is at all times clear that his mission and capability are not to eliminate all of these, but rather to optimize the rational component in the process, he can work comfortably and usefully.[34]

PLANNING DESIGNS

In order to demonstrate the relationships among elements of planning methodology and to integrate them into a coherent process, the course should include consideration of a number of planning "models" or "designs" that are available in the literature. A few illustrations will be outlined in this section in order to suggest a pattern for their inclusion in the course.

The model proposed by Harvey Perloff is a very ambitious program for a systematic accumulation of much more extensive data than are now generally available for planning purposes.[35] In Perloff's own view, this is an "ideal" model which cannot be implemented immediately or completely but would have to be modified on the basis of community variations, feasibility, and degree of community acceptance. The Perloff model leans heavily on the construction of a comprehensive body of data obtained at a number of levels in such a way that connections can be made among different kinds of information.

Information to be obtained at the level of individual households is to be combined into "household welfare indices," which would reveal the existence of social problems and thereby help determine objectives for planning. The indices are based on income, level of self-support, and extent of employment. Estimates are made of those who are potentially self-supporting, and information is obtained concerning the extent and adequacy of existing employment (including measures of under-employment), income, and numbers receiving aid of different types. A suggested long-term measure is an index of lifetime earning power which would differentiate between temporary periods of low income and the existence of a chronic situation characterized by lack of adequate income or employment.

---

[34] Kahn, *op. cit.*, p. 261.

[35] Harvey S. Perloff, "New Directions in Social Planning," *Journal of the American Institute of Planners*, Vol. 31, No. 4 (November, 1965), pp. 297-304.

From the household level we move to a description of the social structure and institutional situation. A system of regional accounts would give a continuous picture of the state of earnings and employment opportunities within the region. An analysis of the social structure would include substantial amounts of information concerning a variety of groups within the population. Information would be differentiated by socio-economic status and also by age in order to pinpoint the characteristics and needs of different populations at risk. Detailed breakdowns of the regional figures would provide a picture of the concentration of problem situations within particular sub-sections of the region so that these problems could then be related to information concerning the physical environment and other aspects of the community situation. Comprehensive information would also be obtained on all kinds of community services and facilities, including education, health, recreation and youth and welfare services; and on the physical condition of houses, streets, and other aspects of the physical setting.

One of the general problems in the use of data for planning purposes is the lack of effective correlation between information concerning the general population and information available to service agencies and organizations concerning their activities and the people they reach. The Perloff model provides for an integration of these different bodies of data. It proposes that there be a comprehensive inventory of program information indicating expenditures on education, health, welfare, recreation, housing, law enforcement, and other activities. This is to be obtained by the use of program budgeting techniques and an analysis of both income and expenditures indicating the purposes of expenditures and the various sources of income.

Perloff's model visualizes a combination of extensive central data gathering, technical planning, and projection of overall guidelines together with a diffusion of planning processes through various groups in the community. It calls for an extensive metering and reporting system set up on a regional basis. Such a central service, in addition to maintaining a continuous flow of information, would undertake special research projects in order to analyze problems, suggest alternative solutions, and work with relevant groups in an attempt to improve the attacks upon such problems. The central planning unit would also prepare a general community policy plan, including overall capital and operating budgets for the social services and neighborhood improvement programs, and relating a variety of needs to one another and indicating the priority choices that have to be made. This would be done by an interdisciplinary group operating centrally and combining the various skills that are required for technical planning tasks. The group would include physical planners, social scientists, experts in particular fields such as health and education, mental health personnel, social workers, lawyers, and others. The planning process would use a variety of approaches, such as experimental pilot projects in order to experiment with new approaches for preventing and solving problems.

Although this is a highly technical and centralized model, Perloff places a great deal of emphasis on the need for public participation at every level in the development of the system. This would call for participation both by central leadership at the metropolitan level and by neighborhood groups. It is also proposed that the planning and programming work of individual agencies in the community be strengthened by technical assistance from the central group through information, funds, personnel, and training.

Finally, the central planning group would be a source of regular reporting to the general public. It would have responsibility for evaluating progress in the planning done by various segments of the community and report on the degree of achievement of community objectives.

The model proposed by Zweig and Morris is less extensive than Perloff's and not necessarily related to central planning on a metropolitan or regional level but to the design of any planning project sponsored by a particular group.[36] It suggests a number of interrelated steps in the planning process. First comes the statement of the problem describing the nature of the situation which is being addressed, the societal value which is implicated in the problem, and the degree of recognition which exists in the community concerning its existence. The description is to be made in relation to a number of specific dimensions such as the quantitative extent of the problem, its duration over time, and the geographical scale of both the problem and the intervention effort which is being contemplated (this scale is to be determined by the level at which the planner is located).

Theories of causation provide the next stage in the development of the design. Here the attempt is made to bring to bear on the problem whatever knowledge exists concerning the possible causes of the condition. Such a statement provides the basis for consideration of strategy and the choice among different types of intervention that might be considered. A statement concerning the modes of intervention which are possible follows immediately from the discussion of causation. Previous results of alternative forms of intervention are considered and the possible consequences of the different alternatives in relation to the problems in hand are projected. Such analysis is based on the characteristics of people affected by the problem being addressed, available resources within the population, and whatever normative standards exist concerning the desirable states toward which the effort should be directed.

Value considerations are to be considered explicitly since they form a necessary bridge between the design of a plan and its implementation.

---

[36] Franklin M. Zweig and Robert Morris, "The Social Planning Design Guide: Process and Proposal," *Social Work*, Vol. 11, No. 2 (April, 1966), pp. 13-21.

Zweig and Morris use the concept of "branching" to describe the movement of a planning design.[37] The design begins with a single problem which then branches into multiple possible causations, each of which branches into a series of intervention possibilities, which then in turn can be traced through different target populations. Choices are involved at every stage of the process. Evaluation, which is the final step, provides a necessary feedback as to the actual effectiveness of the plan after it has been adopted and put into action.

One of these models or others that involve similar procedures can provide a useful field exercise. For example, students might be assigned to explore the feasibility of the Perloff model in a concrete community situation. This would involve gathering whatever data already exist in accordance with the requirements of the Perloff model, indicating where the gaps are, and making estimates of what would have to be done in order to carry out the requirements of that program.

Depending on the state of relationships between the school and resources within the community, further steps might be taken in an attempt by the class actually to establish a program or parts of it within the community situation. Similarly, the Zweig-Morris planning design could be used as a guide for a class which undertakes to conduct a project for a community organization or agency.

---

[37] *Ibid.*

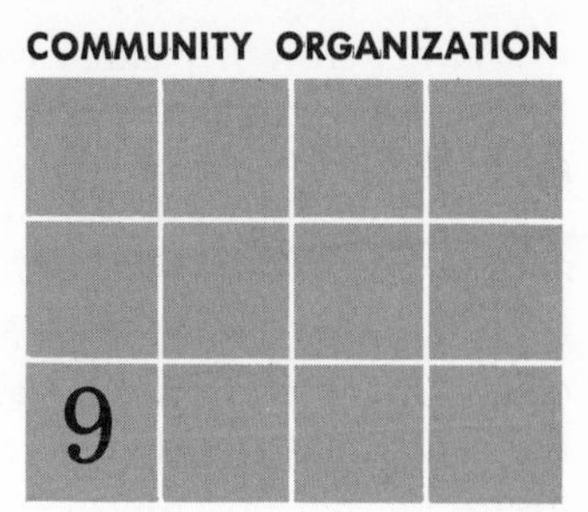

Specialized Courses

INTRODUCTION

PART OF THE CURRICULUM should provide an opportunity for the student to acquire expertness in a particular social problem area or field of service. Each school of social work, in accordance with the interests of its faculty and its relationship with the community in which it is located, tends to develop particular emphases in one or another area of social welfare activity, such as public welfare, rehabilitation, juvenile delinquency, race relations and intergroup relations, employment and training, housing, medical care, and the like.

Recently there has been a revival of emphasis in schools of social work on including in the curriculum certain problem or content areas. Social work education began as apprenticeship training related very closely to specific service organizations. In the course of attempting to establish more clearly both the unity of the profession and its broad academic base, there was a negative reaction to courses devoted to particular fields of service. The aim was to develop expertness in general methods of professional practice rather than in the specific organizational and administrative requirements of a particular service system. More recently it has been recognized that methodology may have been emphasized at the expense of content. The issue became particularly sharp during the past decade with the eruptions in American society in relation to problems of poverty and racism. There was parallel concern in the field of social work education that these major problem areas had been neglected in the education of social workers.

As in any cyclical process, the revived emphasis upon fields and content areas does not mean that social work education is returning automatically to its previous forms of training. Education in specialized areas today is obviously more informed, sophisticated, and theoretically based than was the older apprenticeship system. The purpose is not to convey factual information and operational procedures that are indigenous to a particular type of service. The earlier argument against such narrow training—that these specifics are more effectively learned on the job and do not belong in the university context—continues to have validity. Today, however, teaching in specialized areas draws on theoretical and research literature that has grown up in the various fields. Content courses provide one of the points in the curriculum where relevant bodies of knowledge drawn from the social sciences and other professional fields can be integrated with social policy and practice methods to provide the student with at least a beginning expertness in a specific area of practice.

Although the discussion in this report focuses on content areas as an element in the educational program for students who will be specialists in community organization and social planning, the specialized courses represent one of the points in the curriculum where students concentrating in different modes of intervention can be brought together for a common educational experience. Course content should include a survey of the nature of the social problems being dealt with and the policy issues involved, as well as a searching examination of the different modes of intervention that are available for dealing with the problems and their relationship to one another. Our conception of the problem area courses is very similar to the one proposed by Studt for an integrated approach to "Social Problem, Social Task, and Service System."[1]

There are several ways in which specialized course content can be organized. The suggestions which follow are based on a number of different dimensions. Some courses are based on the geographical level of organizing and planning which is under consideration (e.g., from neighborhood to national planning). Another way of dividing the field is to develop courses which deal with specific problem entities and/or segments of the population and the methods of intervention relevant to each. A combination of both approaches will give a school's program versatility and options that will help it to meet the variations of student background and interests. In either or both types of formats, the school will necessarily be selective because not all possible areas of content can be covered effectively. In

[1] Elliott Studt, *A Conceptual Approach to Teaching Materials: Illustrations from the Field of Corrections* (New York: Council on Social Work Education, 1965).

making such selections, a school would be well-advised to work from its field placement possibilities so that the areas chosen for specialized course development are consistent with the field training resources that the school has available.

Several possible courses are outlined briefly as indications of the kinds of specialized offerings that schools may choose to develop. In each of them, we point to a number of major topics that would provide organizing themes for the course and that are particularly relevant to education for practice. References to bibliography are made selectively in order to call attention to recent and particularly useful items that would provide valuable source materials for each of the courses.

NEIGHBORHOOD ORGANIZATION AND PLANNING

The focus of this course is on the neighborhood—that is, the small geographic community—as an arena in which the practice of community organization and social planning takes place in efforts to achieve social objectives. Such a focus cuts across the dimensions that have been employed in other courses. All contexts of practice are touched upon, because voluntary associations, direct service agencies, and planning and allocating organizations are all represented at the neighborhood level. Similarly, methods both of organizing and of planning come into play in neighborhood work.

Since specialized courses are meant to perform an integrating function in the curriculum, the material to be covered in them will overlap to some extent that of the survey and methods courses, subject, however, to reinterpretation within the perspective of the substantive field of work under consideration. In regard to neighborhood organization and planning, the area of overlap is greatest in relation to the core course on methods of organizing. However, it is the relationship of those methods to the broader constellation of practice within a neighborhood that becomes the issue to be considered in this course.

THEORETICAL ISSUES

Ideally, practice in neighborhood organization and planning should rest upon a body of knowledge concerning the nature of the small community. Many basic issues in this field are, however, problematic. It is therefore one of the functions of the course to offer a critical review and analysis of the theoretical issues that are implicit in neighborhood organization approaches and an evaluation of whatever evidence is available in relation to them.

Theoretical approaches to the neighborhood come in part from the concepts of primary groups. These concepts go back to Cooley and have been revived recently by sociologists who have studied the continuing functions of primary group relationships in the mass society.[2] Another orientation might be termed ecological, in that it focuses on the social functions which are located and organized within a small geographic unit. The overall problem, as generally recognized, is the long-term decline in the relative importance of the local neighborhood (as against the larger society) in relation to *both* social organization functions and processes of identification.[3] Keller's analysis points also to the difficulty of defining a neighborhood because of the different dimensions involved and their failure to coincide:

> . . . the boundaries of neighbors with whom active relations are maintained do not coincide with historical, official, or physical boundaries of neighborhoods, nor with those of local facilities, nor with attachment to the local settings.[4]

As against this general picture (which is not substantially in dispute) there arise many specific questions as to *variability* in the *degree* to which the neighborhood can be a useful context for organized efforts to improve social conditions and relationships. The starting point for the course is the recognition that there *is* such variation, which means that neighborhood organization is not a universal methodology that is always suitable, but that it can be a methodology of choice under certain circumstances. Given the limitations of existing knowledge, the course can at least separate out the elements of ideology and value commitments from the more empirical hypotheses intertwined in the literature on neighborhood organization. A comprehensive critique which can serve as a useful guide on this scope is provided by Bloomberg.[5]

Contributions to the subject are being made daily by reports of experiences in neighborhood organization and, increasingly, by more systematic research. Of particular relevance are studies of the neighborhood organization efforts which have taken place as part of the anti-poverty programs in the United States in the 1960's.[6] These studies as well as others

---

[2] See, for example: Eugene Litwak and Ivan Szelenvi, "Primary Group Structures and Their Functions: Kin, Neighbors and Friends, "*American Sociological Review*, Vol. 34 (August, 1969), pp. 465-481.

[3] Roland L. Warren, *The Community in America* (Chicago: Rand McNally & Co., 1963); and Suzanne Keller, *The Urban Neighborhood: A Sociological Perspective* (New York: Random House, 1968).

[4] Keller, *op. cit.*, pp. 156-157.

[5] Warner Bloomberg, Jr., "Community Organization," in Howard S. Becker, (ed.), *Social Problems: A Modern Approach* (New York: John Wiley & Sons, Inc., 1966), pp. 359-406. Reprinted in Ralph M. Kramer and Harry Specht, *Readings in Community Organization Practice* (Englewood Cliffs, N.J.: Prentice Hall, 1969).

[6] George A. Brager and Francis C. Purcell, (eds.), *Community Action Against Poverty: Readings from the Mobilization Experience* (New Haven, Conn.: College and

have highlighted the fact that community organization at the neighborhood level is affected fundamentally by the class and ethnic characteristics of the neighborhood in which it is taking place. Neighborhood organization has been of significance primarily in those areas where it has been one aspect of the more general politicalization of minority groups—and especially the black population in urban ghettos. The neighborhood context becomes one form of group identification based on race or race and class rather than on essentially local interests. The segregation of the population and the immediate unmet needs which do have a local nexus in the physical and social services provide the basis for neighborhood organization efforts. Whether or not there is a viable basis for organization of neighborhoods with other population characteristics is uncertain; it would rest on different strategies and approaches.

TYPES OF ORGANIZING EFFORTS

Some efforts are directed to a population at large—that is, to a population that is not organized in any visible way (although there undoubtedly are always networks of informal relationships) and with whom the practitioner works toward the achievement of some mode of more formal organization based on a pursuit of common interests. Others are based on a series of organized interest groups who are being brought into some new set of relationships with one another, whether for confrontation and conflict or cooperation or some mixture of both over a period of time. A third form is a general framework or organization which is not based on the integration of a variety of interest groups but is rather a direct form of participation by the individual on the basis of his citizenship in the community—a type of town meeting approach.

At different times and in different circumstances, neighborhood organization may be directed either to the strengthening of horizontal relationships within a particular neighborhood or to the strengthening of vertical relationships between the people being organized in a neighborhood and those who are outside the area. It is possible that both types of oganization may be pursued together within a common plan. Thus, an organizational effort which starts with direct organization of unorganized people

---

University Press, 1967); David M. Austin, "Dilemmas of Participation," paper presented at the National Conference on Social Welfare, New York, May, 1969 (mimeographed); Ralph M. Kramer, *Participation of the Poor: Comparative Community Case Studies in the War on Poverty* (Englewood Cliffs, N.J.: Prentice-Hall, Inc., 1969); Peter Marris and Martin Rein, *Dilemmas of Social Reform* (New York: Atherton Press, 1967); John Turner, (ed.), *Neighborhood Organization for Community Action* (New York: National Association of Social Workers, 1968); Roland L. Warren, "Model Cities First Round: Politics, Planning, and Participation," *Journal of the American Institute of Planners,* Vol. XXXV, No. 4 (July, 1969), pp. 245-252; and Harold H. Weissman, (ed.), *Community Development in the Mobilization for Youth Experience,* Vol. 2, *The New Social Work Series* (New York: Association Press, 1969).

on a local neighborhood basis and by exploring common interests without specifying particular goals can develop eventually into a interest-focused organization that forms links with wider movements outside of the local neighborhood. This is essentially the kind of process that has been taking place in the growth of the Welfare Rights Organization, which has by now taken on the character of a national movement even though its early beginnings were in a series of neighborhood-based organizational efforts.

Another major type of activity at the neighborhood level is the coordination and organization of services. Here, the work of the organizer is related to agencies and service organizations rather than directly to the population.

Most typically, the services which are operating on a neighborhood level are not indigenous to the neighborhood and not confined to it. They are, rather, extensions of more centrally organized services which need to reach clientele at the neighborhood level. The basis for attempting to achieve organization among them is the need to provide people living within the neighborhood with greater access to the services and to help the services achieve greater effectiveness in meeting people's needs.

Two forms of organization are particularly important to the service type of neighborhood organization. These are neighborhood service centers and neighborhood councils. In the case of the center, there is an attempt to bring services and the clientele into a better set of relationships. It is a direct service agency and is characterized by the issues and processes which prevail in that context of c.o. work.[7] Perlman and Jones offer a comprehensive discussion of the work of such centers and the issues involved. Their report includes useful case studies.[8]

The neighborhood council brings together a number of different agencies not to provide the direct service but rather to coordinate their policy and planning functions and to engage in a variety of joint activities ranging from coordination or clearance at the case level to merging of some activities.

SKILLS AND TECHNIQUES

Neighborhood work includes processes of both organizing and planning and calls for a range of analytical and interactional skills. For example, in efforts that are directed toward building a new neighborhood organization the initial steps of establishing contact are accompanied by analysis of problems and needs which might provide the focus for such a project. Similar interaction is evident in the selection of goals and

[7] See Chapter 6, pp. 101-103.

[8] Robert Perlman and David Jones, *Neighborhood Service Centers* (Washington, D.C.: U.S. Government Printing Office, 1967).

strategies, in building organizational structure, and in program development.

The building and maintenance of structure and program development are closely related and account for the major portion of neighborhood work. Structure emerges gradually out of initial organizing efforts and its character is determined by the general goals and strategies that have been selected. It is part of the development of an organizational structure, however, to move through a program of activities which assigns tasks and roles to members of the organization and, by its very development, helps to build the structure of the organization itself. Practice involves continuously the development both of the program content (representing concrete activities directed toward the achievement of the adopted goals) and the building of membership and leadership to sustain the organization and to increase its effectiveness in achieving its objectives.

Skills training in neighborhood organization and planning can be organized into units which are roughly parallel to the chronological development of an organizing project at the neighborhood level. The first phase of neighborhood organization involves skills in fact-finding and policy analysis combined with skills in the steps of initial organizational work. On the other hand, if the neighborhood effort is an on-going project, the emphasis would shift to such organizing skills as committee technology, leadership development, training and supervision of professional indigenous professionals, and the design and implementation of alternatives strategies together with promotional and educational techniques.

Neighborhood work today is concerned primarily with the needs of low-income groups. It would therefore be appropriate either to have an entire course dealing with this type of neighborhood organization or, at least, to devote a very substantial section of a general course to the specific issues and methodologies related to low-income neighborhoods.

In addition to the material already outlined, the course should deal more specifically with the characteristics of low-income populations and neighborhoods, including examination of studies on social structure, life style, organizational behavior, citizen participation, etc., and their implications for community organization. Particular attention should be given to emerging social movements and their ideological objectives. Neighborhood work in low-income areas has political implications, either explicitly or implicitly, which need to be clarified.

A word of caution is perhaps in order at this point. While it is desirable to give priority to the needs of poor people in poor neighborhoods in teaching neighborhood work, it does not follow that the problems of poverty can be met entirely or even to a major extent at the neighborhood level. Therefore, it is desirable to avoid an identification of anti-poverty intervention with neighborhood organization. In planning the curriculum it is desirable that poverty be approached as one of the substantive social problems that are dealt with in problem-oriented courses which touch on a variety of levels of intervention.

URBAN COMMUNITY PLANNING

This course would approach the tasks of community organization and social planning from the perspective of a central planning structure in the urban community. It is a course which could be given jointly with other departments in the university, such as a department of urban planning. Since urban community planning is necessarily interdisciplinary, this is a desirable area in which to establish relationships with other disciplines. Particularly relevant would be the participation of representatives from political science, economics, and sociology.

The general framework for the course is the urban community as a social and economic system and as the physical environment in which needs are met. Major sources of relevant knowledge are economics of the urban community; those aspects of sociology which are particularly focused on urban affairs such as ecology, demography, and urban sociology; urban politics; and the field of physical planning. In each of these fields there is strong interest at this time in urban planning and therefore a substantial volume of relevant literature, some of which was cited in Chapter 3.

Perhaps more important than the emerging concepts concerning the nature of the urban community as a social system is material on various substantive problems and developments. There is a very substantial literature in the field of housing, urban renewal, and relocation, from which lessons may be drawn that are pertinent to the practice of community organization and social planning. Over a period of time, the emphasis in these programs has shifted from exclusive concern with the physical environment to the major issues of social policy and the value choices which they involve. A substantial portion of the course might well be used to examine the implications of the issues that have arisen during the history of urban renewal programs. However, the course should move from a criticism of those programs to the positive issue of how to build social provisions into physical plans. It is at this point that practice exercises in the development of social plans should be provided. Students might collaborate with physical planners in working out the social aspects of a proposed change in the physical environment. One of the typical ways in which this can be accomplished is by developing a joint physical planning-social planning team to work in urban renewal projects either as actual participants in projects which are under way or in the form of simulated exercises. Similar types of exercises can be organized in relation to proposals for the construction of new towns rather than the renewal of old neighborhoods. Contrasting the two situations can be useful as a learning experience which involves the general principle of adjusting rational plans to the constraints of existing situations.

Interwoven with these considerations of the physical environment are major questions of economic policy and organization. It is now recognized that problems of physical blight are inseparable from other characteristics of low-income urban areas, such as lack of economic opportunity, poor educational achievement, lack of skills, and the like. It has also become clear that the strictly physical elements in this complex have tended to be exaggerated and the issue of adequate income and the social deprivations surrounding inadequate income are probably more basic. In urban communities in the United States, the central issue of racial discrimination compounds the combination of problems and deprivations besetting the blacks and other minority groups.

In order to begin a process of reform and improvement in urban communities, social planners need to have some conception of the general physical *and* economic framework in which improvements can take place. The course should deal in depth with a variety of economic issues, such as the level of economic enterprise that is or can be made available within the urban community, the problems of public transportation and other aspects of the relationship between place of residence and place of work, and similar issues.

CHARACTERISTICS OF CENTRAL PLANNING

A distinctive aspect of a course in urban planning is that it deals with planning at the central community level as contrasted, for example, with planning on behalf of a neighborhood group that is seeking resources or policy changes from a central body. There are, admittedly, difficulties in such a definition. It has been observed accurately that there is not one center, but a variety of planning centers in a community, each of which actually represents a particular interest rather than a general "public" interest. There is also difficulty with the very concept of central planning, since centrality, or the lack of it, is a relative term and a matter of perspective. Similarly, there is a multiplicity of community and subcommunity levels for planning—regional, metropolitan, city, neighborhood, "catchment" areas, etc.

Accepting the need for some degree of arbitrariness in selecting boundaries, we suggest the following as the distinctive elements which will identify urban community planning within the context of this course:

1. Planning within a geographical area that is coterminous with a *politically* defined locality.

2. Planning in which there is a common framework for consideration of physical environment, economic development, and social services in a specified geographical area.

3. Social planning which reaches for some degree of "comprehensive-

ness" across a number of service fields, organizational structures, and interest groups.

Both public and voluntary central planning bodies (or some combination of the two) may meet the above criteria.

The social planner's special responsibility in urban community planning is to plan for the effective organization, development, and coordination of the social services in relation to the physical and economic planning of the community.

Three elements are involved in this responsibility:

1. the network of the social services themselves,

2. the population being served, and

3. the decision-making authority (ultimately the political authority) which has responsibility for taking action, with or without plans.

Since the total population of the community is not a viable group for participation in planning processes, relationships between the "community" and service agencies take place through a variety of representative structures. The broadest of these is the general electorate, which expresses itself through the political process. However, as a practical matter the constituencies of service agencies are a small fraction of the total electorate. They may be consumers—that is, people who are direct users of the service being provided—or citizens who support the goals of the agency whether or not it serves them directly. There are many instances in which these roles are distinct but others (and perhaps a growing number) in which the constituents of service agencies are simultaneously consumers and citizen supporters. This tendency is particularly marked as services become broader and aspire to serve the entire population rather than particular groups. The merging of roles between consumers and citizens is also an aspect of recent attempts to provide consumers of social services with an opportunity to influence the directions of the programs being conducted on their behalf.

In centralized urban community planning the issues of participation are more complex than they are for a single service agency. A variety of groups and their interests need to be concerted around the formulation and execution of a centralized plan. There is no single constituency but rather a multiplicity of constituencies. They differ in their values and objectives, make competing claims, and offer conflicting proposals in regard to priorities and programs.

The decision-making authority which receives the plans considers them within the framework of its total responsibilities and constraints. Power relationships and command over resources are critical variables in both governmental and voluntary bodies.

There are also authorities and agencies beyond the local community which set the policies and command the resources for specific service structures within the local community and, in some respect, for the local authority as a whole. National decisionmaking bodies impinge both on the local authority and through specialized service programs on many of the components of the local network of social services. National bodies also have constituencies within the citizen and consumer groups within the local community, so that there may frequently be a combination of national and local partisan or specialized pressures upon a central planning body of the local community. On the other hand, citizen and consumer groups, in pursuing their own objectives exert pressures both on local community service agencies and on corresponding national bodies.

PLANNING ISSUES

Within the limitations of the foregoing constraints, the planning body attempts to reach solutions to a number of typical recurring issues that should be explored in the course.

Patterns of Organizing Social Services. The social planner is presumably a specialist on the specific substantive issues involved in organizing the social services. Various patterns exist, each of which has strengths and weaknesses. Some are based on a dominant professional field (e.g., health), others on a particular segment of the population (e.g., aging) or on a specific function (e.g., the provision of financial assistance). The choice of a particular pattern depends on the purpose to be served. For example, it would be appropriate to use aging as a basis for integrating various services if the aim is to give the needs of older people a certain amount of priority over the other claims which are made on each of the services separately.

Since any of these choices involves gains in one direction at the expense of losses in another direction, no solution to the problem of organization is adequate for all time. The problem needs to be addressed repeatedly as the dysfunctions of one solution become too costly and therefore call for a shift in emphasis to a neglected area through a re-organization of the structure.

In the most recent period there has been a tendency to move toward larger groupings which bring together a number of human service areas such as health, education, welfare, housing, employment, and re-training. Terms such as "human resources" or "human services" have come into use to describe the efforts to weld together the many fields that comprise the social sector. The impetus to such a development comes from growing recognition that a variety of measures need to be brought to bear simultaneously on the social problems of the urban community and that fragmentary, isolated measures cannot be effective. A "human resources" approach also ties in with the growing interest on the part of economic planners in the subject of investment in human capital and its place in economic development.

There are at least three ways in which different service systems within the social sector are brought together. One is through the establishment of coordinating committees or commissions in which the service systems have equal authority. Another is through super-agencies or departments in which all are subject to a higher authority. The third is to combine services on an *ad hoc* basis instead of undertaking the change of permanent structures. In the anti-poverty programs of recent years experimentation took place with various structural patterns. New agencies have been created which combine various governmental and voluntary elements. For the most part, they have tended to become responsible for certain service functions financed by the federal government under the new programs rather than serving as broad coordinating and planning instrumentalities for the human service programs of the community. In the latest of the federal programs (Model Cities), emphasis has been placed on centering responsibility in the city administration itself in order to achieve more comprehensive coordination. In a broad discussion of the structural issues, Kahn concludes that "statutory planning should be a staff function in the office of the executive —with only occasional exceptions."[9]

There are, however, great difficulties in the way of achieving effective coordination among all the elements involved in large service systems. The experience of the U.S. Department of Health, Education, and Welfare illustrates the problems. For most of the time that these elements have been combined in a single governmental department they have tended, nevertheless, to operate very much as a separate entity, and central planning is still largely undeveloped despite a number of re-organizations.

Centralization and Decentralization. The issue of centralization versus decentralization is growing in importance as functions become more complex and conflicts of interest more sharp in urban communities. The issue has both functional and political dimensions. On the functional side are questions of economy of scale—the criteria for determining the geographical and size-of-population scope of a given service. The dilemma here is the need for a large enough unit to command sufficient resources to provide a proper level of service while avoiding the dysfunctions of size—the complexities of administration and depersonalization of service. Finding the proper mix of centralization and decentralization means struggling with the classic problem of how to maximize the benefits of bureaucratization without suffering from an undue measure of its costs.

Another issue of the functional side is access to service and effective ser-

---

[9] Alfred J. Kahn, *Studies in Social Policy and Planning* (New York: Russell Sage Foundation, 1969), p. 314.

vice delivery. The kinds of questions that come under consideration are whether a service in a neighborhood is more visible to the people who need it most and more likely to be used by them than one which is located centrally.

The political dimension refers not to the intrinsic merits or demerits of a centralized versus decentralized service but rather to the issue of control on the part of different groups.

From the point of view of rational planning, the question of decentralization would be determined primarily by the functional criteria and control would be vested in groups best able to provide the particular service. However, the two dimensions do not always mesh so consistently. The choice will sometimes have to be made on the basis of political criteria with some loss in regard to optimizing the gains on the side of service effectiveness, or vice versa. As in all such cases of choices among conflicting purposes, it is the function of the planner to identify the choices that have to be made and to attempt a meaningful calculation of the costs involved.

Participation. Many detailed questions regarding participation need to be determined as part of urban community planning. Both in centralized and in decentralized aspects of the service structure, provisions have to be made for the selection of the participants. Deliberate steps are also necessary to make sure that there is actual meaningful participation by those who carry responsibility for deciding upon or influencing policies and programs. Distinctions need to be made between participation at the policy-making level in the broad management control of the service as against participation through voluntary activity or paid activity in the rendering of the service itself.

One of the broadest issues is the relationship between governmental service agencies and the general political structure through which the community is governed—e.g., whether the elected authorities or citizen groups are to have ultimate authority over governmental functions that are financed through taxation. These are essentially political questions where the planner will be governed by the political policies of the local authority of which he is a part. His contribution will lie primarily in suggesting policies and procedures—and also implementing them—which are calculated to facilitate the kind of participation that will be most helpful in rendering the services most effective.

There has been a period of experimentation under the United States anti-poverty program with the creation of structures in which local government, service agencies, and citizen and consumer groups were all represented. There are apparently weaknesses in this approach if the purpose is to maximize opportunities for the expression of interest on the part of wide segments of the population and have these views considered seriously in the determination of policy.[10] The organization of citizen participation on a more independent and more frankly adversary basis is an alternative approach.

Governmental and Nongovernmental Functions. Among the considerations that enter into the planning of local services is the distribution of functions between governmental and nongovernmental agencies. The traditional lines of division between governmental and voluntary agencies have become less meaningful over time in view of the extension of governmental functions into areas that were previously reserved for voluntary agencies. However, on the other hand, there is a growing concern with the participation of citizens in policymaking and in assuming responsibility for control over services. The result is a variety of mixed patterns which offer the possibility of many different combinations, depending on both the functional and political criteria. Increasingly, social services are being rendered through the private market by individual or group enterprises that offer services for fees on a commercial basis. It is likely that the use of private enterprises for social programs will increase both through direct government contracts and through provision of social benefits that individuals will be free to use as they wish (as in Medicare). Local planning will therefore need to take into account the private sector in its deliberations.

METHODS AND SKILLS

Planners in the local urban community need to employ all of the skills that were described in the outline for the core course on planning. They also need to draw on many organizing methods and techniques, especially in such areas as the management of committee processes and the use of various methods of negotiation.

SOCIAL DEVELOPMENT

Although there are many elements of practice in community organization and social planning which are common to the local community and to non-local settings, there are enough distinctive features to warrant a separate course which focuses on the non-local level of intervention as a framework for organizing and planning.

We have chosen to use the term social development for this unit although other titles, such as "national planning" or "national and regional planning," are, of course, possible. The term social development was chosen deliberately because it is the term being used by the United Nations

---

[10] Melvin Mogulof, "Coalition to Adversary: Citizen Participation in Three Federal Programs," *Journal of the American Institute of Planners,* Vol. XXXV, No. 4 (July, 1969), pp. 225-232.

to identify a useful set of emerging concepts. U.N. material in this field covers both underdeveloped and developing countries and therefore has relevance for national social planning in advanced industrial countries such as the United States.

Just as the frame of reference for social planning in the local urban community is the physical environment of the locality, the framework for social development at the national and regional level is the economic structure of the society. The concept of social development has at its core a close integration of social planning with economic planning. This course should therefore acquaint the student with the kinds of policy issues that enter into economic planning and with the tools that are used in that field.

At the national level, just as in the local community, the social planner's distinctive responsibility is for policies and programs that involve the social services. A program of social development sets the sights for the country in regard to levels of employment, production goals, and rate of economic growth. To some extent social services are geared to the contribution which they can make toward the achievement of those national goals. Educational and training policies particularly are affected by these considerations.

The United Nations 1961 *Report on the World Social Situation* advances the concept of "balance and integration of economic and social development," arguing as follows:

> Instead of treating social policy as a housemaid whose function is to tidy up human suffering and insecurity left in the wake of economic development, social objectives should be built in on an equal footing with economic objectives into comprehensive social and economic planning.[11]

Three aspects of the interrelationship between social and economic planning are identified: (1) the need to deal with the social *consequences* of economic development, (2) programs to overcome the social *obstacles* to economic development, and (3) the *positive role* of social factors in furthering economic development.

In approaching these tasks, it must be recognized that "there are at present no quantitative criteria derivable from theoretical, logical, or mathematical analysis by which the amount of attention to be devoted to a particular field of social development can be indicated."[12] The 1961 U.N. report suggests the need for empirical studies which will help build a body of knowledge on the ways in which social and economic developments interact empirically. Similar studies are needed on the interrelationships of fields within the social sector. On the basis of limited empirical studies, the following guidelines are suggested:

---

[11] *Report on a Co-ordinated Policy Regarding Family Levels of Living,* United Nations Publication Sales No. 57. IV. 7, p. 18. Quoted in *Report on the World Social Situation,* (New York: United Nations, 1961), p. 23.

[12] *Report on World Situation. . . ,* p. 38.

1. It is fallacious to attempt to justify all social goals on the basis of economic benefits. Many cannot be stated in economic terms but are still basic commitments of the society.

2. That in no way justifies, however, the failure to calculate the economic costs and consequences of social programs.

3. By the same token, it is necessary to attempt to identify and as far as possible to measure the social costs and consequences of economic policies.

4. While there is a general indication that expenditures for social and economic purposes tend to rise together and that the proportion of national income spent on social purposes rises with rising total income, it is not valid to assume total compatibility between economic and social development. Comparative studies point to areas of imbalance and differences in rates of growth on various economic and social measures. Much more detailed study is required before conclusions can be reached.

5. Since general guides will not be available in the immediate future, planning decisions need to be made on the basis of past experience, political priorities, and special studies.

6. There are some programs which are strategically placed and therefore merit priority in development planning. These are social programs that reinforce economic progress and economic programs that are most likely to contribute to the solution of urgent social problems.

In addition to being part of the economic planning framework of the country, the social sector is also an integral aspect of the country's political structure. The issues of centralization and decentralization arise here as they did in the discussion of urban community planning. Differences in political philosophies will affect the distribution of functions between government levels. They will also determine how citizens participate in the political process and also in the organization and planning of services at both national and local levels.

There has been a tendency, in the post-war period, for highly centralized governments to move toward decentralization in some of their functions, while those having more diffuse political power structures, like the United States, seek to achieve more centralized planning in major spheres of social policy.[13]

While social development, in its broadest aspects, involves the integration of social and economic planning, social planners deal primarily with planning issues within the social sector. The course in social development should therefore give attention to what has been termed "sectoral" planning at the national level, which refers to planning in relation to a particular social problem, and the field or fields of service related to it.

---

[13] *International Survey of Programmes of Social Development* (New York: United Nations, 1959), pp. 122-125.

In a complex political and social structure such as that of the United States, such planning involves a great many different types of organizations—national and local, governmental and voluntary. A national program is concerned with the vertical relationships that extend along specialized program or field of service lines from the national body to local constituencies, with horizontal relationships at the national level, and with local horizontal structures in which service systems are brought into relationship with one another within the framework of locally determined policies and programs.

For example, in the United States, the national program of mental health services has set guidelines on a comprehensive basis for the development of community mental health services throughout the nation. Through a combination of national legislation, budgetary appropriations, and national administrative regulations, both resources and guidelines are made available to the respective states and through them to local communities for a pattern of organization of mental health services. This is a field in which national resources have been substantial and the impact of national policy more decisive than in a number of other areas. However, areas of discretion are left open within the national program for determination by decentralized planning groups. Thus, mental health agencies and other public and voluntary services and a wide range of consumer and citizen groups are brought into the process of deciding on the ways in which a program will be implemented in their localities.

A national program may have several different goals. Its central purpose may be to provide a general level of service for the entire population (as in the case of a basic income-maintenance program). In this case, its major concern is coverage and equal treatment to those being served. It achieves the objective by setting minimum standards and making provision for their enforcement. Such an objective and such a strategy are appropriate when both the goal and the mode of intervention are clearly defined.

On the other hand, many of the most difficult current problems are those for which there are no clear, generally accepted remedies. This has given rise to attempts to follow strategies of experimentation, with the role of the national program one of stimulator and supporter of a search for better solutions. Such a strategy calls for maximizing innovation at every level of the program—a strategy that has not always been followed, due to political and other constraints. Nor have demonstration projects always been appropriately used, since they have tended to become inadequate substitutes for more comprehensive social provisions.[14]

---

[14] Martin Rein and S. M. Miller, "The Demonstration Project as a Strategy of Change," in Mayer N. Zald, (ed.), *Organizing for Community Welfare* (Chicago: Quadrangle Books, 1967).

Structures for planning should be appraised in relation to goals and strategies. In the United States, the 1960's have seen the use of many different types of planning instrumentalities at the national level, such as task forces within and between departments, interdepartmental committees or commissions, planning departments of operating agencies, the growth of planning functions in relation to budgeting procedures, etc. These provide useful case examples for consideration in the course. Material can be drawn both from documents and from live contacts with actors in past and present planning operations.

The course in social development provides another opportunity to reinforce a broad perspective toward community organization and social planning—one in which the connections among different levels of intervention and fields of activity are kept constantly in view. It offers another vantage point from which to appraise local efforts to bring about community change through neighborhood work and similar "grass roots" activities. Community development, as practiced in developing countries, is a field of activity which is very much at the "grass roots" level—mostly in rural villages, dealing with people on a face-to-face basis to change habits and attitudes and to motivate self-help activities toward the improvement of conditions. On the other hand, it is defined officially as "processes by which the efforts of the people themselves are united with those of governmental authorities to improve the economic, social, and cultural conditions of communities, to integrate these communities into the life of the nation, and to enable them to contribute fully to national progress."[15] In recent appraisals of community development work, attention is being given to the need for greater integration of local community development projects with national social policy. Similarly, there is widespread agreement that the recent community action programs in the United States have suffered from the absence of adequate national social development policies.[16]

METHODS AND SKILLS

The methodology of planning at the non-local level follows the pattern outlined in the core course on methods of planning and also includes a number of organizing methods and skills.[17] Knowledge and use of national

[15] *Report on Concepts and Principles of Community Development*, Annex 2 (New York: United Nations, 1956).

[16] Louis A. Ferman, (ed.), *Evaluating the War on Poverty, The Annals*, Vol. 385 (September, 1969).

[17] Arnold Gurin, "Community Organization Methods and Skills in the Programs of National Agencies" in Harry L. Lurie, (ed.), *The Community Organization Method in Social Work Education*, Vol. IV of the *Social Work Curriculum Study* (New York: Council on Social Work Education, 1959), pp. 133-147.

social statistical materials should be one of the aims of the course. Efforts to develop social indicators should be reviewed at a more advanced level than in the core course. There should also be further grounding in the methods of collecting data in specific fields, the difficulties of obtaining data nationally from a large number of local jurisdictions, and techniques being used to improve both the coverage and the reliability of such information.

Policy analysis deals with choices as to the scope and character of national intervention, including such recurring issues as cash versus service benefits; the use of governmental, nonprofit, or private resources for the rendering of service; and the population groups to be reached and priorities among them, as well as questions of strategy outlined earlier.

Program development involves a spelling out of the various components of the service and the marshalling of resources at different levels of the operation. Particular attention should be paid to the interrelationships among legislation (including the process of its development from early planning through the final stages of a bill), administrative regulations, and budgetary planning.[18]

ADMINISTRATIVE PLANNING

It is suggested that a course on administrative planning be considered, possibly as a joint offering with a concentration on administration (if that should exist within the school) or with a department of public administration or business administration in the university.

Theoretical and research material relevant to such a course may be drawn from sociological and social psychological studies of organization and from the field of administrative science. Special attention should be given to the growing literature that deals directly with organizational and administrative issues in voluntary associations and service agencies. (For references, see Chapters 3 and 4.)

This course would develop in greater detail the material included in the survey course on the practice of community organization and social planning in a direct service agency. It differs from a course in the administration of social agencies (although it borders on such a course and overlaps it to some extent) in that its focus is on the external relationships of the service agency rather than on internal management.

All phases of planning involve some type of interaction between the organization and the external environment. In regard to goal setting and policy formation, the planning function calls for an examination of rele-

---

[18] Charles I. Schottland, "Administrative Decisions and Fund Allocation in Social Welfare," in Leonard H. Goodman, (ed.), *Economic Progress and Social Welfare* (New York: Columbia University Press, 1966).

vant data describing conditions and problems in the community for which the organization has theoretical responsibility. This kind of exploration is combined with an identification of the relevant groups and social systems to which the organization is related and the value preferences, political pressures, and other factors which impinge upon the organization and affect its functions and policies. These external demands are evaluated in relation to the various constraints to which the organization is subject and to issues of feasibility that arise in the implementation of policies and programs.

All service agencies are part of a network of organizations linked by interdependent relationships and exchange arrangements in the management of resources and service to clients. A major task in administrative planning is the maintenance of relationships between the organization and its clientele and constituency. The primary instrument incorporating this function is the Board of Directors, which at least in theory represents whatever "community" provides the legitimation for the organization to carry out its functions. Questions as to the composition of the Board involve considerations both of linkages with relevant segments of the community and competence in the performance of the policymaking functions which the organization requires. Also involved here are general organizational questions concerning the relationship among Board, administration, and staff. While these issues generally are of concern to the administrator, the planning person has special responsibility for determining the effects of the different levels of the organization on the external relationships of the organization. It is the administrator's general task to integrate various elements in the organization in order to maximize effective performance. It is the administrative planner's *specific* responsibility to help maximize the kind of performance which meets community needs.

In order to define those needs, administrative planning calls for the use of a variety of channels for obtaining consultation and advice from relevant groups in the community. Such relationships are based on two-way communication—the community groups help to inform the organization concerning the needs and conditions toward which it has a responsibility, while at the same time they act as a channel of communication to the community from the organization itself.

There would be more emphasis on administrative skills in this course than in some of the others; these skills would include the collection and use of service data, program monitoring and evaluation, and budgeting and finance. Skills in committee technology are required in several contexts. They are employed by the planner in developing working groups within his organization which involve the Board and staff, other agencies, clients, and citizen groups. Another aspect is the effective representation of organizational interests in coordinating and planning bodies where the agency participates along with other agencies and wider community groups in more comprehensive planning functions.

COURSES IN PROBLEM OR PROGRAM FIELDS

As indicated in the introduction to this chapter, it is recommended that schools consider a number of courses which focus on a particular social problem area. Such courses help the students to develop expertise in a substantive area of work and also offer another way of illustrating and reinforcing the general concepts and skills of practice in community organization and social planning.

A large number of problem areas lend themselves to this kind of treatment. A major criterion in selecting which to pursue is the availability of theoretical and research literature which can be drawn upon as background for education for practice. Accessibility to relevant interdisciplinary resources is also essential.

Although the courses cover a variety of substantive subject matter, they can nevertheless follow a common format. A general outline providing some consistency of orientation can be developed for all of the courses. This should, however, be sufficiently flexible to allow for differences among instructors in philosophy and approach to practice.

Elements of methodology in both organizing and planning need to be integrated into the construction of the proposed format. The following covers a number of the major elements:

1. Analysis and delineation of the dimensions of the problems being addressed.
2. Analysis of relevant theoretical background material and research.
3. Delineation of various approaches that are derived from different theories of causation and from the body of knowledge that is relevant to the problem.
4. A system analysis of the population groups and organizational structures that are relevant to dealing with the problem.
5. Policy formation involving selection of levels and methods of intervention.
6. Development of specific programmatic implementation of policy.
7. Evaluation and feedback in order to correct and modify policy decisions as well as programmatic measures.

This model is to be interpreted as involving both planning and organizing responsibilities. It is not limited to an analytic exercise in which the dimensions of the problem are identified and alternative plans are evaluated and chosen. On the contrary, the student would be expected to take active responsibility for carrying out the program within his specialized area. The courses are therefore tied very closely to the practicum in the specialized field.

POVERTY AND RACE RELATIONS

While we are not attempting to recommend specific problem areas, there are two which are so pervasive in the current historical period that they merit special attention and visibility within the curriculum. These are *poverty* and *race relations*.[19] Since both subjects are receiving widespread attention, there is an abundance of material from which to construct a course and no need to deal in this report with the content in any detail. The few comments which follow are designed merely to suggest the kind of focus which would be particularly relevant to the concerns of the concentration in community organization and social planning, following the format that has been suggested for problem-oriented couses.

POVERTY

Definitions and Dimensions. The different ways of conceptualizing the problem of poverty and the implications of such differences in relation to social values, goals, and major lines of intervention are to be identified. Major questions are whether poverty is to be defined in absolute or in relative terms, which raises the value isssue of whether the stress is to be placed on minimum standards of living or on equality.

As the discussion has developed in the United States, emphasis has shifted increasingly to issues of equality rather than absolute standard of living, although the official definitions of poverty fall under the latter. Equality also has two aspects—equality of condition or equality of opportunity.

Measurement of poverty depends upon the concepts and definitions used. Whichever approach is taken, it is important to examine different rates of poverty among different groups within a population, differences over time, differences in relation to space (different rates of different geographical areas), and differences across generations. The substantial data already available should be reviewed, with attention called to the questions which remain unanswered as well as to the insights which are provided concerning various dimensions of poverty.

Theoretical Orientations. Recognizing that poverty involves a complex interaction of economic, social, and psychological factors, there are several major theoretical orientations which have been influential in guiding policy and programs. They relate to the possible causes of poverty, its

[19] Intergroup relations or community relations are other terms used to describe the area we have in mind; these terms are preferred by some as dealing with race relations in the broader framework of religious and other kinds of intergroup differences. We have chosen to retain the term race in order to focus attention on the most serious of intergroup problems, while proposing that the course also include consideration of other types of intergroup relations.

correlates with other social phenomena, and the types of remedies that would be appropriate. The major theoretical issue is to understand the nature of the relationship between the individual and the social structure in the phenomenon of poverty. Broad theoretical approaches such as "culture of poverty," "opportunity," and "powerlessness" offer different vantage points from which to view the problem, but none of them is rigorous in providing a definitive set of propositions and even less in demonstrating validity through actual empirical studies. There is, however, a very substantial and useful literature setting forth the different notions involved in these approaches and also a critical literature in which the assumptions of the different approaches are challenged.

The focus for this course would be not only on the concepts themselves but on the implications of various concepts for the derivation of action goals and strategies of intervention.

While the material on theoretical orientations is lacking in conclusiveness, there is a growing body of factual data concerning the correlates of poverty. Particularly important in the context of this discussion are the close connections between poverty and minority status, especially in regard to color. Measures of such phenomena as income, education, health, housing, and so forth help to identify what is known about these interrelationships and also to identify areas where the precise nature of the connections needs further examination.

Interventional approaches are based in part on theoretical orientations, but there is also a strong element of ideological value judgment both in the choice of theories and in the selection of intervention strategies. All of the major strategies—individual improvement to enhance opportunities for mobility, additional social provisions such as family allowances, or mass organization for fundamental social change—need to be reviewed in detail.

It would be useful at this point in the course to give close attention to the material that is available in the form of general evaluations, critiques, and case studies of recent experience in anti-poverty programs. Such a review helps to focus and sharpen the theoretical issues, to make possible some distinctions between ideological commitments and empirical approaches, and to identify the major unresolved issues facing the organizer and planner who enters the anti-poverty field.

Policy Issues. It is very clear in this field that the definition of the nature of the problem and the group or groups to be affected by the intervention are crucial questions which determine the nature of the program that is undertaken. As put by one of the earliest critiques of the anti-poverty program, the question is "what war and which poverty?"[20] Typo-

[20] Earl Raab, "What War and Which Poverty?" *The Public Interest*, No. 3 (Spring, 1966).

logies of the poor are useful in defining the groups for whom alternative policies might or might not be helpful—for example, "the working poor" as compared with those who have no attachment to the labor market, the poor in the different age groups, and those who are members of different communities and sub-communities. Also to be explicated are the ideological and political issues involved in each of the policy choices.

Programmatic Approaches. Just as the issues of causation and policy are multi-dimensional, the specifics of dealing with poverty involve many different programs in a variety of fields. Compilations are available which outline the specific measures that have been tried in fields such as youth employment, training programs, information and referral services, legal services, organization of personal services under new types of structures such as multi-service centers, community health and mental health programs, legal services, and many others. There are also experiments underway on different methods of using income maintenance supports in order to counteract some of the effects of poverty.

The course should place particular emphasis on the ways in which different programs are connected with one another. Some of the general dimensions to be considered are adequacy of the resources provided and the scope of the program undertaken, the degree to which the people for whom the programs are intended are actually reached, and the degree to which program measures are sufficiently comprehensive. Experience indicates the problems that arise from attempting to deal with one facet of a situation (e.g., training) without having available another closely related resource on which the first program is dependent (e.g., jobs).

Program content also needs to be related very closely to the organizational issues that were discussed earlier and particularly to the question of participation of the poor in anti-poverty programs on which there has been extensive experience which is now beginning to be evaluated.

Literature. The literature on poverty is vast and most of the major works are widely known and extensively used in schools of social work. Because there is so much literature, the problem is one of selection. A few of the most recent works are particularly useful because of their coverage of different facets of the subject, and because they reflect actual experience that is relevant to the particular concerns of community organization and social planning.

Poverty and Human Resources Abstracts, published since 1966, is a basic bibliographic resource. Several collections cover various facets of poverty, such as definitions of the problem, statistical material on different dimensions of poverty, policy, issues, theories of causation, and so forth. Of particular interest are the works now appearing which are reports on actual programs of various types which attempted to deal with poverty in the past few years. Some of these are explicit efforts at evaluation, but even those which aim only to report carry implications for evaluation and can therefore contribute usefully to courses in which the focus is on applications to practice. A recent issue of *The Annals* is devoted to a collection of articles which attempt evaluation of various facets of the American anti-poverty program.[21] Levitan covers similar ground more comprehensively.[22] A shorter treatment, but one whose approach is particularly appropriate to this curriculum is Kahn.[23] Several works deal with specific local programs that were part of the "war on poverty." They provide useful material and also contribute to discussion of theoretical issues. Marris and Rein appraised some of the earlier community action programs and delineated a number of the basic contradictions in American social policy in the poverty area that have become increasingly clear since that time.[24] Substantial reports are now available on the experience of Mobilization for Youth, the earliest and most extensive of the local community action projects.[25]

RACE RELATIONS

Dimensions. There are now available extensive data on the disabilities suffered by minority groups who are subject to discrimination. Particularly extensive is the material concerning the conditions of the black minority in the United States and the extent to which it is disadvantaged on the basis of all indices which measure economic and social progress. Particular attention should be given to the measures of change in these conditions and to the various interpretations that are available as to the extent of progress which is or is not being made in alleviating the consequences of long-term discrimination. Greater clarity concerning these issues can be achieved by dealing not only with aggregate figures but with more specific measures that show differences among some groups within the minority population.

---

[21] Ferman, *Evaluating the War on Poverty, op. cit.*

[22] Sar A. Levitan, *The Great Society's Poor Laws: A New Approach to Poverty* (Baltimore, Md.: John Hopkins Press, 1968).

[23] Kahn, *Studies in Social Policy and Planning, op. cit.*

[24] Marris and Rein, *Dilemmas of Social Reform, op. cit.*

[25] Brager and Purcell, *Community Action . . . , op. cit.;* Harold H. Weissman, (ed.), *The New Social Work Series,* Vol. 1, *Individual and Group Services in the Mobilization for Youth Experience,* Vol. 2, *Community Development in the Mobilization for Youth Experience,* Vol. 3, *Employment and Educational Services in the Mobilization for Youth Experience,* and Vol. 4, *Justice and the Law in the Mobilization for Youth Experience* (New York: Association Press, 1969); Irwin Deutscher and Elizabeth Thompsons (eds.), *Among the People: Encounters with the Poor* (New York: Basic Books, 1968); and Kramer, *Participation of the Poor. . . , op. cit.*

Another dimension focuses not on the minority but on the discriminating majority. An attempt is made to discover more precisely where and how discrimination takes place, who the people are who discriminate, and how they practice this discrimination.

Theoretical and Research Backgrounds. Different streams of social science theory and research have contributed different insights and points of view to the issues of intergroup relations. Psychologically oriented theories stress attitudes and interpersonal relationships. Those which take a cultural approach have placed the emphasis on values and belief systems while social structural approaches stress the effect of class position and access to resources on the maintenance of discrimination and the resulting disabilities suffered by minority groups. Although there has been in the past some polarization among these different viewpoints, recent developments stress the interrelationships among various factors and the inadequacy of dealing with the problem effectively if a monistic approach is used. Specifically, it now seems clear that attitudes and behavior are not completely interdependent but can change independently of each other, and that individual capacities, motivations, and behavior cannot be understood in isolation from the social structure through which they are generated.

Within the framework of these broad generalizations, there continues to be a host of unknowns as to the precise interrelationships among the multiple factors involved in these problems and the influence of attempted intervention in one area upon results in other areas. In this field, as in others, action choices must be based not only on the limited knowledge available but also on value judgments and ideological orientations.

Definition of the Field. As with community organization, in general it is somewhat difficult to define the boundaries of the field of intergroup relations and particularly to answer the conceptual question as to whether it should be visualized as a separate field or as an aspect of all the organized activities within the community that bring groups together.

As a practical matter, however, there are certain specialized functions which do have an organizational framework. The field may be defined roughly as including organized efforts to deal with specific problems of prejudice, discrimination, and segregation which affect racial, religious, and ethnic groups. Organized efforts that deal specifically with such problems may be found both in government and in various voluntary groups, some of which are sectarian in the sense that they are instruments of the minority itself, whereas others cut across various racial, ethnic, and religious lines.

Strategies. Different theoretical orientations have their reflection in the choices of strategy that are available. Some of the dichotomies that were identified in other areas come to a sharp focus in the field of race relations. Although there may be general agreement as to the interrelationships between individual psychological and social structure factors, differences in degree of emphasis on one or the other have implications for a choice of strategies. Orientations which emphasize the individual level will focus on changes in attitudes, opinions, and behavior, whereas structural approaches will attempt to emphasize institutional change. Similar choices are involved in the relative emphasis upon strategies of consensus as against those of conflict.

Richard English, in a paper prepared for the Curriculum Project, reviewed the work of a number of writers in the area and developed a beginning typology which attempts to link organizational purposes with such dimensions as target of change, assumptions underlying strategy, selection of problem focus, goal of change effort, and strategy of change. Paraphrasing his scheme, the following typology offers the beginning of a framework for studying the field.

1. *Group welfare.* This refers to self-help efforts directed to members of minority groups in which the emphasis is on changing the abilities and behavior of members of the groups so that they may be in a better position to overcome their disabilities. The primary strategy of change here is provision of services for the development of increased skills and resources.
2. *Education.* Agencies organized for educational purposes are based primarily on the "melting pot" theory of intergroup relations. They are directed both to members of minority groups and to the majority groups in an attempt to build relationships among them. The major strategy is fact-finding and investigation, on the theory that accurate information will help to overcome the prejudices of people and the false images that groups have of one another. The ultimate social goal of such programs is assimilation and integration.
3. *Minority-group integration.* In contrast with the melting pot approach, the strategy which emphasizes integration within the minority group itself is based on the theoretical position that such internal strengthening is a necessary precondition for overcoming the disabilities resulting from discrimination and for establishing satisfactory relationships with the majority group. It aims to build a strong sense of solidarity and group identification among the members of the minority and also to create institutions that will advance their economic, social, and political position.
4. *Defense and protection.* This refers to efforts to achieve changes in the conditions and institutions which promote discrimination. Strategies of change include legal action and political activity of various

degrees of protest and militance or reform tactics. Targets are major institutional programs such as education, employment, housing, and public accommodations, as well as the operation of the legal and political system.

Race relations today occupy a central position among the problems causing tension and conflict in American society. Course content is necessarily affected by the climate of the times and should be both reflective of and responsive to that climate. At the same time, it should be recognized that ideological positions have been shifting in short periods of time, and that today's formulations may become obsolete very quickly. Historical perspective as well as contemporary analysis are therefore necessary for a proper understanding of the ideological positions and the problems to which they propose solutions.

In the field of race relations, the major shift in the recent past has been from a philosophy of integration to one that stresses the need to strengthen the solidarity of the minority group and to build its separate and distinctive resources ("black power," in the case of the black minority). This is not a new issue. It goes back to earlier philosophical formulations such as the "melting pot" and "cultural pluralism." Most fundamentally, it raises questions as to the nature of American society. Not only philosophy but also experience plays a role—with the tendency toward minority-group solidarity representing at least in part a reaction against the failure of the "American Dream" of individual mobility to deliver on its promises.

While emphases may shift, the duality between integration and building minority institutions is a recurring one, which means that neither polar position is completely adequate. Programs of intergroup relations therefore must be concerned over a period of time both with strengthening minority groups internally and with opening up to an ever-increasing extent the opportunities for members of minorities to participate on an equal footing in the benefits and institutions of the total society.

Note on Literature. As in the case of poverty, the literature in the field of race relations is vast, and these notes will refer only to a few recent and particularly relevant sources.

For a broad, overall view of relationships among ethnic groups of all types, Williams is the most comprehensive.[26] Glazer and Moynihan, although limited to New York City, offer interesting material on comparisons between different groups.[27] There are many volumes that focus particularly on the problems of the black minority and on racism in white

[26] Robin M. Williams, *Strangers Next Door: Ethnic Relations in American Communities* (Englewood Cliffs, N.J.: Prentice-Hall, Inc., 1964).

[27] Nathan Glazer and Daniel P. Moynihan, *Beyond the Melting Pot* (Cambridge, Mass.: Massachusetts Institute of Technology Press, 1963).

society. The Report of the National Advisory Committee on Civil Disorder is fundamental to the entire discussion.[28]

Supplementing the classic work of Myrdal are a number of recent compilations on the Negro in America.[29]

A number of articles describe and attempt to define the field of intergroup relations, indicating the organizations involved, their goals and strategies, and specific programs. Examples are Aaronson, Culberson, Field, and Young.[30]

---

[28] *Report of the National Advisory Commission on Civil Disorder* (New York: Dutton, 1968).

[29] Gunnar Myrdal, *An American Dilemma* (New York: Harper and Row, 1944); Talcott Parsons and K. B. Clarke, (eds.), *The Negro American* (Boston: The Beacon Press, 1965); and *Daedalus*, "The Negro American," 1 (Fall, 1965), and "The Negro American," 2 (Winter, 1966).

[30] Arnold Aaronson, "Organization of the Community Relations Field," *Journal of Intergroup Relations*, Vol. 1 (Spring, 1960), pp. 18-32; George W. Culberson, "Intergroup Relations and Community Welfare Planning," in *Community Organization* (New York: Columbia University Press, 1961), pp. 132-145; John Field, "The Emerging Intergroup Profession," *Journal of Intergroup Relations*, Vol. 1 (Summer, 1960), pp. 61-65; and Whitney Young, "Intergroup Relations and Social Work Practice," *The Social Welfare Forum, 1960* (New York: Columbia University Press, 1960), pp. 146-153.

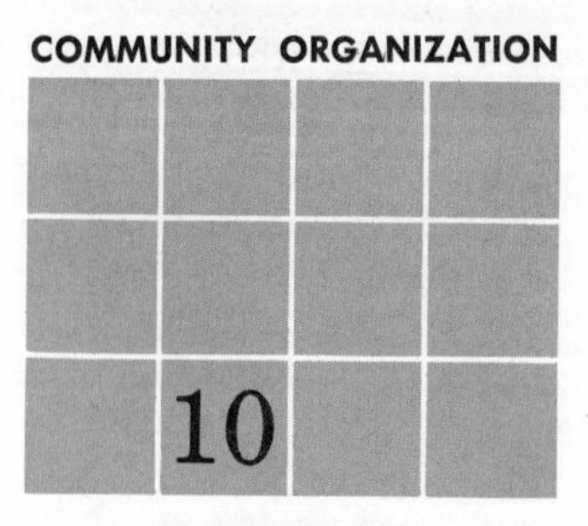

Practicum

IN ADDITION TO THE COURSE WORK with its associated field experiences and skills training units, education for practice includes a practicum. The nature and purposes of the practicum are substantially different from the other parts of the curriculum. The emphasis in the courses is on structured units of learning, but the emphasis in the practicum is on holistic aspects of a process in community organization and social planning. The purpose of the courses is to help the student acquire certain bodies of knowledge and skills; in the practicum the purpose is to help develop both confidence and competence in carrying responsibility for performance. The practicum provides an opportunity for the student to become a practitioner, to take on a professional identity. It is a socializing experience as well as an intellectual learning experience.

Depth in particular areas of social planning and community organization is to be obtained from the specialized courses that have been described. In the practicum the student undertakes a defined responsibility in one of the substantive areas in which the school offers training, or in some combination of them.

PRACTICUM SETTINGS

A number of different settings can be used for the practicum. It need not be thought of in the usual sense of agency field placements, although some agencies can very well provide the setting for a practicum. In the programs of many schools today, the range of settings being used for placements is much wider than in professionally staffed social agencies. Government departments of various types—and not only those which are within the professional orbit of social work functions—are and should be used. Also, the range of voluntary associations that can provide useful training sites is broader than those which have had professional social work service. Thus, in recent years, schools have placed students with trade unions, civil rights organizations, and other types of "cause" organizations or social movements. Placements have also been made with members of city councils, state legislature, and Congress, and in the offices of mayors and governors.

The point was made earlier in this Report that the research-training center type of setting operated directly by the school is a preferred model because it seems to offer the best opportunities for achieving the flexible and experimentally innovative approach to the educational tasks that is needed in a still-emerging field. Many benefits converge in such a model. In a field where there is very little to draw on in the way of definite principles and validated knowledge, the school-operated center offers a very important opportunity fo combining practice and knowledge-building. It will make the theoretical teaching much more alive and immediate and will help to overcome the constant danger of abstraction which besets the curriculum. It also brings into play the practice experience and talents of those faculty members (of whom there are many) who have such experience and who can sometimes teach more effectively as supervisors in a working situation than as lecturers dealing with practice on a theoretical level.

Whether in school-operated centers or not, it is desirable that the students be grouped into units for training purposes. Such units are to be organized around a common area of interest. If the general line of building specialized training around certain problem fields is followed, then the units will parallel such a structure. A group of students whose practicum is in the same project or in a number of closely related projects within the same field would make up such a unit. They would work with faculty who are experts in the area. The practicum should be accompanied by a seminar which relates the work of the field projects to theoretical and research material and which provides an opportunity for reflection by the students on the theoretical implications of their field experiences. For greater range and deeper immersion in the chosen area, students would also have available a substantial number of choices among elective courses in the school, in other departments, or even in other universities. Finally, the program should also include a series of papers in the field of specialization. These might or might not be research reports, depending upon the needs and interests of the students and on the character of the project. Clearly, if the practicum is located in a research project, then the student would be receiving additional training in research and would therefore produce research reports.

We consider it virtually essential that a school which is offering a c.o. concentration have some ongoing projects under its own auspices through which it can gain knowledge concerning substantive problems, practice principles and methodology, and educational processes. However, not all students can be placed in this manner, nor is it necessarily desirable that all of the training be bounded by the university itself.

Nevertheless, the model of the university-sponsored teaching-research center is useful as a guide to the use of other settings. The notion of a unit of students can be applied to an outside agency or organization. It is also possible for students who are located in different settings to be treated by the school as a unit, participating in a seminar or a joint tutorial on the basis of elements which their placements have in common. For example, they may be located in different parts of a service network, within a particular problem field, or in different, though interrelated, structures involved in urban planning. The seminar, conducted by the school or by an outside organization (which could be the case in a setting which conducts training programs) or through some combination of forces of school and agency, is a key point in the process. The seminar should be in the nature of a tutorial, with the number of participants very small and the work intensive in its pursuit of the implications of the practicum experience.

PRACTICUM PROJECTS

There remain to be considered criteria for the kinds of project which students should be expected to undertake in their practicum.

A first premise is that it is not adequate for the student to be assigned to some agency (or school training center, or "cause" organization, or politican, etc.) on a *general* basis, simply to participate in the work of that body, to learn its ways, and to engage in the work as it comes along. While there is undoubtedly some learning in such an open arrangement, and while it does have the advantage of being close to reality, there are losses of time, energy, and stimulation. That is evident from some of the reports we have gathered on student experiences. There should therefore be a definition of what the student is to be responsible for—subject to modifications as necessary, but at least providing a basis for control over the learning experiences to be provided.

Such an approach places a burden on the school to formulate much more clearly and specifically than has generally been done just what the student is expected to gain from the practicum experience. It also calls for much more individualized planning than has usually been the case, so that the practicum will build upon the student's previous experience to fill gaps and to provide strengthening and more depth where needed. It is assumed that the student will himself be an active participant in developing such a program.

The specific content of the student assignments can cover as wide a range as the imagination of faculty and the availability of resources, both human and financial, will permit. Provided that the tasks are meaningful ones, significantly related to important social issues, and that the setting is one in which the student can assume substantial responsibility in carrying out a project, there are many settings which can offer useful learning experiences. Following are a few illustrations among many that might be considered.

Neighborhood Work

Building a neighborhood organization—participation in the underlying planning of the organization; determination of membership, purposes, strategy; experience in direct organizational work. Should include study, analysis, planning, and organizing-negotiating experiences.

Neighborhood services—planning and/or implementation of neighborhood services, involving creation of new services or changes in existing ones. Auspices can be a local unit of a non-local organization, a community corporation, or neighborhood association conducting a single service program or a multi-service center. Experiences to include such matters as establishing support and legitimation, mobilizing resources, working out relationships with other service systems.

Neighborhood planning—organizing and planning responsibilities with neighborhood councils or other mechanisms for the development of neighborhood services and resources. Experience should include program development and management of procedures for participation and decision-making.

Service Agency Assignments

Study-evaluation-reappraisal of agency program or some segment of it. Use of agency data, development of administrative research procedures and proposals for improvement of information processes. Use of administrative analysis techniques such as cost-benefit analysis. Development of appropriate administrative channels for conducting study and acting upon findings.

Community projects—modification in agency services involving new forms of relationship with community such as home care, halfway houses, consultation services, formation of neighborhood groups and organizations, educational programs, etc. Usually such modifications involve an attempt to facilitate communication with clients and to make services more accessible and more appropriate to them. Experiences should include elements of both planning the service modification (data base, rationale, choice of strategy and program, etc.) and the organizational work involved in bringing the plans to fruition through interaction with relevant elements of the community.

Participation in community-wide bodies—participation with others in community-wide projects under such auspices as community councils which call for special studies and planning in particular service fields, such as aging, youth, relocation, etc.

Legislative programs and campaigns to achieve improvements in specific service areas.

Local Community Planning

Central planning body—either governmental or voluntary. Project for restructuring or improving services in a specific field, including modifications in the distribution of responsibilities and resources among agencies and in their interrelationships. Improvement in coordination is thus one of the modifications that may be under consideration. Assignments can include either study or implementation or some combination of both. The project can be built around proposals for new services or changes in existing ones. Studies plus programmatic work with committees and community groups.

Organized interest group—a group that is community-wide in scope and has organizational and planning functions, but in relation to a special "cause" or interest rather than a central planning type of responsibility (e.g., unions, civil rights organizations, membership associations concerned with citizen action, etc.). Study of issues, selection of priorities, strategies, and tactics, and campaign management are some of the skills to be learned.

Non-Local Settings

Sectoral—within a program field, or
Comprehensive planning.
Both involve data-gathering, bringing together relevant planning groups, development of legislative proposals and administrative regulations. The governmental task force is a particularly useful framework for a placement, because it is an occasion for broad consideration of important policy issues and involves a wide range of planning and organizational tasks.

Political Placements

Students can be placed at different geographical levels with political officials—councilmen, legislators, Congressmen. Functions include serving as administrative aide to a political official in regard to social service matters. Meeting with community groups to exchange views; studies of issues; formulations of proposals for legislation and administrative regulation.

To summarize what the practicum is expected to provide in the student's educational program: It is an opportunity for a *sustained* experience in carrying out a responsibility over a period of time. It is also an experience in *process*, as contrasted with the more segmented experience in the core courses, which were geared to specific elements of skill. The emphasis in the practicum is on the interrelatedness of elements in organizing and planning.

While no single setting can provide all the training opportunities that might be considered relevant even to a specialized area of practice, a practicum should be able to provide some range of experience covering a number of the following typical elements: collection and use of data; organizing groups in the form of committees or work groups or associations; definition of group tasks; formulation of alternative policies, strategies, and tactics; conduct of negotiations with other groups that are relevant to the task objectives; and performing administrative operations in the implementation and monitoring of programs.

ORGANIZATION OF PRACTICUM

In the spirit of helping the student to obtain as independent an experience as possible, based on assuming genuine responsibility for his performance, it is recommended that the timing of the field assignment be highly flexible and not tied to the traditional format of specified hours and days per week. It is particularly true in community organization and social planning that the flow of work is irregular. The schedule should be flexible enough to permit the student to fit in with the requirements of the assignment, which might mean some periods of very intensive activity, much of which would be outside of usual daytime office hours, and periods of relative inactivity.

As a general approach, subject to modification in the light of each school's circumstances, it is proposed that the assignment of the student be settled at the end of the first year and that the summer period be used for initial orientation in the assignment, if possible on the basis of paid employment or a stipend. The student would then carry his assignment into the second year, adjusting hours to the requirements of the project. All of these arrangements would, as indicated, be subject to faculty supervision and consultation. For administrative purposes, some minimum number of hours might be specified by the school as fulfilling the practicum requirements. The present field work standard of 500 or 600 hours for the academic year might be taken as a rough rule of thumb. However, it is most likely that assignments of the type outlined in these recommendations will greatly exceed any such minimum.

PART IV

IMPLEMENTATION OF CURRICULUM RECOMMENDATIONS

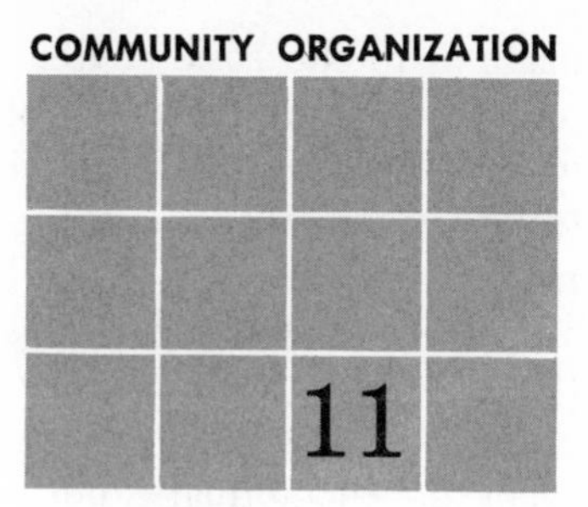

Organization of the Curriculum

AN EFFORT HAS BEEN MADE throughout this report to avoid the recommendation of a blueprint and to emphasize the need for maintaining a high degree of flexibility and for keeping many options open in the development of a curriculum for community organization and social planning. The rationale for such an approach is to be found in the nature of the field at the present time. Community organization and social planning is a field made up of a wide range of activities which are quite diverse in many ways, although it is our view that these activities do belong within a common curriculum in the professional education of social workers. This is also a field which is lacking in clear definition and in which specific content and methodology are still evolving. Under these circumstances, the student is necessarily being educated for undefined and uncertain potentialities. There is a paucity of tested principles of practice, but there is a variety of value assumptions, ideological commitments, and methodological approaches that have been employed in many different types of organizational settings and under a wide range of sponsorships. Having stressed that it is both necessary and desirable that each school develop its own approach to the curriculum on the basis of its interests and capacities, we kept the proposed requirements to a minimum, allowing for a variety of options both for individual students and for schools as a whole.

On the other hand, a number of specific recommendations have been made as to the basic content which should be covered within the community organization–social planning concentration, and the lines along which different options can be developed. At this point we shall draw these various recommendations together in order to indicate how such a curriculum would be organized. The purpose here is to show the relationships among the various suggestions that have been made and to indicate what the implementation of such a program would involve in the way of organizational arrangements within a school. However, it should be stressed again that this format is not proposed for general adoption. It is presented for illustrative purposes.

The recommendations are presented within the framework of the two-year master's degree program. This has been done as a matter of convenience and in order to avoid consideration of issues which lie beyond the c.o. concentration but refer to social work training more generally. It is not meant to imply that a two-year program is necessary in order to accomplish the objectives of the curriculum recommendations. They could be adapted to the requirements of an accelerated graduate program or a five-year undergraduate combination. However, the two-year master's curriculum is still the prevalent pattern in graduate social work education and the recommendations will therefore be summarized in relation to that pattern. Similarly, we shall use two semesters per year as the basis for presenting the recommendations, while recognizing that a number of schools operate on a trimester or quarter system. Each school can make the necessary translation to its own pattern.

REQUIREMENTS AND ELECTIVES

The recommendations that have been set forth in earlier chapters of this report call for a program of core courses which are considered to incorporate the basic knowledge that is needed by all the students in community organization and social planning, regardless of the areas of specialization which they decide to pursue. The core curriculum as recommended consists of the following:

Foundation Courses		Practice Courses	
Social science	2	Survey	1
Social research	2	Methods of organizing	1
Social welfare and social policy	2	Methods of planning	1

The core curriculum thus consists of nine courses. They are required courses in the sense that the students will be expected to have mastered their content as outlined in the specific recommendations. To the extent that the students are able to demonstrate that they have already covered the material presented in such courses (an option which should be available at all levels in the curriculum), they will be free to use a portion of the time reserved for core courses to pursue areas of special interest and specialization. However, the listed requirements provide a norm and a guidepost in the formulation of student programs.

If we assume a normal course load of four courses per semester for four semesters, then the total program would be made up of sixteen semester courses, not including the practicum or the field experiences that are related to the core methods courses. Of this total of sixteen, the core required courses would constitute nine, or just a little over one-half. This means that approximately one-half of the student's total time in the program would be planned individually on an elective basis in order to provide him with considerable freedom in following a program that will be suitable to his individual interests and career goals.

SEQUENCE AND SCHEDULING

Given the format of a two-year graduate program, we see the core requirements generally as comprising the major portion of the first year's program. The overall purpose of the core requirements is to provide the student with a general view of the entire area that is being covered. They call for an acquaintance with the relevant bodies of knowledge underlying practice in community organization and social planning, with the fields of work involved in that practice and also with the basic methodology and skills employed within it. There is, therefore, some logic in having this material covered first, before the student begins to specialize within particular fields of work. It could be argued that he is in a better position to choose such an area of specialization if he will first have obtained the broad coverage provided by the core courses.

On the other hand, it is recognized that a full year devoted to required courses can be too rigid a mold for some students and can involve undesirable delays in the opportunities provided to students to explore their individual interests. It seems particularly desirable that at least the survey course in the practice area and a portion of the foundation material be covered in the first year so that the more specialized practice courses which have been recommended can be planned with the knowledge that the students have covered a body of basic material. Since there are differences in emphasis among specialized courses, they may be arranged to carry different prerequisites in both foundation and practice courses so that a student need not take all of the core courses before beginning to choose electives.

On the assumption, however, that most of the core material will have been covered in the first year, the second year would be devoted primarily to areas of specialization in which the further grounding that the student receives in relevant social science courses, advanced research, and practice courses in specific areas combine with the practicum to develop competence within a field of practice.

As recent reviews of field instruction have noted, learning experiences can be organized in relation either to a "method" or a "problem" or both.[1] As has been indicated earlier, the approach to community organization and social planning being taken in this report is based on both concepts. The focus that a student will select for concentration in the second year will therefore include components of problem orientation, field of service, and methodology. The specialized courses outlined in Chapter 9 indicate the approximate range of possibilities now available or likely to develop in various schools. Specialization may also take the form of combined concentrations, including both elements of the c.o. curriculum and other practice methods. A number of possibilities of this type will be outlined in Chapter 12.

INDIVIDUALIZATION

Because of the diversity of practice for which the program is designed to prepare students, the wide range of subject matter to be covered, and the differences among students entering the program, there is need for a high degree of individualization in the planning of student programs. The curriculum should be designed in such a way that it will use the specific background of education and experience which the student brings and will provide him with opportunities both to deepen the exposures that he has already had and to fill in knowledge about other areas in which he has no background.

The study of student backgrounds and characteristics conducted as part of this Project has made it clear once more that there is no single road into social work education.[2] Students come from a variety of personal backgrounds and follow different routes of undergraduate education or preprofessional work experience. It would therefore be premature to establish any single pattern of prerequisites for graduate education. For some time to come the field will need to draw upon people who enter at different stages in their life experience and through a variety of academic channels. In the recommendations which have been made here, we have

---

[1] See, for example: Margaret Schubert, "An Overview of Field Instruction," in Betty Lacy Jones, (ed.), *Current Patterns in Field Instruction in Graduate Social Work Education* (New York: Council on Social Work Education, 1969), pp. 3-11.

[2] D. Golden, A. Pins, and W. Jones, *Students in Schools of Social Work: A Study of Characteristics and Factors Affecting Career Choice and Practice Concentration* (New York: Council on Social Work Education, 1970).

taken as a model the student who comes with a strong undergraduate background in the social sciences and who has had experience either during his college career or afterwards as a nonprofessional worker and/or volunteer in an area that is related to social work. That description is true to a growing extent of most of the students who will be found in a c.o. concentration. However, it is not true of all of them, and individualized arrangements therefore will have to be made in order to adapt both the prerequisites and the curriculum to such variations in the student body.

We believe that it is sound to build the curriculum on the basis of what most students will bring to graduate education by way of previous background in order to avoid unnecessary duplication of material and to set the level of graduate work at a standard which will be challenging to the most highly qualified students entering. It has therefore been recommended that prerequisites be established in the major foundation areas of social science and social research. For those that come into the program lacking such backgound, provision can be made for make-up work on a individualized basis as necessary. Experience has indicated, however, that it is frequently possible for people with good undergraduate education that does not include specialization in the social sciences to meet the requirements of graduate courses, so that make-up work is not necessarily the only way in which people may find it possible to qualify. This is a matter of individual capacity which can be determined on a case-by-case basis.

At the other end of the spectrum are a certain number of students whose background has been so extensive that it may be unnecessary for them to take some of the material which has been recommended for the core requirements. For these students the program can be adjusted in such a way as to permit them to move more quickly into more specialized content both in the foundation and practice areas. Adjustments for individual students should not pose inordinate organizational problems for the school, because the program as outlined already calls for making available a substantial number of electives.

ORGANIZATION OF SCHOOL RESOURCES

To carry out the full range of the program that has been outlined in these recommendations would call for a diversity of resources in teaching faculty, training laboratories, and field placements. In line with the general objectives of the first year of the program which is to provide a broad coverage of all aspects of the field through opportunities for wide observation and prestructured experience, a combination of resources are to be used. In the Rothman-Jones volume, which is offered as a suggestive guide, it is recommended that students be anchored within an agency for the semester in which they are taking the survey course so that they have a framework in which to make an analysis of various aspects of practice.[3] It is also recommended, however, that these anchor placements be supplemented with other experiences organized by the school itself through some type of laboratory resources.

The general model which we have used and which forms the framework for the Rothman-Jones volume consists of the following:

1. A survey course, the major purpose of which is to introduce the student to the field, supported by a laboratory-observatory based on a combination of agency placements and school-directed exercises.

2. Two courses—one in organizing and one in planning—supported by a skills laboratory which provides a range of skill training under school direction.

These recommendations involve a certain risk. It was noted earlier that most social work students seem to find greater stimulation and satisfaction in their field work than in the classroom, and this is true, as far as we can judge from our investigations, in c.o. programs as well as in others. In calling for a shift to greater centrality of the class, we run the risk, at least in the short run, of weakening the total program. Yet it is important that future developments be in that direction. Field work placements are uneven, and, though they provide the stimulation of contact with reality, they do not necessarily offer the kind of training which is desired for future practitioners in community organization and social planning. Unless the school specifies and controls the content of the training, it can have no assurance that its students will be afforded the opportunity to gain the knowledge and skills that are the objectives of the program.

There is, however, no justification to shift from agency placements to school-directed field instruction unless the school can provide richer, deeper, and more rounded opportunities for training than are available in the agencies. The word of caution which must be sounded is that these recommendations call for substantial development of the school's resources. Ideally, this should take the form of research and consultation projects which continuously provide the school with sites and action situations that offer students opportunities for meaningful field experiences in addition to the kinds of laboratory experiences suggested in the Rothman-Jones volume.[4] Since schools cannot achieve all of their goals at once, the recommendations are offered as directions toward which to work, with the recognition that many transitional arrangements will be necessary. One

---

[3] J. Rothman and W. Jones, *A New Look at Field Instruction: Education for Application of Practice Skills in Community Organization and Social Planning* (New York: Association Press, 1970).

[4] *Ibid.*

immediate step is for a school to evaluate its existing placements in relation to the kinds of learning experiences that have been proposed and to select those which are most promising as centers for the school's investment.

The following guidelines are suggested in the use of outside agencies for field instruction in both the core courses and the practicum:

1. That the school specify the content and phasing of the experiences.
2. That the placement offer learning opportunities in a range of skills in organizing and planning.
3. That the training provided be in elements of methodology and skill such as those outlined in the course recommendations, with adequate supervision under school direction.

Another type of resource which requires some planning and organization on the part of the school, but does not have to be operated directly by the school itself, is paid employment. If the format for the program covers the standard two academic years, then the summer in between is a time that can be used carefully to enhance the student's equipment. One way in which this can be done is through paid employment which is undertaken not only for financial reasons but as a planned work experience selected by the student in consultation with the faculty. Wherever feasible, it would be well to relate such employment to the practicum requirements. One type of arrangement which would be highly desirable is for the student to enter his practicum during the summer (wherever possible on a paid basis) and to begin to assume responsibilities which he would then carry throughout the subsequent academic year. Such an arrangement might be particularly feasible on projects which are themselves sponsored and directed by the school, but such possibilities could also be worked out with other agencies and organizations that are serving as sites for the practicum.

FACULTY RESOURCES

It is implicit in the kinds of recommendations that have been made that there be represented within the faculty a combination of competencies and specializations to cover at least some of the areas that have been outlined. Each specialized program within the broad spectrum of community organization and social planning calls for collaboration among representatives of the relevant fields of social science, research, and practice.

There is no way of saying what "critical mass" is needed in numbers of students and in size of faculty to make for a viable concentration. It is probably inevitable that there will be a selective process, with both students and faculty attracted to centers which become known for competence in certain areas. That is true in all fields and disciplines and social work has been no exception. It seems in the nature of the situation that strong concentrations in one or another form of community organization and social planning will be developed in some, but not all, schools of social work. In the others, the mission of faculty with commitments to community organization and social planning would seem to lie less in providing specialized training for the relatively few students who might be seeking it in such schools and more in the integration of relevant c.o. components into the central mission of the school, whatever it may be.

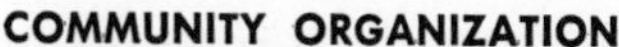

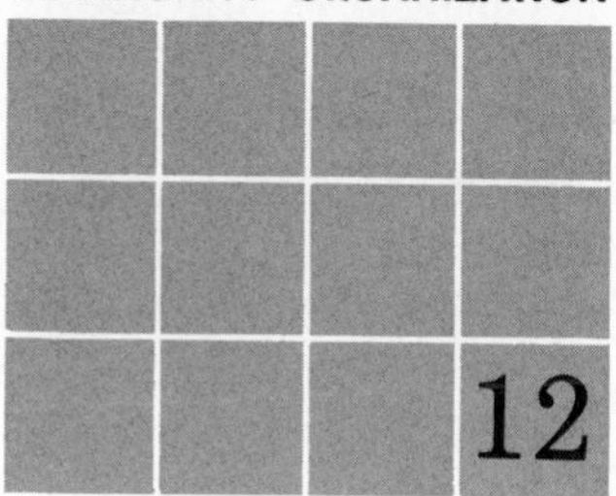

Implications for Social Work Education

THIS REPORT APPEARS at a time of very rapid change in social work and social work education. The Community Organization Curriculum Development Project itself was an important indicator of the forces impinging on social work education during the decade of the 1960's, and the pace of development has accelerated even more quickly than was anticipated when the Project was first conceived. Issues which seemed important in the middle of the decade have been settled by time and experience, whereas others have arisen. Thus, there is no longer serious difference of opinion about the legitimacy of a two-year concentration in community organization. There is, however, growing interest in attempts to reconceptualize all of social work practice so that distinctions between the methods are blunted in favor of a more comprehensive professional methodology.

Of greater importance than any specific substantive issue, however, is the general spirit of change and experimentation. It has become clear that social work education cannot and will not follow any single model in this turbulent period. That conclusion is evident in the direction taken by recent revisions in the Curriculum Policy Statement of the Council on Social Work Education.[1] Unlike former statements, the new statement avoids specifying content and mode of organization of curriculum. The

[1] *Curriculum Policy Statement* (New York: Council on Social Work Education, 1969).

statement deals instead with general objectives that will be implemented by each school in accordance with its design, which it is expected to justify with an explicit rationale. Diversity among schools "in the kinds and number of concentrations offered as well as in their designations, and in the instructional activities and learning experiences provided" is recognized, legitimated, and institutionalized.

The present situation and the future outlook were well-described by Herman Stein in his presidential address to the Seventeenth Annual Program Meeting of the Council on Social Work Education at the beginning of 1969:

> Our educational institutions will individually have to select the kinds of expertise on which they will concentrate, aside from the basic underpinnings. Schools will therefore differ considerably, depending on their interests, resources, and priority commitments to social goals. . . . Common cores of competence and much overlap will continue to exist, but with much greater variation than we are accustomed to now. It is no longer experimentation with curriculum innovation that I am referring to, but large-scale changes through painstaking development by schools, which can justify society's confidence in the capacity of the profession to produce expertise for existing and for emerging new areas of practice.[2]

Because of the diversity among schools, there is no single framework into which the recommendations of this Project can be fitted. In attempting to answer the question which has been posed as to how the recommendations will affect the total program of schools of social work, the answer at this point must begin with a question in reply—which programs and which schools? Whether schools can and will use all or part of the recommendations—and how they use them—will depend on what they are trying to do generally and also on the characteristics and interests of their students and faculties.

The proposed curriculum as a whole would fit best those schools which offer a two-year concentration in community organization and social planning, as those terms have been described in this report. Some schools will undoubtedly fit this model, but by no means all of them. Hopefully, parts of the recommendations may commend themselves to faculties who have other commitments and to schools whose patterns do not permit acceptance of the entire range of recommendations.

METHODS COMBINATIONS

One of the variations in curriculum development in recent years has been a growth in the number of concentrations offered by some schools.

---

[2] Herman D. Stein, "Reflections on Competence and Ideology in Social Work Education," *Journal of Education for Social Work*, Vol. 5, No. 1 (Spring, 1969), p. 86.

Concentrations now exist not only in casework, group work, and community organization, but also in research, administration, and social policy. Also of interest is the grouping together of two or more methods into combined concentrations. Among such combinations the methods frequently brought together are casework and group work. Programs described as "generic" or "inter-methodological" often are essentially a combination of casework and group work.

One of the options which should be considered in relation to the recommendations of this report is the possibility of offering joint concentrations, in which some elements of the material proposed for community organization and social planning are combined with elements of other concentrations in a program that will attempt to train students for one of the kinds of expertise suggested by Stein. Such joint concentrations fit very well with these recommendations, which have pointed to the diversity of settings, tasks, and methods that have been grouped together under the category of community organization and social planning. Combinations with other concentrations would provide the opportunity for intensifying one or another phase of this broad spectrum, thus hopefully enhancing the possibilities for the development of expertise on the part of the student.[3]

In describing a proposed joint methods concentration in community organization and administration, Kramer has suggested that two approaches are possible.[4] One, which he labels "separate but equal," would call for students to take an equal amount of work in required courses and obtain field instruction in *both* areas, with reliance on some joint offerings and/or a special seminar to help in the process of integration. The alternative, which Kramer calls "integration," would provide a unified program geared specifically to the needs of students whose practice goals cut across two methods. It would call for a new set of course offerings and field experience, though in relation to the needs of students interested in both.

The "separate but equal" approach has actually existed for some time in schools of social work in the form of one-year concentrations. Many c.o. programs are still of this type, providing for a second-year concentration in community organization, preceded by a year of concentration in either casework or group work. In the past, most of these programs were based on general notions as to the desirability of providing all social workers with a common base in "direct" practice (as represented by casework or group work). Today that is no longer a prevalent point of view.

It would be consistent with the recommendations of this report to favor

[3] For a summary and analysis of recent developments, see: *Innovations in Teaching Social Work Practice*, edited by Lilian Ripple (New York: Council on Social Work Education, 1970).

[4] Ralph M. Kramer, "Community Organization and Administration: Integration or Separate but Equal?" *Journal of Education for Social Work*, Vol. 2, No. 2 (Fall, 1966), pp. 48-56.

an "integrated" rather than a "separate but equal" approach to the combination of concentrations. An integrated program would call for making explicit the specific areas of competence which the student is expected to acquire. An integrated program calls for selection in all areas of the curriculum. Some of the social science offerings would be more relevant than others. Different combined specializations would call for different degrees of involvement in research, in the pursuit of social policy issues, and in particular components of practice methods and skills. Each combination would have its own "package," made up, as is the case in the "general" model, of a minimum number of core requirements and wide opportunities for the choice of individual options.

Among the combined concentrations that have been suggested, the group-work community-organization combination is the one most in use at the present time in one form or another. At the boundary, in such a field as neighborhood organization, it is sometimes hard to distinguish between programs that may be organized, respectively, in a community organization or group work sequence. It would also be difficult to differentiate some of the field placements. Recognizing the closeness of the two fields both historically and in contemporary forms of practice, a joint program would be aimed at preparing students primarily for community organization work at the "grass roots" level, in what has been described here as working with voluntary associations.

The social science offerings described earlier under the "behavioral" category, the core course in methods of organizing, and the specialized course in neighborhood organization would be particularly relevant and would probably overlap some of the material normally included in a group work concentration. On the other hand, intensive exposure to theory, research, and practice relating to group process which would normally be provided by the group work program to a greater extent than in a community organization concentration would become part of the joint concentration.

The possibility of some combination between community organization and administration was raised in the 1958 curriculum study and at various times since then.[5] Kramer's analysis of the relationships between the two areas pointed out that a rationale for a combined program exists in a common knowledge base and in the reciprocal nature of the career lines of organizers, planners, and administrators.[6] The recommendations in this report support that view. For example, organizational analysis, which is a

---

[5] Sue W. Spencer, *The Administrative Method in Social Work Education,* Vol. III of the *Social Work Curriculum Study* (New York: Council on Social Work Education, 1959); and Harry L. Lurie, *The Community Organization Method in Social Work Education,* Vol. IV of the *Social Work Curriculum Study* (New York: Council on Social Work Education, 1959).

[6] Kramer, *op. cit.*

basic element in the body of knowledge underlying administration, is reflected in the recommendations that have been made both as to social science foundations and practice. That portion of the survey course which deals with direct service agencies and the specialized course in administrative planning are most directly related to administration and could just as well serve as teaching units within a concentration in administration.

There are other possibilities which are equally plausible and which are beginning to appear as schools experiment with new approaches. A research concentration, for example, provides opportunities for sub-specialization depending on the substantive focus of the research. Within a framework of specialization in research methods, a combined program would be directed to students who wish to prepare themselves for careers as researchers and social planners. Similarly, a feasible link could be made between social planning and social policy, while combining elements of methodology in both policy analysis and planning.

The problem that arises in the proliferation of specializations and sub-specializations is the danger that students will be prepared for only a very narrow band of activities in the world of actual practice. Fear has been expressed that students will lack flexibility and versatility in adapting methods of work to the needs of the situation which they find; that they will find it difficult to move among a range of positions within the field, to the detriment of both themselves and the needs that they should be serving.

These are important problems that cannot be ignored. It is not possible to avoid completely the hazards of specialization nor to allay completely legitimate concerns about the dangers of over-specialization. In the evaluation of costs and benefits on both sides, we have come down on the side of specialization as required in order to meet the needs described by Stein for competence and expertise. That having been said, it then becomes necessary to consider the dangers of over-specialization and to seek measures which will help to reduce them.

Part of the answer is to be found in the point of view which prevails in the curriculum. If the faculty has a broad view of the field and its variations, it may convey this view without necessarily providing actual skills training in all aspects of the work. In these curriculum recommendations the survey course has been proposed for the core curriculum as a basic introduction to and overview of all aspects of community organization and social planning. It is suggested that such a survey be retained as one of the core courses in a combined concentration so that the student obtains an overview of the broader range of activities than those in which he will have an opportunity to engage directly. It is also desirable that the range of methods included in the two core methods courses become part of all students' equipment, regardless of the areas they determine to pursue more intensively. Some of the material included in the methods courses may overlap that in the other concentrations. Elements of each may appear in new combinations in the joint concentrations. The Project's recommendations may be used as a check list in order to assure curriculum planners that various types of knowledge and skill have been considered and, if held to be relevant to the objectives of the program, included in some way in the course offerings.

A further protection against undue narrowness is provided by the intermixing of problem-oriented and method-oriented elements, both in the course work and in field instruction. Methods cut across problem areas, whereas a focus on problem areas brings a number of different methodologies together.

In a time such as the present, when practice is changing so rapidly, the practitioner's growth and movement into new areas will take place in the course of his career development in ways which cannot be anticipated while he is a student, no matter how broad the curriculum may be. The issue then is a general one of helping the students to acquire attitudes and skills that are amenable to continuing search and innovation. At the same time, it is necessary that he be equipped with some specific competence to function in existing areas of practice. It is the purpose of these recommendations to strengthen the area of competence so that the practitioner may find a place, because of the expert contribution he can make, in ongoing efforts to achieve better solutions to social problems. The hope is that, armed with such an area of competence, with an appreciation of the broader framework of which his efforts are a part, and with the attitudes and skills necessary to learn from experience, he will have the capacity to discover better ways of tackling new problems.

GENERIC APPROACHES

Running counter to the kinds of specializations and sub-specializations discussed above is the growing popularity of efforts to find a common base in the social work curriculum that will unify all social work methods. Such efforts take several forms. Many are, in essence, a broadening of the casework methods curriculum to include some work with groups and to focus more sharply on the community context in which the casework service is given. Others involve an effort to move away from a "methods" orientation altogether and to build curriculum on the basis of problem-oriented material, showing the use of different modes of intervention in dealing with problems.

Much of the motivation for these efforts stems from the concern about the limitations of the classic casework model of one-to-one treatment and the recognition that broader approaches are required in order to cope with the needs of the most disadvantaged elements of the population. Schools have created field work training centers in low-income neighborhoods which provide a range of experience, including dealing with individual needs, groups, and community action projects. They have argued that current demands upon practitioners are such as to require competence in all of these areas.

While the issues are admittedly debatable, it has been the conclusion of the staff of this Project, on the basis of its examination of actual experience, that there continues to be an important and meaningful differentiation between intervention at the case level and intervention at the organizational level. The term "case level" is used instead of "individual" because this seems to be closer to the real issue. As various new approaches develop in dealing with the problems of clients, mixtures of one-to-one and group approaches will be used. Similarly, some aspects of what has usually been considered community organization, for example, referral systems and case committees, belong together with diagnostic and therapeutic techniques as part of the equipment of the social worker who is dealing with case situations. But the distinction between bringing resources to bear in a specific case situation and working on the general issue of providing resources for a population continues to be a meaningful one. The Project's own study of neighborhood service centers has in fact pointed to the conflicts between service needs and the objectives of organizational development, suggesting that some separation between the two activities is necessary if both objectives are to be achieved.[7]

FRAGMENTATION

One of the issues on which concern has been expressed is that the process of specialization may lead to such separation among curriculum "tracks" that there will be a loss in professional identity—a fragmentation of the profession. It has been argued here that specialization is important in order to develop the capacities of the profession in areas where demands are being made and where its contributions have not yet played a significant role. The recommendations are designed to help students achieve a type of competence which may be different from those of students in other programs. However, to quote Stein again, "It should not be identical targets for training in competence that unites schools of social work, but commonly accepted premises of social purpose, values, and commitment. . . .[8]

Despite the emphasis on specialization which permeates this entire re-

---

[7] Robert Perlman and David Jones, *Neighborhood Service Centers* (Washington, D.C.: U.S. Government Printing Office, 1967).

[8] Stein, *op. cit.*, p.90.

port, there are a number of points at which the recommendations call explicitly for integration with the total curriculum. Of particular importance is the area of social policy, which incorporates what Stein has pinpointed as the element that should unite all schools (as well as all concentrations). Another point of integration is to be found in the suggested specialization in problem areas. To the extent that schools adopt such an approach for their curriculum planning generally, they will be required to bring together students who are concentrating in different methods. It is also anticipated that the growth of school-sponsored training centers will provide additional opportunities for interaction among students in relation to shared concerns, even though they may be acquiring different types of skills.

On a broader plane, it is hoped that the approaches which the Project has employed in reaching its recommendations may prove useful to curriculum planners concerned with the total curriculum and its various objectives, which will differ from school to school. For example, the approaches followed in the selection of material from the social sciences and from social research methodologies, the attempts to integrate class and field instruction, and the use of diversified learning experiences in both class and field are applicable to other areas of concentration as well as to community organization and social planning. Because of the diversity of objectives and curriculum patterns in schools of social work, there seems no basis for specifying any uniform content of community organization and social planning that is applicable to the total curriculum. Various components of the curriculum as set forth in these recommendations will have to be reviewed by each school to see what parts fit—and in what way—into its own objectives and frame of reference.

EDUCATION OUTSIDE MASTER'S PROGRAMS

The Curriculum Project has given no special study to undergraduate education, to advanced education, to continuing education or to in-service training. In conclusion, a few observations will be offered on these points. They are based not on original study but on the staff's exposure to these issues during the course of the Project and in their other roles.

In regard to undergraduate education, the major recommendation is for entering students to have maximum grounding in the various social sciences. Some of the recommended practice materials, particularly the survey course, could become part of an undergraduate program in social welfare. Should this become general, the graduate program could begin at a more advanced level, giving more time to methods and skills and to the deepening of theoretical knowledge and the application of theory, research, and practice skills to specific problem areas.

In regard to advanced education, it may be noted that many of these curriculum recommendations are modeled on the doctoral programs that have developed in schools of social work during the past decade. It seems inevitable that social work education, like all professional education, will continue to experience a rapid upgrading in its curriculum at all levels. What is now taught at the doctoral level will soon be covered in the master's program and what is now taught at the master's level will increasingly be taught in undergraduate programs. The future role of doctoral programs will increasingly focus on theory building and research rather than on preparation for advanced positions in practice.

In-service training also becomes a more important element in the total program as knowledge grows and technologies become more complicated. These processes combine to make knowledge obsolescent at a very early stage in the practitioner's career. Should the present curriculum recommendations prove effective, they may help the schools to meet the needs of agencies for in-service training. A school that has developed the resources required to implement the recommendations should be in a good position to offer agencies brief training courses made up of elements of its curriculum.

FOLLOW-UP AND IMPLEMENTATION

In presenting this report, it is recognized that a host of questions are left unanswered and that many judgments which seem reasonable at the moment may be changed very quickly by experience in the volatile situation which characterizes social work education today. Provision must therefore be made for a continuing process of exchange and consultation in which experience can be examined and evaluated for its potential contributions to better solutions.

During the course of the Project, the staff received a number of useful suggestions from faculties, students, and practitioners concerning possible follow-up activities. One type of suggestion was that there be a series of conferences, perhaps on a regional level, in order to examine the Project's recommendations and to fill out certain areas of its report through a closer examination of actual experience in curriculum construction and teaching. It has also been proposed that arrangements be made for exchange and sharing of resources in the building of community organization and social planning programs. Especially for smaller schools that may be limited in the number and variety of staff which they can command for specialized areas, it might be feasible to develop regional arrangements for the sharing of training center facilities and the pooling of some faculty resources. Exchange visits by faculty and perhaps even students among schools were also proposed.

The Council on Social Work Education, through its mechanisms of consultation, publications, conferences, and other modes of communication among faculties and schools, provides the continuing channel for the translation of these and subsequent recommendations into activities for the strengthening of education for practice in community organization and social planning.

APPENDIXES

APPENDIX I

FULL-TIME STUDENT ENROLLMENT IN MASTER'S DEGREE PROGRAM AND ENROLLMENT IN COMMUNITY ORGANIZATION CONCENTRATION, 1960-1969

Year	Total full-time enrollment	Enrollment in c.o.	Percentage of all students in c.o.	Percentage increase over previous year in	
				total enrollment	c.o.
1960	5,461	85	1.5	—	—
1961	5,864	100	1.7	7.38	17.65
1962	6,490	141	2.2	7.88	41.00
1963	7,074	201	2.9	9.00	42.55
1964	7,925	297	3.8	12.03	47.76
1965	8,989	442	4.9	13.43	48.82
1966	10,131	789	7.8	12.70	78.51
1967	10,961	897	8.2	8.19	13.69
1968	11,700	1,017	8.7	6.74	13.38
1969	12,551	1,125	9.0	7.27	10.62

Source: **Statistics on Social Work Education,** 1960 through 1969.

APPENDIX II

FULL-TIME STUDENTS IN MASTER'S DEGREE PROGRAM, BY CONCENTRATION, 1960-1969

	ENROLLMENT				PERCENTAGE OF TOTAL ENROLLMENT			
Year	Casework	Group work	c.o.	All other	Casework	Group work	c.o.	All other
1960	4,493	507	85	376	82.2	9.7	1.5	6.8
1961	4,691	520	100	553	80.0	9.0	1.7	9.4
1962	5,159	564	141	626	79.5	8.7	2.2	9.6
1963	5,735	622	201	516	81.1	8.8	2.9	7.3
1964	6,744	703	297	181	85.1	8.8	3.8	2.3
1965	7,394	841	442	312	82.3	9.4	4.9	3.5
1966	7,633	953	789	756	75.3	9.4	7.8	7.5
1967	7,806	1072	897	1186	71.2	9.8	8.2	10.8
1968	6,966	1006	1017	2711	59.5	8.6	8.7	23.2
1969	5,609	1156	1125	4661	44.7	9.2	9.0	37.1

Source: **Statistics on Social Work Education,** 1960 through 1969.

APPENDIX III

*COMMUNITY ORGANIZATION CURRICULUM DEVELOPMENT PROJECT ADVISORY COMMITTEE**

Chairman: ALFRED J. KAHN

Arnold Aronson
Director of Program Planning and Evaluation
National Community Relations Advisory Council
55 West 42 Street
New York, N.Y. 10036

James G. Banks
Consultant, United Planning Organization of the Washington Metropolitan Area
1420 New York Avenue, N.W.
Washington, D.C.

Philip Bernstein
Executive Director
Council of Jewish Federations and Welfare Funds
315 Park Avenue South
New York, N.Y. 10010

Margaret Berry
Executive Director
National Federation of Settlements
232 Madison Avenue
New York, N.Y. 10016

Milton Chernin
Dean, School of Social Welfare
University of California
Berkeley, California 94720

Marshall B. Clinard
Professor, Department of Sociology
University of Wisconsin
Madison, Wisconsin 53706

Maurice F. Connery
Associate Dean
School of Social Welfare
University of California
Los Angeles, California 90024

Very Rev. Msgr. Lawrence J. Corcoran
Secretary, National Conference of Catholic Charities
1346 Connecticut Avenue, N.W.
Washington, D.C. 20036

Leonard S. Cottrell, Jr.
Russell Sage Foundation
230 Park Avenue
New York, N.Y. 10017

Arthur J. Edmunds
Executive Director
Urban League of Pittsburgh
200 Ross Street
Pittsburgh, Pennsylvania 15219

Lyman S. Ford
Executive Director
United Community Funds and Councils of America
345 East 46th Street
New York, N.Y. 10017

Nathan Glazer
Professor of Sociology
University of California
Berkeley, California 94704

Shelton B. Granger
Deputy Assistant Secretary
Department of Health, Education, and Welfare
Washington, D.C. 20201

* Affiliations shown for committee members were those at the time of participation on the Project Advisory Committee.

Charles E. Hendry
Director, School of Social Work
University of Toronto
Toronto 5, Canada

Morris Janowitz
Department of Sociology
University of Chicago
Chicago, Illinois 60637

Ray Johns
General Executive
Boston YMCA
316 Huntington Avenue
Boston, Massachusetts 02115

Alfred J. Kahn
Professor of Social Work
Columbia University School of Social Work
2 East 91st Street
New York, N.Y. 10028

Glen Leet
Executive Director
Community Development Foundation
345 East 46th Street
New York, N.Y. 10017

Norman V. Lourie
Deputy Secretary
Pennsylvania Department of Public Welfare
Harrisburg, Pennsylvania 17105

Leonard W. May
Professor of Human Development
Colby College, Lovejoy Hall
Waterville, Maine 04900

C. F. McNeil
Director
National Social Welfare Assembly
345 East 46th Street
New York, N.Y. 10017

Rev. Almon R. Pepper
23 Lewis Avenue
Hartsdale, New York 10530

Leo Perlis
Director, AFL-CIO Community Services Activities
815 16th Street, N.W.
Washington, D.C. 20006

Helen U. Phillips
Professor, School of Social Work
University of Pennsylvania
3701 Locust Street
Philadelphia, Pennsylvania 19104

Milton G. Rector
Director, National Council on Crime and Delinquency
44 East 23rd Street
New York, N.Y. 10010

Jack Rothman
Professor of Community Organization
School of Social Work
University of Michigan
Ann Arbor, Michigan 48104

Eli A. Rubinstein, M.D.
Director of Manpower and Training Programs
National Institute of Mental Health
5454 Wisconsin Avenue
Chevy Chase, Maryland 20203

Meyer Schwartz
Professor of Community Organization
Graduate School of Social Work
University of Pittsburgh
Pittsburgh, Pennsylvania 15213

Ernest F. Witte
Dean, School of Social Work
San Diego State College
San Diego, California 92115

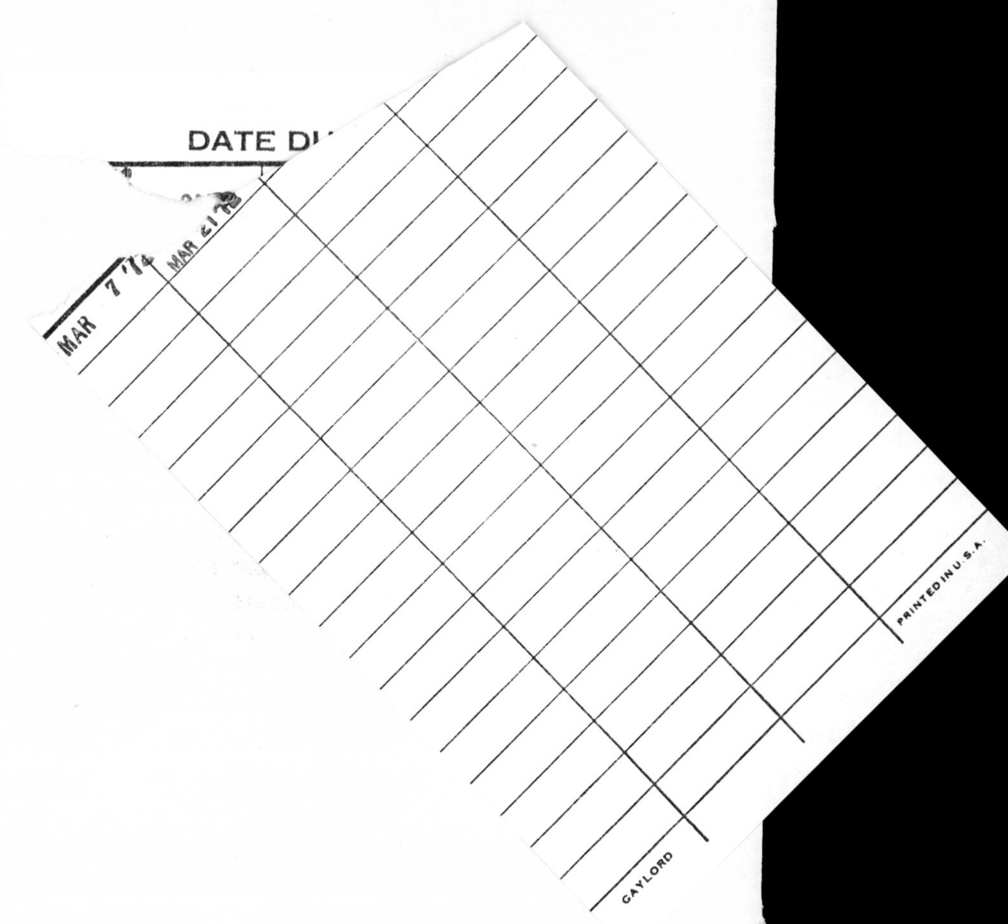
DATE DU
MAR 7 '78
MAR 21 '78
GAYLORD
PRINTED IN U.S.A.